THE TWELVE STEPS TO A LIFE OF EXEMPLARY EXCELLENCE

THIRD IMPROVED EDITION

M. U. SHAH

Chennai • Bangalore

CLEVER FOX PUBLISHING
Chennai, India

Published by CLEVER FOX PUBLISHING 2023
Copyright © M. U. SHAH 2023

All Rights Reserved.
ISBN: 978-93-56487-09-3

This book has been published with all reasonable efforts taken to make the material error-free after the consent of the author. No part of this book shall be used, reproduced in any manner whatsoever without written permission from the author, except in the case of brief quotations embodied in critical articles and reviews.

The Author of this book is solely responsible and liable for its content including but not limited to the views, representations, descriptions, statements, information, opinions and references ["Content"]. The Content of this book shall not constitute or be construed or deemed to reflect the opinion or expression of the Publisher or Editor. Neither the Publisher nor Editor endorse or approve the Content of this book or guarantee the reliability, accuracy or completeness of the Content published herein and do not make any representations or warranties of any kind, express or implied, including but not limited to the implied warranties of merchantability, fitness for a particular purpose. The Publisher and Editor shall not be liable whatsoever for any errors, omissions, whether such errors or omissions result from negligence, accident, or any other cause or claims for loss or damages of any kind, including without limitation, indirect or consequential loss or damage arising out of use, inability to use, or about the reliability, accuracy or sufficiency of the information contained in this book.

First Published in November, 2019
Second Edition Published in August, 2021
Third Edition Published in November, 2023

Thank You, Esteemed Readers!

"Thanks a lot for your wonderful gift, 'The Twelve Steps to a Life of Exemplary Excellence'. This life-enhancing book is immensely useful for the entire span of life, from studentship to retirement. I will not be surprised if this book is recommended as a reference manual in many educational institutes and corporate organisations."

– A. B. Desai, CEO, Gammon India Ltd., Mumbai

"Thank you very much for sharing your knowledge. A priceless resource, the book has enlightened us all, for which we are grateful to you forever. This book will create not only many time-efficient and successful executives but also great human beings. Perhaps no book has highlighted the importance of a principle-centered life so impactfully."

– M. Sambasiva Rao, Managing Director,
Techno Unique Infratech, Hyderabad

"If you are experiencing stress arising from multi-faceted demands on your time and struggling to balance your commitments pertaining to your profession, family, health and spiritual aspects, this book is for you."

– Mukesh Gupta, Jt. Managing Director,
IRB Infra, Mumbai

"Thanks for sharing some great tips."

– Girish Bhat, Operating Partner, Samara Capital, Mumbai

"Thanks for sharing the gift you have worked so hard to refine. A valuable guide, the book provides a priceless compass enabling us to live a life of exemplary excellence. A must-read for all corporate executives."

— R. B. Sainani, Sr. Vice President, Gammon Engineers & Contractors Pvt. Ltd., Mumbai

"Packed with pearls of priceless wisdom, your treatise has a life-transforming power. It can trigger a virtuous cycle of incredible excellence."

— H. Jayakrishna, Head Quality Control, Dubai

"Excellent people management tips. The book shows how to create powerful synergies and achieve excellence in life. A thought-provoking work, indeed!"

— Chetan Ghelani, Chartered Accountant, Ahmedabad

"Profound and powerful, this book provides effective tools and techniques for achieving excellence. Great tips for drafting Personal Mission Statement. Practical and insightful wisdom at its best."

— S. Biswas, Project Director, Kolkata

"An inspiring game plan for the best use of your time. Also, a great tool for achieving exemplary professional success and fulfilling life through enriching interpersonal relationships."

— Chintan Shah, Proprietor, Handy Logistics, Mumbai

"A book with a writing style that is unique and fascinating with the power to transform the reader's life. Merits worldwide distribution."

— N. Acharya, General Manager (Engineering), Tripoli

"Thanks for sharing the gift you have worked so hard to refine. A valuable guide, the book provides a priceless compass enabling us to live a life of exemplary excellence. A must-read for all corporate executives."

— R. B. Sainani, Sr. Vice President, Gammon Engineers & Contractors Pvt. Ltd., Mumbai

"Packed with pearls of priceless wisdom, your treatise has a life-transforming power. It can trigger a virtuous cycle of incredible excellence."

— H. Jayakrishna, Head Quality Control, Dubai

"Excellent people management tips. The book shows how to create powerful synergies and achieve excellence in life. A thought-provoking work, indeed!"

— Chetan Ghelani, Chartered Accountant, Ahmedabad

"Profound and powerful, this book provides effective tools and techniques for achieving excellence. Great tips for drafting Personal Mission Statement. Practical and insightful wisdom at its best."

— S. Biswas, Project Director, Kolkata

"An inspiring game plan for the best use of your time. Also, a great tool for achieving exemplary professional success and fulfilling life through enriching interpersonal relationships."

— Chintan Shah, Proprietor, Handy Logistics, Mumbai

"A book with a writing style that is unique and fascinating with the power to transform the reader's life. Merits worldwide distribution."

— N. Acharya, General Manager (Engineering), Tripoli

Thank You, Esteemed Readers!

"Thanks a lot for your wonderful gift, **'The Twelve Steps to a Life of Exemplary Excellence'.** This life-enhancing book is immensely useful for the entire span of life, from studentship to retirement. I will not be surprised if this book is recommended as a reference manual in many educational institutes and corporate organisations."

— A. B. Desai, CEO, Gammon India Ltd., Mumbai

"Thank you very much for sharing your knowledge. A priceless resource, the book has enlightened us all, for which we are grateful to you forever. This book will create not only many time-efficient and successful executives but also great human beings. Perhaps no book has highlighted the importance of a principle-centered life so impactfully."

— M. Sambasiva Rao, Managing Director, Techno Unique Infratech, Hyderabad

"If you are experiencing stress arising from multi-faceted demands on your time and struggling to balance your commitments pertaining to your profession, family, health and spiritual aspects, this book is for you."

— Mukesh Gupta, Jt. Managing Director, IRB Infra, Mumbai

"Thanks for sharing some great tips."

— Girish Bhat, Operating Partner, Samara Capital, Mumbai

"A book that will truly unleash the fire within you and satisfy the basic human needs to love, grow and leave a life of legacy — a life of enduring meaning. An enlightening, down-to-earth and paradigm-shifting piece of work."

— Satyanarayan Shetty, Project Coordinator, Bengaluru

"A practical, direct-action personal improvement manual exquisitely covering management of time, life and people. Perhaps no book has stressed the need for people management so comprehensively."

— Jayesh Patil, IT Consultant, Pune

"A valuable resource, the book lucidly explains the complex process of achieving excellence in personal and professional lives. A master piece and a beacon of wisdom, it is indeed a life-transforming book."

— Kinjal Shah, Director, Kipraa Enterprise, Mumbai

"Timeless wisdom packaged in an understandable and useable fashion with plenty of quintessential, relatable examples. The book provides a holistic approach to achieving excellence.."

— Manoj Shah, Executive Engineer, Ahmedabad

"Deep meaning in short write-ups. Very effective tips for meeting deadlines. A one-stop shop for all desirous to achieve excellence in personal and professional lives."

— Riddhesh Mehta, Business Development, Amiand Consulting, Mumbai

"The twelve steps described in the book comprehensively covers all that is required for excelling in life. A guaranted receipe for exemplary excellence. A must-read if you want to achieve excellence in life."

—Rohit Tandon, Consulting Engineer, Chandigarh

"My life got completely transformed for good when I read the best-selling book titled 'The Power Of Positive Thinking' by Dr. Norman Vincent Peale. Your book has similar life-transforming power though it deals with the different topic. The tips and ideas presented in the book are worth implementing. The young generation can derive maximum benefit from the book."

—Dilip Desai, Sr. Vice President, Gammon India Ltd., Mumbai

" Superb insights. Simple yet powerful tips to transform our lives. A noble contribution."

—Pankaj Shah, Dy. Executive Engineer, Ahmedabad

Contents

Foreword .... *viii*
Preamble .... *x*
Preface .... *xi*
The Layered Learning Technique .... *xii*

1. What This Book Can Do For You 1
2. The Twelve-Step Formula: A Master Key to Excellence 3
3. The Five Core Elements of True Wealth 15
4. The Science Behind Living a Life of Excellence 41
5. The Art of Living a Life of Excellence: Laudable Philosophies and Avoidable Syndromes 70
6. Know Thyself And Focus More On Self-Improvement 97
7. The Art of People Management 125
8. Powerful Quotes 148
9. What Successful People Do 157
10. The Twenty Common Myths About Excellence 163
11. Philanthropy: A Precious Philosophy 166
12. Conclusion 169
13. Appendices 174
14. Bibliography 255

About The Author *256*

FOREWORD

It gives me a great pleasure to write this Foreword for the book **'The Twelve Steps to a Life of Exemplary Excellence'** by M. U. Shah.

My association with the author spans over two decades. The topic of achieving excellence in life has been close to the author's heart. A perpetual student of faculty of excellence and a consummate team player, the author walks his talk. The tips prescribed by the author have been put into practice by him and found to have worked with amazing success, making him a holistically successful corporate executive. The author shared this painstakingly acquired knowledge with fellow executives through PowerPoint presentations and workshops throughout the country and abroad. The phenomenal success of these workshops and their popularity inspired him to compose this wonderful book.

Comprehensive yet concise, this book stands out among many books on this subject. Blessed with unique writing talent, the author has used bullet points starting with verbs to offer readily actionable tips and avoided long essays. Whether it is the science behind living a life of excellence or creating a Personal Mission Statement, the message is sent across with impactful clarity.

Acknowledging the importance of enriching interpersonal relationships in successful personal and professional lives, the author has prescribed several useful people management tips to help readers develop a people-focused culture.

I have no hesitation in recommending this book as a valuable guide to those desirous of taking their personal and professional lives to the next level by excelling in every facet of life.

Dr. N. V. Nayak, Former Dy. Managing Director, Gammon India Ltd. and Principal Advisor, Gammon Engineers and Contractors Pvt. Ltd., Mumbai

PREAMBLE

*H*ave we ever wondered why some people are outstanding achievers and others are not? Why are only some people happy and others are not? How can we place ourselves in the first category rather than the second? How can we transform our lives to achieve excellence in whatever we do? How can we achieve true happiness in life?

Can we analyse the success stories of outstanding achievers in the world? Are there any common secrets to these successes? Can we identify the most common underlying factors in these successes? Can we replicate these successes? Is it possible to achieve excellence without paying a price in terms of deteriorating health or compromising the quality of family life?

If these questions arise in your mind, you are not in a minority. These are the most common questions that arise in everyone's mind at some stage or the other in their lives and answers are sought from different sources. This book was conceived to make available answers to such common questions that arise in everyone's mind.

The initial version of the book was in the form of Powerpoint presentations delivered to fellow corporate executives who were desirious to pursue excellence as a habit and were looking for a systematic approach which is replicable. This improved edition of the book addresses the above need and presents a thoughtfully conceived, scientifically designed and painstakingly refined twelve-step process to facilitate achieving exemplary excellence in personal and professional lives.

Acknowledging the importance of enriching interpersonal relationships in successful personal and professional lives, the author has prescribed several useful people management tips to help readers develop a people-focused culture.

I have no hesitation in recommending this book as a valuable guide to those desirous of taking their personal and professional lives to the next level by excelling in every facet of life.

Dr. N. V. Nayak, Former Dy. Managing Director, Gammon India Ltd. and Principal Advisor, Gammon Engineers and Contractors Pvt. Ltd., Mumbai

PREAMBLE

Have we ever wondered why some people are outstanding achievers and others are not? Why are only some people happy and others are not? How can we place ourselves in the first category rather than the second? How can we transform our lives to achieve excellence in whatever we do? How can we achieve true happiness in life?

Can we analyse the success stories of outstanding achievers in the world? Are there any common secrets to these successes? Can we identify the most common underlying factors in these successes? Can we replicate these successes? Is it possible to achieve excellence without paying a price in terms of deteriorating health or compromising the quality of family life?

If these questions arise in your mind, you are not in a minority. These are the most common questions that arise in everyone's mind at some stage or the other in their lives and answers are sought from different sources. This book was conceived to make available answers to such common questions that arise in everyone's mind.

The initial version of the book was in the form of Powerpoint presentations delivered to fellow corporate executives who were desirious to pursue excellence as a habit and were looking for a systematic approach which is replicable. This improved edition of the book addresses the above need and presents a thoughtfully conceived, scientifically designed and painstakingly refined twelve-step process to facilitate achieving exemplary excellence in personal and professional lives.

PREFACE

We all have the potential for a perfect life that is filled with happiness, joy, accomplishments and pure bliss. This potential may slumber deep inside us, waiting only to be tapped and unleashed. The noblest of pursuits is to ignite this fire for living a life of excellence. A life-transforming change towards personal excellence can happen in a blink of an eye if we commit to unleashing latent power slumbering deep inside us. For this to happen, every second of our time from now onwards counts.

Time is one of life's greatest equalizers. Everyone, no matter how intelligent or ignorant, accomplished or unskilled, rich or poor, receives the same twenty-four-hour gift every day. No one receives more; no one receives less. However, utilisation of this twenty-four-hour gift varies from person to person. This utilisation separates peak performers from weak performers or outstanding achievers from average achievers. Whereas weak performers always struggle to balance multi-faceted demands on their time and feel perpetually exhausted, peak performers take charge of their lives and proactively shape the events of their lives with ease. They are successful because they excel in whatever they do. Also, they achieve achieve such exemplary excellence with serenity and peace of mind.

This book is for those for whom good enough is not good enough. Prepared after extensive research of the available literature on the subject and decades of self-learning, this thought-stimulating book is designed to help readers in accelerating their journey towards a life of exemplary excellence.

THE LAYERED LEARNING TECHNIQUE

Consider using the Layered Learning Technique suggested below to derive the maximum benefit from this book:

Layer 1: The first time you read the book, you only get an overview. A few specifics may stand out but, by and large, the book's message will fade quite fast unless you layer it on some more.

Layer 2: The book's central idea is now clear to you and will not fade quickly. At this stage, highlight the points that appeal to you.

Layer 3: Upon the third reading, you understand the book well and the details stand out for you. You are now able to recite the insights of narration. The impressions created in your subconscious mind are now available when needed. This is the time to pause and listen to your heart and mind. You can now relate the materials to your life and see their practical applications. Your mind now slowly begins to function at an active 'how–to–apply' level. Prepare a written time-bound Action Plan for ideas or tips you feel are worth implementing.

Refresh your memory by periodic review of the highlighted portion of the book and quantitatively evaluate the progress achieved on the personal Action Plan prepared by you.

Update yourself periodically with the latest materials on the subject.

Multiply the knowledge gained by sharing it with others.

1

WHAT THIS BOOK CAN DO FOR YOU

This book is for you if you want to achieve exemplary excellence in your personal and professional lives with serenity and peace of mind.

The book supplies guidance in adopting and executing strategies that will enable living an enriching and fulfilling life leading to excellence. The book will also help you appreciate the difference between being rich and being wealthy. Whereas riches are about excesses and indulgences, being wealthy is about acquiring all elements of true wealth in a judiciously balanced manner.

Using this thought–stimulating book as a guide, you can improve your ability to do the following:

- Appreciate the importance of altruistic philosophy in life.
- Discover your passion and weave your life around your passion.
- Establish a strong and nobly altruistic 'why factor' that keeps driving you towards your mission even when the going gets tough.
- Achieve holistic success by judiciously balancing all elements of true wealth rather than an undue focus on monetary wealth.
- Develop a feeling of gratitude for the blessings showered on you.
- Develop a strong, positive attitude.
- Appreciate the value of time in your life and develop a deep personal sense of time.
- Organise your life around key priorities while eliminating non-essentials.

- Proactively take charge of your life by preparing an inspiring and empowering Personal Mission Statement (PMS) and plans covering the long, medium and short-term horizons.
- Deal more effectively with your family, friends, colleagues, boss and others and develop enriching relationships through transformational rather than transactional interaction.
- Delight your boss and customers - both internal and external with increased satisfaction.
- Increase your value manifold and empower yourself with the ultimate goal of 'moving the fulcrum over' and becoming a change catalyst for your family, team and organisation.
- Expanding your creativity and gaining more time for yourself to pursue your interests and passion.
- Live a life of legacy, a life of enduring meaning.

Packed with priceless wisdom, the book provides a compass to set the righteous direction in your life. It also offers many effective tools to realise your life's goals as per your priorities. This book is about fulfilment and freedom through sustainable techniques. This life-enhancing book will reignite the fire of meaning and purpose in your life and help you move ahead and scale new heights in your personal, professional, social and community lives.

That you have decided to invest your time in reading this book sets you apart from the vast majority of people. It shows that you are determined to take charge of your life. You deserve far more happiness, joy, accomplishments and pure bliss in your life. You can quickly have it if you keep practising each principle covered in the book until it becomes a part of your personality and habit in doing.

This book will do wonders for you. It will supercharge your life. Read it, apply it and share it. A perfect life - a life of exemplary excellence is yours for the taking.

2

THE TWELVE-STEP FORMULA: A MASTER KEY TO EXCELLENCE

*M*any of us treat excellence as synonymous with success. However, excellence is quite different from success. Success is how good you are in relation to the rest of the world. It is a comparison. Success is getting good grades, winning medals in competitions, etc. It requires external validation. Success doesn't necessarily mean doing one's best or doing one's best as a habit. Excellence, on the other hand, is how good you are in relation to how good you individually can be. Achieving excellence is being the best version of yourself each day. It's you continually improving and unleashing your limitless potential as a natural habit. Success has a finish line; there is no such finish line in a journey to excellence. Chasing success gives you only limited incremental gains with respect to the past benchmark. However, making excellence a habit will springboard you to limitless greatness of the next level. Excellence means the manufacture of mighty miracles. While success is characterised by the attachment to results, excellence is characterised by detachment. When you run after success, you always strive but never arrive. When you excel, you experience the utmost satisfaction. Success is transactional. Excellence is never transactional; it is always systematic.

While success may be achieved even by shortcuts, no shortcuts are available on the path to excellence. If you want to excel, you need to live a principle-centered life and build an impeccable character with spotless integrity. You need to painstakingly develop a culture of excellence which requires deep, structural-level transformations in your thoughts, mindset, attitudes, rituals, routines, habits, desires, actions and lifestyle. While success may be selfishly self-centric, excellence is always generously or magnanimously altruistic. Excellence means selflessly seeking ways to impact the lives of those around you. Success may make you a master, but excellence will make you a legend. Hence, don't madly run after success. Pursue excellence without confusing it with worldly success. Once you pursue excellence, success is bound to follow you.

The principles covered in the book apply to individuals as well as organisations. Living a life of excellence at the individual level means always striving to make a difference in whatever we do or wherever we go. Living a life of excellence is about the fanatical and passionate pursuit of daily improvements. We achieve excellence when we make every job, whether small or big, a self-portrait of ourselves. Each task we do should carry our brand. Each job we do should be our signature job. Excellence means surpassing the highest standards of expectations as a natural habit. It is a relentless hunger to continually strive to do better and better. It means always making exemplary contribution and making it so impactful that it is remembered for years to come.

At an organisational level, excellence means articulating an integrated approach that results in:

1) delivery of ever-improving value to the customers and stakeholders duly contributing to organisational sustainability and growth
2) improvement of overall organisational effectiveness and capabilities
3) organisational and personal learning.

The entire process of living a life of excellence is broken down into twelve simple and readily actionable steps. Though these steps substantially overlap and operate as a dynamic loop, these steps are presented as distinct steps only for ease of understanding.

While a detailed explanation of the above steps follows in subsequent chapters, a synopsis is presented below:

The Twelve-Step Formula: A Master Key to Excellence

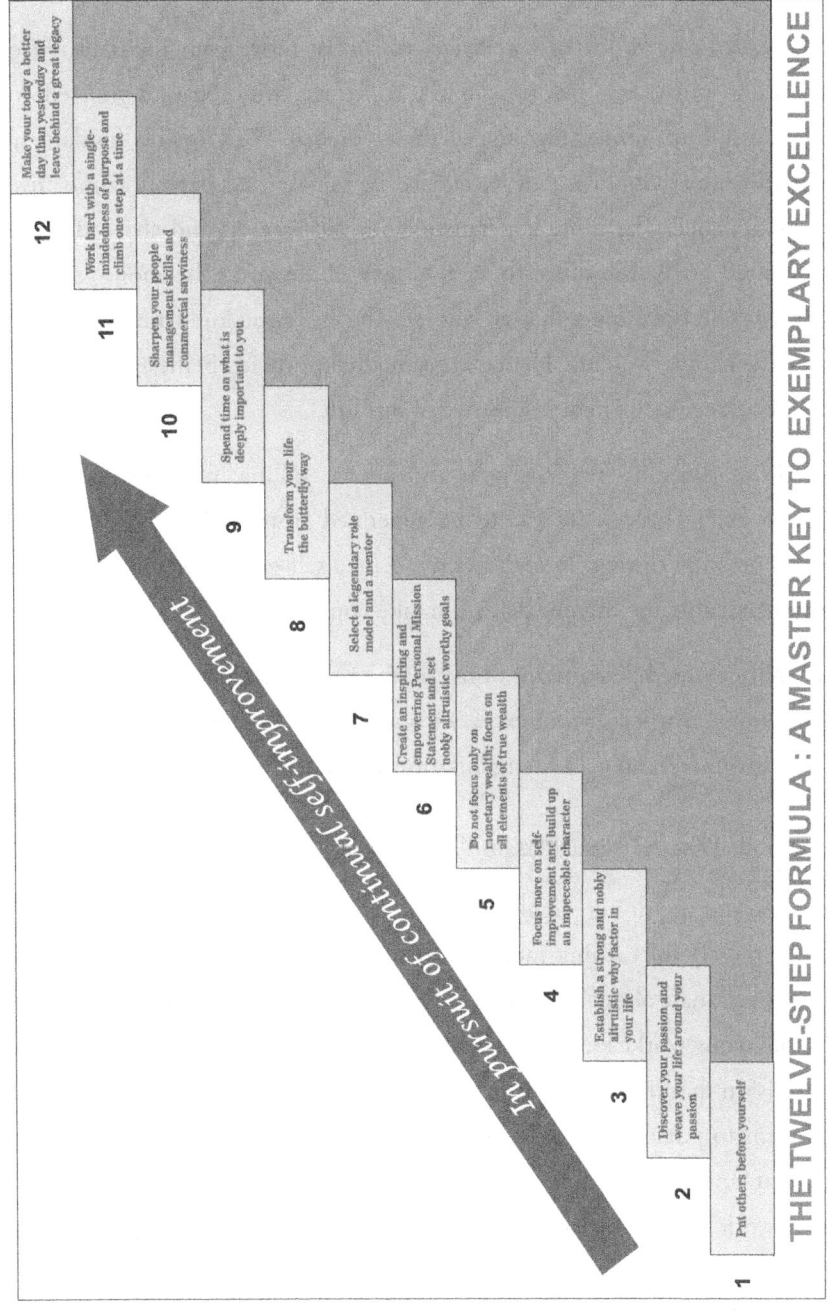

Step No. 1: Put others before yourself

If you want to live a life of excellence, you must move your focus away from yourself and put others before yourself. You must think beyond yourself. You must commit to something bigger than yourself. This is the fundamental prerequisite for living a life of excellence. A self-centred person cannot live a life of excellence. The more you pursue your self-interest and chase after your self-oriented goals, the more these aims will elude you. The more you think about yourself, the more unhappy you are. The more you lose yourself in serving others, the happier you are. Hence, continually improving Selflessness Quotient should become the primary objective of our life.

Apart from the shift in focus, you also need a killing instinct and a strong desire to excel. This desire has to be generated from within. No amount of external pressure can ignite such desire. Only a self-generated burning desire - an unquenchable fire in your belly, can take you to the top.

Like a self-centered person cannot live a life of excellence, an internally focused organisation can't become an excellent one. External focus, for example, focus on the customers, can lead to organisational excellence.

Step No. 2: Discover your passion and weave your life around your passion

The work you are doing should not be done merely for the sake of doing the work or merely for earning money. You should do it more for the reason that you are passionate about it. If you are not passionate about your work, you will not enjoy your work. Hence, discover your passion and create an empowering future vision that translates this passion into reality. Treat your job or profession as a means to pursue your passion; not a means to earn a livelihood. Once you find what you truly love doing, you will never have to work another day for the sake of work. Also, don't make money the center of your life. Money is bound to flow automatically on its own if your professional life is woven around your passion.

Step No. 3: Establish a strong and nobly altruistic why factor in your life

While IQ is important, we must also focus on YQ (Why Quotient), i.e., the why factor or why part of our life. Unless a strong why factor drives activities in our lives, we are likely to abandon our efforts midway when the going gets tough. Also, the why factor must be nobly altruistic – something bigger than ourselves. This is because a self-centric why factor is incapable of driving us through tough times. For example, a person who pursues solving some national or global burning issue is more likely to excel than a person who merely pursues his self-interest.

Perhaps the best example of a strong YQ is a poor single mother struggling to educate her children for a better future. She picks up household work to earn some money and pay her children's school fees. She continues to work even in her old age because the only objective of her life is to educate her children. One day, she is sick, having a fever with a 102-degree temperature. She is unable to get up from the bed. For a moment, a thought comes to her mind to stop working. She even questions herself, "Why am I doing all this?" A big tug-of-war takes place in her mind. However, eventually, the strong YQ wins and the next moment, she gets up from the bed and goes to work despite her fever. She could do this because she was not pursuing her self-interest; she was pursuing something bigger than herself. Though she is illiterate and her IQ is too low, she scores nine out of ten on YQ. She has no financial assets, but she possesses abundant contribution assets.

We need a reason to live - a compelling reason. Hence, establish some nobly altruistic why factor in your life that is so strong that it can keep driving you towards your mission even when the going gets tough.

Step No. 4: Focus more on self-improvement and build up an impeccable character

Improving ourselves is within our circle of influence. Changing others is outside our circle of influence and, hence, futile. Learn to accept others as they are.

Instead of struggling to change others, divert this energy to self-improvement. You will experience inner peace of mind if you focus on self-improvement traits like a positive attitude, a strong self-belief, an altruistic mindset, integrity, trustworthiness, humility, benevolence, kindness, gratitude and love. These are vital ingredients for the recipe of excellence.

Character is the noblest of all possessions. The essence of a person is his character. Our character shouldn't be a pack of cards. It should be built on rock. Building a character is a lifelong process. It is built up by the influence of the endless chain of choices or decisions we are called upon to make during our lives. If we want to excel, we need to painstakingly build (and maintain) our character piece by piece, making it impeccable, unblemished and spotless.

Step No. 5: Do not focus only on monetary wealth; focus on all elements of true wealth

True wealth comprises five core elements, viz. physical wealth, social wealth, time wealth, spiritual wealth and monetary wealth. Monetary wealth ranks last in the priority. Health is on top of the list. This is because physical excellence precedes mental excellence.

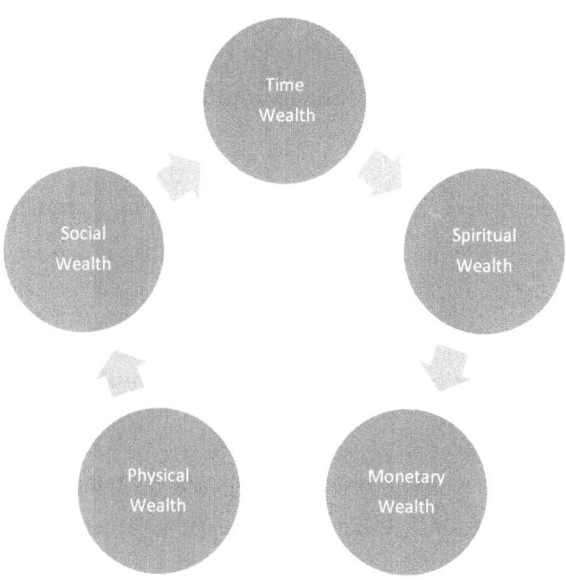

The analogy of a juggler smartly balancing five or more balls in his hands aptly explains our struggle to achieve a judicious balance between these five core elements of true wealth.

Material abundance is not the true success. Material abundance happens to be one of those things that makes the journey of life more enjoyable. But true success, apart from material abundance, also includes an exemplary, passion-driven professional career, good health, a fulfilling family life, enriching personal and professional relationships, knowledge, wisdom, a sound foundation of worthy principles, emotional and psychological stability, spiritual enlightenment, a philanthropically sensitive heart, eventual level of creative freedom as regards all five elements of true wealth and a sense of well-being with serenity and peace of mind. It is an incessant flow of all good things in abundance. The wealth of fulfilment occurs when the above five elements of true wealth intersect and are constantly being improved upon. When we are able to continually expand happiness and relentlessly pursue progressive realisation of nobly altruistic worthy goals with effortless ease duly embracing others around us, we achieve excellence. Excellence is a journey and not a destination. The relentless hunger to be the best version of ourselves each day leads us to an exciting and rewarding journey towards a life of exemplary excellence.

Step No. 6: Create an inspiring and empowering Personal Mission Statement and set nobly altruistic worthy goals

A PMS is a capsule statement of our life's predominant purpose. Inspiring and empowering, the PMS is the best drawing-board tool to systematically plan, design and articulate our lives. It allows you to envision a bigger picture of your life in an integrated manner. However, don't restrict your vision to yourself or your self-interest; magnanimously expand it to encompass nobly altruistic objectives. Also, remember, whatever our mind can conceive and believe, the mind can achieve. Hence, adopt blue-sky thinking and aim for the stars. Dream big. Be passionate about your dreams. Dreams are not to be seen while sleeping; they are ones which do not allow you to sleep.

Apart from the future path, the PMS should also lay down core values and principles around which you want to build your life. This will keep you on track whenever there are distractions. Once you have painted the picture of your life's mission, you can add a quantitative flavour to your vision by establishing challenging goals covering long, medium and short-term horizons. Setting ambitious goals with challenging deadlines and your firm resolve to achieve them makes your life interesting. Without worthy goals backed by a firm commitment, our life becomes dull and we have nothing to look up to. Hence, proactively take charge of your life with the help of a well-conceived PMS.

Step No. 7: Select a legendary role model and a mentor

If, for example, I want to become a cricketer, Sachin Tendulkar could be my role model. R. K. Laxman could be my role model if I want to become a cartoonist. If I want to become an eminent Civil Engineer, M. Visvesvaraya could be my role model. Role models could be active or passive. Our parents, teachers, or boss could be our active role models. Outstanding personalities of the world or the authors of the best-selling books could be our passive role models.

After selecting a suitable role model, start thinking and acting like him. We also need a mentor to guide us through our journey in life.

Step No. 8: Transform your life the butterfly way

To live a life of excellence, we will need changes or transformations that are radical or paradigm in nature; superficial transformations will not do. We will need changes that are structural in nature. These changes should take place at the blood level. It should take place at the level of the genes. It should take place at the DNA level.

We often use the butterfly analogy to explain the process of transformation. If we want to achieve any large-scale meaningful improvements in our lives, we must radically transform ourselves the way an ugly caterpillar transforms itself into a beautiful butterfly through an extremely painful metamorphosis process.

Step No. 9: Spend time on what is deeply important to you

Life is all about priorities. Hence, put first things first. The most important activities in our lives belong to Quadrant II of the Time Management Matrix. However, most of the time, we are busy fighting a fire or resolving some crisis that was preventable in the first place, leaving hardly any time for really important things. We often ignore activities like, preventive medical check-ups, building and nurturing relationships, or training employees. It is Quadrant II activities that will take our lives to new heights. We must ask ourselves what one thing we could do in our personal and professional lives that could make an atomic and positive impact on our lives if we do it regularly. Quadrant II activities have that kind of impact. Hence, eliminate all non-essentials and shift your focus from urgency to importance by subordinating the clock to the compass.

Step No. 10: Sharpen your people management skills and commercial savviness

Technical excellence or domain expertise alone is not enough to take us to the top. Apart from technical excellence, we also need people management skills and commercial savviness of the highest order. While technical excellence is important for the first few years of our professional career, people management skills and commercial savviness take precedence as we move up in the hierarchy.

Research on this subject reveals that in overall success, people management skills and commercial savviness occupy the lion's share.

Attribute	% Contribution in overall success
Technical excellence or domain expertise	20%
People Management skills	35%
Commercial savviness	45%
Total	100%

After gaining domain expertise, if we develop a people-focused culture and mastermind grand alliances, we achieve mind-boggling leverage. When this is further combined with commercial savviness of the highest order, we are bound to achieve outstanding success.

Step No. 11: Work hard with a single-mindedness of purpose and climb one step at a time

The road to success is always uphill and there is no shortcut. No escalator is available to reach the top. We need to take a staircase and painstakingly climb one step at a time with due pauses. Nothing good ever comes easy. If you want to excel, you have to be willing to do what average people are unwilling to do. We must come out of our comfort zone and stretch ourselves beyond our elastic limits. We must work hard with a single-mindedness of purpose. There is no substitute for hard work. Pursuing excellence requires developing a hustle involving many sacrifices, sweat, hard work, long days and a strong determination. Remember, if you are determined to put in hard work and possess unwavering self-confidence, even a mountain is not unconquerable because it isn't taller than your confidence. It will be under your feet when you reach the top.

Step No. 12: Make your today a better day than yesterday and leave behind a great legacy

What we do today is what matters most. However, it is our biggest defeat if we are the same as yesterday. Our today should be better than yesterday. Our aim for today should be higher than the achievement of yesterday. We must improve ourselves every day. We must continually upgrade our intellectual capacity, uplift the level of spiritual enlightenment and learn and practice something good every day. If we can get one percent better each day for one year, we will end up 37 percent better at the end of the year. Hence, learn to crave for excellence as a habit.

So far, about 120 billion people have lived on this earth, including the current population of nearly ten billion. Out of these 120 billion people, we remember only those 400 to 500 people who made outstanding contributions to the world; the rest are forgotten. Thus, on average, only one person out of 250 million persons is remembered.

Eminent personalities like Isaac Newton, Albert Einstein, Nelson Mandela, Helen Keller and Mother Teresa will be remembered for many centuries to come.

They were all ordinary people like us, with no privileges. Then, what was the secret of their outstanding success? Do we find anything common in this elite club of 500 eminent people? The most important thing in common among them is that they lived their life for the benefit of others. None of them was self-centered. They could conquer great heights because they passionately pursued a noble cause instead of their self-interest. The driving force behind their success was their altruistic intentions. These success stories reinforce our central idea that puts a strong emphasis on serving others. Another thing in common among them is their hard work and perseverance. They stretched themselves beyond elastic limits. Despite many obstacles and multiple failures, they never gave up nor enforced any artificial limits on their thinking. They had an unwavering belief in themselves.

Thoughtfully conceived, scientifically designed and painstakingly refined, this twelve-step formula is the master key to excellence. Thousands of readers of this book and participants of the workshops conducted by the author have accelerated their journey towards a life of excellence by following these steps.

You, too, can become a member of an elite club of such top achievers and leave behind a great legacy. You have everything in you to achieve outstanding success.

At first glance, readers may find incongruities in these steps. You may find that the requirements of one step conflict with those of other steps. However, such contradictions will disappear if you think deeply enough and hard enough. Also, even if you find some contradictory directions from two or more steps in some peculiar situations, these contradictions are to be resolved by giving overriding power to one of the considerations, which is relatively more important.

While these twelve steps are presented sequentially in the above synopsis, the detailed explanation of each step is placed in the appropriate chapters, not necessarily in the same sequence.

3

THE FIVE CORE ELEMENTS OF TRUE WEALTH

There is no universally accepted definition of wealth. People define wealth depending on what is considered desirable by them. If we go by the most common definition, wealth means a plentiful supply of desirable things. Wealth means an abundance of valuable possessions, resources or money. Most people relate wealth to material prosperity or the state of being rich and accordingly they assign unduly excessive importance to material possessions, like big houses or luxury cars. Of course, money is very much necessary in our lives and we need to have enough money to secure sufficient food and clothing for us and our family, provide a roof over our heads and meet other basic needs to free us from undue anxiety. Hence, money should be treated as a necessary resource that should serve individuals and families as they seek happiness, fulfilment, and meaning in life. Money is merely a vehicle or tool to achieve financial freedom. With money, we can pursue our passion and go after our dreams. We can design our life to make us feel alive and fulfilled. In that sense, the desire to maximise monetary wealth is understandable, but should this be the only purpose of our life? Many desirable aspects of life have nothing to do with money. There is a lot more to wealth than just money. Monetary wealth is not true wealth. True wealth includes those things that we value more than money. However, in our mad pursuit to run after money, we often neglect essential activities, like caring for our health, spending time with our loved ones, or pursuing our spiritual well-being.

This book will enlighten you about true wealth and show you how to compound the same in your life. You will understand how to treasure the things that give you immense happiness, something that is not achievable through monetary wealth.

3.1 TODAY'S BLESSED GENERATION

We are the most blessed generation in the history of human beings. Never before has there been so much material prosperity, such generous freedom of thought and the vastness of opportunities available. Today, many people have access to luxury items, like lavishly furnished large houses, expensive cars, supercomputers and smart mobile phones. A generation ago, access to such material wealth was available only to a handful of wealthy people. Similarly, today it is possible for people to express themselves freely and as regards the availability of opportunities, the sky is the limit for fulfilling one's aspirations. There are several examples where ordinary people from poor backgrounds have reached the top in various fields, including politics. However, despite all the material prosperity, freedom of thought, and vast opportunities, the modern generation is perhaps the unhappiest generation of all time. It is suffering from ills, like poor health, obesity, stress at the workplace, insomnia, absence of serenity and peace of mind, and poor interpersonal relationships. This surely needs introspection individually and also collectively as a society.

3.2 INCREASING UNHAPPINESS: MALADIES AND REMEDIES

Why are people not so happy in the present times despite so much material wealth? What is preventing them from treasuring true happiness? Well, the list is quite long. However, a few critical things that make people unhappy are enumerated below, together with corresponding remedies:

3.2.1 Mad pursuit of success

We often associate happiness with success. We are happy if we achieve what we desire; otherwise, we feel unhappy. Associating happiness with success is a trap that takes joy away from us. This is because it is not possible to achieve success all the time. There will always be some failures. It is a law of nature. Also, even when we achieve a certain level of success, we are not satisfied and desire more success. We keep setting higher parameters of success until we can no longer achieve it. Despite many accomplishments, we remain perpetually unhappy because we focus on what is not achieved.

In उपनिषद (India's ancient Sanskrit text of spiritual teaching), the rishis have given a metaphor of a mirage to explain the dilemma that human beings face when they spend their lifetime here on this earth. If you travel on a tarmac road on a hot sunny day in summer, you may get an illusory impression, as if there is a small pool of water or oil ahead of you at some distance, though there is no such water or oil. These kinds of illusions are called mirages. A thirsty deer gets trapped in the hot summer by such shimmering but illusive water glaze. He runs from one glaze to another with no success and eventually falls down tired, more thirsty, dehydrated, and disappointed. Hindus call this मृग-तृष्णा -an insatiable, deer-like desire that can never be fulfilled.

Like the deer, we also fall into the trap of mirage as we are prone to get enticed and deluded by the illusion of happiness created by greed and lust inside us. We madly run after position, status, money, people, and many other ephemeral things, though we know we can never satisfy our greed or lust even if we spend our entire life chasing such things. The person who lives like a deer running for one mirage after the other is likely to be disappointed over time. The mirage or illusion means that which appears real but is non-existent. In the absence of enlightenment, we run after such a false illusion. Lord Buddha stressed that such desire is the root cause of our suffering and many incarnations. The enlightened person calls it माया (an alluring worldly charm) and its attraction, being like a mirage, is not worth chasing. He, therefore, wishes to acquire only those things that are not short-lived, do not give sorrow or grief and, above all, do not compel him to attachment or bondage. Therefore, he seeks freedom and lasting happiness instead of bondage and suffering. He does not fall prey to the false glitter and charm of the physical world. Neither is the enlightened person sorrowful at the loss of the unreal things of the physical world nor is he overly joyful or arrogant when he receives such things. This is because the enlightened person practices detachment.

We can learn to detach ourselves from the illusory माया of the transitory world by having the right perspective and seeing the actual state of things as they are and by shifting the focus and mind's attention from temporary to everlasting elements. We can create awareness and control what we think all day and what goes on behind our current thoughts in our subconscious minds. Through various spiritual and yogic activities, we can eliminate and exterminate those recurring thoughts of illusion and replace them with divine thoughts by reflection, introspection, and contemplation of the almighty God. Slowly, the restless and wandering mind calms down and does not stir unnecessarily.

3.2.2 The habit of unhealthy comparison

From childhood, our mind is conditioned to believe that we must be better than others. Though only one out of thirty to forty students in a class can get 1st rank, all parents expect their child to get 1st rank. This builds up undue pressure on a child's mind. The child who gets the 2nd rank does not feel happy about his achievement but curses himself for missing the 1st rank. This childhood habit continues even in adulthood. We keep comparing ourselves to others and become unhappy when we come across a relatively more successful person.

When we focus on competing with relatives, friends, colleagues or neighbours, trying to outperform them, or trying to prove our superiority or importance, we miss on our happiness within our surroundings. We spend our time and energy chasing them at the cost of our happiness. The problem with unhealthy competition is that it never ends. There will always be someone ahead of us with more education, a better job, a nicer car, a larger bank balance, a prettier spouse, better-behaved children, etc.

Remember, a comparison is the surest way to a perpetual unhappiness. No one compares himself to someone who is lower down and comes out even. Nine times out of ten, we compare ourselves to people who are better than us and in the process; we end up feeling more inadequate and develop an inferiority complex. While comparison with a positive approach to achieving excellence is fine, it is not in order if it makes you feel inferior. If, for example, your neighbour's latest model of Mercedes car makes you unhappy and feel inferior though you possess an economy sedan, then there is a need to introspect. If we are in a continuous state of unhappiness because of such comparisons, we must reorient our minds as to how we view and interpret comparisons. Remember, you can be the best when you are not competing with anyone. Some people are insecure because they pay too much attention to what others are and what others are doing.

Accept whatever you have and be grateful that you are blessed. Count your blessings. The phrase 'Count your blessings' is more than just an empty platitude. It's a philosophy to live by. There is no competition in destiny. Each has his own. Comparisons and competitions are the biggest thieves of joy. It kills the joy of living your own life. Hence, feel blessed by comparing yourself with those below you rather than feeling inferior by comparing to those above you.

3.2.3 Excessive materialism

Most rich people value themselves not based on human qualities, but on what they possess. They seek more wealth and accumulate material things, hoping it will give them more happiness. When they don't get happiness, they seek even more wealth and work even harder. They become part of the rat race that never ends and in the process, they never enjoy life.

If we continue chasing money and material possessions madly, true and lasting happiness will keep eluding us. We must learn to practice contentment and treat money merely as a medium of exchange - a means to a good life and not an end in itself. We must learn to derive happiness in non-material things like love, relationships, friendships, reading, writing, music, or painting. These things need a little money.

3.2.4 External validation

Most people seek happiness through external validation. They seek praise and endorsement of their wealthy status from others. They pay too much attention to the outward appearance of their body. They wear branded clothes and expensive watches and carry the latest smartphones. They give more importance to monetary wealth, material possessions, social status, power, fame, reputation and winning in arguments rather than basic human values like integrity, trust worthiness, humility, benevolence, kindness, gratitude, and love. They feel happy when they are appreciated and unhappy when others ignore or criticise them. Such people's happiness depends on others they try to please. This way, they rarely find lasting happiness since one can't please all the people all the time. Some people are always critical of us. Seeking happiness through external validation by others is like handing over a remote control of our happiness to someone else. They will make us happy or unhappy at their will. Thus, if you are attached to being right or need something external to be at peace or be successful, you will live a life of striving but never arriving.

Instead, we must try to discover happiness within ourselves. Our happiness starts with us, not with our money, job, designation, or external validation. It is easier to find happiness within ourselves. It is rather impossible to find lasting happiness elsewhere. If we know ourselves well and identify our passion, we can live according to our nature and discover the source of joy within us. No one can take away our happiness from us when its origin is within us. Hence, we must direct all our actions towards achieving true happiness from within ourselves. Aristotle wisely said, "Inner happiness is the meaning and the purpose of life, the whole aim, and the end of human existence."

3.2.5 Poor state of mind

Happiness is a state of mind. Many people are unsatisfied even if they possess more money than they could ever spend. They continuously strive to accumulate more and more money. They are caught in a perpetually fearful and poor state of mind. Sadly, they will never have enough because their entire identity is tied to their material wealth, not to who they truly are in each present moment—a realisation they have not discovered.

Normally, we relate poverty to the poverty of monetary wealth. However, when viewed in the context of the overall scheme of life with a broader perspective, the above perception of poverty appears quite narrow and incomplete and needs re-consideration. Financial poverty is not the biggest poverty; the biggest poverty is the poverty of character and values. It is one of the worst diseases that plague different parts of society today. People who don't value character may adopt unfair means initially on a small scale. However, once they get access to easy money, their craving to accumulate more money increases exponentially. Before they realise what is happening, this craving becomes an uncontrollable addiction and they keep accumulating even more money by large-scale unfair means. Similarly, no quality defines poverty as much as poverty of humility. When we think we are bigger than what we really are and worse, when we think we are better than others, we push ourselves over the cliff and into the dark abyss of life. No helping hands are found on the way down because we might have unwittingly rejected them. Even if there are people to help us, our ego will prevent us from breaking the fall and climbing back to our rightful place.

Similar is the case with the poverty of dreams. Life is likened to a feather carried by the aimless winds of life when there is nothing to look forward to and nothing to live and fight for. Hence, discover your purpose. Nothing is more tragic than living without a sense of meaning and purpose. When you hold on with a determination to your higher calling, you can tap into the infinite wealth our creator has generated for you. He has opened a personal checking account with unlimited resources you can draw upon to fulfil his worthwhile causes.

Ultimately, poverty becomes permanent when there is poverty of the right action. If you take the right action, you will live a balanced life. You will live life to the fullest. You can't improve your life if you do not take the right action and enough of them. Somehow, you will be going around in circles and regressing in life and then you may never escape the clutches of poverty. Hence, break this vicious cycle, put yourself on the path to sustainable wealth - true wealth, and see how this virtuous cycle revolutionises your life.

3.3 THE PHILOSOPHY OF TRUE WEALTH

How will you know when you've achieved true wealth? Is it when you have your dream home? Or is it once you own an expensive luxury car? Perhaps the biggest signifier is when you're wealthy enough to have your private jet. A few elite people have multiple mansion-sized homes in different parts of the world, have several luxury sports cars parked in their garages, and own a private jet that takes them to and from their vacation homes. Are such people happy in their lives? Have they achieved such success without causing damage to their health? Such people may not necessarily have access to true wealth. None of these is an indicator of true wealth; at best, these are indicators of monetary wealth and monetary wealth by itself doesn't give lasting happiness.

While many people emphasise the importance of having an abundance of money, few understand the meaning of true wealth. Money and wealth may appear synonymous to many of us. Many factors influence our concepts and opinions about money, riches and wealth. In childhood, we observe how our parents treat money. Then, in school years, folks learn to mentally separate the 'rich kids' from the 'not-so-rich', all while measuring where they fit into this framework. We are incessantly bombarded with advertisements of luxury goods as if possessing such goods is the only objective of life. This divides our society into two sections: those who are proudly possessing such goods and those who can't afford such goods. Thus, the external environment also influences our concepts about money.

What is true wealth, then? To appreciate the righteous philosophy of true wealth, we need to introspect and redefine wealth. As rightly stated by Warren Buffett, wealth is a state of mind. True wealth is having a sense of abundance that we experience rather than possess. True wealth is an inner condition of being. It is about having a contended mind. It means control over insatiable desire. Wealthy people always have enough. People seeking more and more riches never have enough. Richness is not earning more, spending more, or saving more. Richness is when you need no more. So long as there is a desire for more money, one can't be at peace. One will always be craving to get more. One accomplishment will ignite a desire for another one. To some extent, it is understandable so long as your failure to achieve success doesn't make you unhappy, but eventually, one should be free from such desires and transcend to a life of desirelessness. Thus, if an insatiable desire for more money stands in the way of happiness, it is not true wealth.

Most enlightened people believe that true wealth has nothing much to do with money. True wealth means seeking more personal growth (including spiritual growth) and transcending to a life of excellence. It means exploring creative ways to add more meaning to life and leaving behind a great legacy rather than madly running after illusive success. When you follow the above definition of wealth and focus on optimising each element of true wealth, monetary riches are bound to follow. True wealth is the ability to live life on your terms. It's about freedom. It means possessing the ability to enjoy even the small and ordinary pleasures of life. True wealth means treasuring life moment by moment. It is living in the present moment and garlanding it. It means being in life and appreciating all aspects of it. It is about self-awareness, self-enlightenment and living with a purpose. True wealth is about being committed not only to one's happiness but also helping others find theirs. True wealth is the ability to use your available resources, however limited they may be, for the well-being of others. True wealth can be shared with near and dear ones and those who need it the most. While using wealth for oneself may give only momentary pleasure without extinguishing the craving for further wealth; sharing it with others will provide lasting satisfaction. Thus, wealth is not only about money; it's also about embracing the other tenets of true wealth.

3.4 THE FIVE CORE ELEMENTS OF TRUE WEALTH

Besides money, true wealth encompasses many other facets of one's life. The five core elements of true wealth are elucidated below:

3.4.1 Physical Wealth

"Health is a state of complete physical, mental and social well-being and not merely the absence of disease or infirmity."
- World Health Organisation

Our health is our true wealth. Health is the glue that holds the other wealth and one's life together. Without good health and the physical vitality of our bodies, we can't sustainably achieve other wealth. Putting health first is extremely important if you want a fulfilling life. Most people fail to invest in their bodies and minds and don't consider health as a vital component of true wealth. We take our health for granted until we lose it. When we are young, we will compromise our health for monetary wealth, but when we are old, we will gladly sacrifice all of our wealth for just a little bit of our health. As we age and approach the end of our lives, health attains the topmost priority, replacing all those so-called big things we were used to relentlessly chasing in our younger days. Hence, respect your body, fuel your body, challenge your body, move your body and above all, love your body.

Physical wealth comprises understanding and mastering the following fundamentals:

- Disease-free, healthy body and healthy mind with positive thoughts.
- Physical, mental, social and spiritual well-being.
- Proper nutrition, exercise, meditation, yoga, sound sleep etc.
- Proper training and conditioning of the body and its movement.
- An understanding of energy systems (breakdown and repair).
- Healthy environment (people and place) and health literacy.
- Absence of anger, hate, jealousy, fear and all types of negativity.
- Avoiding the temptation to madly run after money at the cost of our health.

3.4.2 Social Wealth

Social wealth or status is one of the most underrated wealth. We rarely think of status as wealth. We understand that status has value, but we never make the connection that it's a type of wealth.

Social wealth largely comes down to how you interact within the social world. Social wealth relates to connectedness and how we fulfil our social and emotional needs by interacting with others. It means sharing and belonging. We feel validated when we are with people. We need each other. Social connection is social wealth. The importance of social wealth can be appreciated from the fact that we can't build other wealth without social wealth and we can't build social wealth alone by ourselves. Spending time with people who care about you makes you feel good. So be open to new relationships, whether it's someone you meet at the office, gymnasium, park, or temple. Maintain those connections lifelong. Studies show the more connected you are, the more happy you are. Social wealth also means what kind of character you build up and how others perceive this character.

Social wealth comprises understanding and mastering the following fundamentals:

- A passion-based, fulfilling professional career.
- An impeccable character and good reputation.
- What you will or will not do to build your monetary wealth.
- Clarity about what you do and don't stand for. Do you stand up for a cause like preserving forests?
- An enriching and fulfilling family life.
- Developing and nurturing enriching personal and professional relationships by understanding human nature and psychology.
- Treating others respectfully, especially those who have less monetary wealth than you do.

3.4.3 Time Wealth

Time wealth means control on your time and the freedom to spend your time as per your desire. It means freedom to spend your time how you want, where you want and with whom you want. Creating a big business empire from a scratch is fine, but if you remain bogged down in its day-to-day affairs on a 24X7 basis, leaving no time to pursue other activities of your interest, you haven't achieved true success. Time wealth is about flexibility and freedom. Your endeavour should be to create the circumstances that enable you to experience life fully regardless of where you fall on the income and wealth spectrum. Most people desperately want such freedom, but it has become rare in the modern day because they spend all of their time (and also other resources) running after money.

Time wealth comprises understanding and mastering the following fundamentals:

- Acknowledging that time is finite.
- Spending time wisely on things that are deeply important to you.
- Deciding your priorities and putting first things first.
- Focusing on Quadrant II of the Time Management Matrix.
- Earning money outside a traditional job structure.
- Understanding how most people trade time for money and avoid this trap. Ensure all of your time isn't spent only on earning money.
- Freedom to retire early without any financial worries.

3.4.4 Spiritual Wealth

The spiritual wealth is the wealth that is dependent on our own state of being rather than material possessions or external circumstances. It is all about self-awareness and enlightenment. Your inner world largely determines your outer world. Your inner world comprises the thoughts that incessantly churn in your subconscious mind, the quality of your thoughts and the resultant peace of mind. It determines your self-worth and your connection to your core. Are you living up to your true values or doing things based out of fear and worry?

Does the internal voice of your soul try to prevent you when you are about to do something dishonest and unfair? Thus, who you are from the inside determines the quality of your life. Also, if your are not spiritually enlightened, your attention may shift according to your self-interest.

Spiritual wealth requires searching for answers to the following introspection-provoking questions:
- Do you honour all religions and those who don't believe in God?
- Do you connect with your higher self?
- Do you pray? Do you meditate? Do you stay in silence? Do you single-task (as opposed to multi-task)?
- What is your practice for connecting with and managing your emotions and feelings? Are your emotions as pure as that of a child? Have you mastered your emotions?
- What do you do to treasure the present moment while you work to design and build your future?
- Have you learnt the art of managing expectations? Can you control your insatiable desire for more and more monetary wealth?
- Have you mastered the art of detachment?

You are spiritually wealthy when you achieve full control over your emotions, stay positive, practice gratitude, connect with others, develop a sense of meaning and purpose and develop coping skills.

3.4.5 Monetary Wealth

Many people erroneously focus only on monetary wealth. Despite the accumulation of ample money and monetary assets, they don't achieve financial freedom. Money is extremely important and makes the world go round and without financial goals, life becomes mundane and boring. Accordingly, becoming a millionaire is a valid desire for everyone, and pursuing the same is advocated rather than discouraged so long as means are honest and fair. However, financial success is only a part of life's purpose, not the only purpose. There is more to life beyond money. There is no higher success than building and maintaining a fulfilling life with meaning and purpose. Achieving financial freedom is more important than merely accumulating money. You should aim to be free from financial turmoil and worries, which is one of the prime causes of suffering in most people's lives. If we madly chase only monetary wealth and invite its undesirable side effects into our lives, is such success worth it?

What's your game plan to secure a financially sound future? Holistically achieving financial freedom comprises understanding and mastering the following fundamentals:

- Living a principle-centered life.
- Adopting altruistic philosophy.
- Building goodwill ahead of earning income.
- Earning income through honest and fair means.
- Long, medium and short-term financial planning.
- Consciously allocating resources, i.e. budgeting.
- Saving a pre-determined amount every month with a disciplined approach.
- Judiciously balancing necessities v/s luxuries, i.e. spending money wisely.
- Financial Literacy, i.e. reading, podcasts, events, etc.
- Surrounding yourself with financial masters.
- Creating and compounding income-generating assets by prudent investing.
- Living a debt-free life.
- Holistic retirement planning from an early age.
- Philanthropically sensitive heart.

Picture yourself in the future, where you never have to worry about money ever again. Imagine how that would make you feel. This will change your family situation and interactions with the world and people around you. It's an amazing feeling. Well, it's possible to achieve this kind of life one day as long as you make a personal commitment to the process of mastering financial wealth. Financial wealth will keep compounding if these fundamentals are constantly worked on and improved upon.

While acknowledging that money is extremely important, remember that people don't seek money to satisfy material needs alone. Craving for money beyond a certain level is because of other uses of money. Also, in a mad pursuit of accumulating excessive wealth, people often compromise their values and ethics. The temptation of easy wealth to a human is unbounded by time or geography.

They say films mirror society. People endorse those films which relate to themselves. Hollywood filmmaker Oliver Stone produced the famous film Wall Street (1984), in which Michael Douglas played Gordon Gekko. He became one of the most memorable characters in US cinema history because he is financially successful. His signature line, 'Greed, for lack of a better word, is good.' became viral. It doesn't matter that he is unethical, selfish, greedy, or a terrible human being. Americans became obsessed with material wealth in the 1980s. People didn't care about a person's values; they cared only about their money. 'Greed is good' was just the validation they needed.

Why do people accumulate so much wealth by unfair means that they couldn't possibly spend in their lifetimes? The root cause is the undue importance our society has attached to money. Money gives stature. You get a certain place in today's society that is above others if your house is big, your car is expensive, or your parties are lavish. We celebrate rich lists and people who live in expensive houses. We make TV shows about extravagant weddings and judge people on their residential addresses. Today, a woman decked in diamond jewellery, carrying a branded designer bag and wearing expensive sandals may be seen as of higher stature than a schoolteacher in a cotton sari who teaches hundreds of kids. People who earn high salaries make more news than selfless doctors who help the poor. In such a societal setup, the temptation to seek wealth, irrespective of the means, is always high. Money also gives a sense of security. This is a genuine benefit of money. Securing retired life is about building assets in your working life to be used later. The irony is, no matter how much you have, if you don't fundamentally value yourself from within, you never feel that status despite the millions stashed away. That is why corrupt people keep on accumulating money until they get caught. They also think that with money, they can escape legal punishments. However, eventually, the crime gnaws at them from within and they can never be at peace.

Those who build monetary wealth by unfair means accumulate money for sure, but they haven't accumulated Lakshmi.

3.5 LAKSHMI

Lakshmi and money may seem similar, but they are not the same. As we pray to the Goddess Lakshmi, the Goddess of material wealth, we must introspect as regards our means of accumulating wealth.

While money can also be accumulated by unfair means, Lakshmi is wealth accumulated through honest and fair means. Money accumulated through unfair means brings unhappiness, fear, sleepless nights and emptiness to the soul. Lakshmi brings serenity, peace of mind and true happiness to the person who painstakingly earns it.

If even by honest and fair means, we can earn so much that we can't spend during our entire life, is there a need to adopt dishonest and unfair means? So, when you pray, ask not for money but Lakshmi – wealth earned through honest and fair means that keeps the mind as peaceful and pias as the lotus. The corrupt who steal from others don't appreciate this difference. No matter how big their parties or how lavish their puja ceremonies are, they do not possess the true Lakshmi.

3.6 BASIC PREREQUISITES FOR LIVING A LIFE OF EXCELLENCE

If we want to experience true wealth and live a life of excellence, we must holistically build our lives. Following are some of the basic prerequisites for living a life of excellence:

3.6.1 Enriching and fulfilling family life

Having loved ones around you and being able to see them whenever you choose is a crucial part of success. Your job or business is extremely important, but a distant second to your family. The greatest support system in the world is good family and friends. You can't be careless here. You need great relationships with your family and friends who make you a better and more complete person. Remember, you can't change your family easily and trying to do so will cause you endless stress and frustration. Love them and appreciate them as they are.

3.6.2 Best professional career which is woven around your passion

The attitude you bring to your days determines your destiny and it's extremely hard to carry a great attitude when you don't enjoy what you do. However, the recent Gallup survey shows nearly 70% of employees are actively disengaged at work.

Think deeply and figure out your strengths. Discover your passion. Purposefully choosing (or creating) your ideal professional career is crucial to a fulfilling life. When you love what you do, you are not working for money but enjoying your work. It's essential to get to the end of your career knowing you gave your best. Never settle low. Of course, life is not easy. It doesn't guarantee a smooth journey. Unexpected circumstances can derail you completely, but how you adapt and adjust yourself will determine what happens next. Be in control of your future by making the right choices

3.6.3 Best circle of genius

Are the people you're associating with contributing to holding you to higher standards and challenging you? If you spend time with people playing at a world-class level, your chances of doing the same increase substantially. Their ways of being will rub off on you. You'll adapt their philosophies and perspectives.

3.6.4 World-class experiences

Life is an adventure. Experiences and memories separate the elite lives from the mediocre. Hence, focus more on producing memorable experiences over material things. You may like both and appreciate the finer things in life, but after studying countless world-class people, it's clear they are constantly creating memorable experiences. What's the point of doing something if you're not having fun?

3.6.5 Philanthropically sensitive heart

Generosity is the key that unlocks happiness. There is no greater feeling than when you help or give something to others without any expectations. Whether it is a compliment or a small gift, do something nice for somebody every day.

3.6.6 Extraordinary impact and legacy

The worthiest aim of life is service to the world around us. How much difference are you making in the world around you? Are you adding consistent value that improves the lives of others?

3.7 WHAT CONSTITUTES TRUE WEALTH

While some richer folks all the time may feel broke, someone with a lower income may think of themselves as wealthy. It ultimately boils down to what you think of your needs, assets and money. However, there is something called true wealth that is vital to make a person wealthy, and true wealth has not so much to do with money as with the state of mind.

Here's what true wealth is all about:

3.7.1 Not the branded clothes, but the healthy body that can wear them is a true wealth

Many of us are madly crazy about the brands. We are so obsessed with the brands that we even flaunt them. If we can't afford the real ones, we buy their first copies or duplicates even if it means lower quality than some non-branded good-quality clothes. We like to put a fad and live that way. However, it is not the brands of our clothes that decide how wealthy we are; the healthy body that allows us to fit into those clothes is the real asset. Being healthy, caring for our body and having good eating habits should be our priority.

3.7.2 Not those expensive mattresses, but the sound sleep you get is a true wealth

Rich people may have expensive mattresses, but do they get sound sleep? Getting sound sleep is what matters, not your mattress's price tag.

3.7.3 Not the lavish royal house, but the people making it home is a true wealth

We often envy people with large houses. We wish we had access to adequate money to own a large house. However, they may have no communication since all are busy in their private rooms and have their own things to do. On the other hand, a smaller yet comfortable house may not have lavish private rooms for all the family members, but the family may be happy and bonded well. The people who live in the house make it a home, not bricks and mortar. Agreed, a house is a basic need, but that need shouldn't be satisfied only by a big house. If you have your family bonded, it is your true wealth, irrespective of the square foot or value of the house. Though real estate is an asset worth acquiring, it is not bigger than family bonding.

3.7.4 Not the new luxury car, but the long drives you share with your loved ones is a true wealth

If you think owning a luxury car is a sign of wealth, you need to rethink. A car is an asset and a means to an end to commuting comfortably. It enables you to go on drives with your loved ones, and it is good to have one. But again, the car's real worth is its utility for sharing with your loved ones. To have people come with you on long drives, to have loved ones smile when they are with you in your car and the wonderful memories are priceless, not the car, per se. A car is a continuously depreciating asset. Let us not judge how wealthy people are by looking at the price tag of their cars.

3.7.5 Not the great status you have in society because of your income, but the blessing of your parents is a true wealth

We often spend most of our lives in our office cubicles to please our bosses, for whom we are merely employees with six-digit codes on the payroll. Though some companies care for employees and are great to work with, the million-dollar question is, 'Are you enjoying your work? If you are a workaholic and working hard, thinking that every next promotion should be yours, well, it is good to have an ambition, but in that ambition, what you are forgoing is what matters. Being able to please others with your designation is good, but not a great way to live. Your life is slipping between cubicles, PowerPoint presentations and airport check-ins. Before you know it, your kids have grown up, your wife may have stopped her life for you and your parents are too old to appreciate your money since they only want to see your face. Having parents to bless you is the biggest asset you can have.

3.7.6 Not the latest expensive smartphone, but having people to call and talk at the other end is a true wealth

Being able to buy the latest gizmos and gadgets is good. That latest smartphone has not even been launched yet in your country and you managed to get hold of it. Great! But do you have people ready to pick up your call and talk to you for fifteen to twenty minutes? Do you have people who will call you to talk just like that for no reason? WhatsApp, Facebook, and other social media applications have killed human contact even while it provides constant communication. Things like birthday wishes are posted on social media walls, as if that matters the most. In today's world, if you still have non-virtual friends and real people eager to talk to you or listen to your voice, you are indeed wealthy.

3.7.7 Not the lavish noisy parties, but the company of that one special person, even when you are alone, is a true wealth

If you feel that being able to go to late-night parties and afford those entry fees of nightclubs or host lavish parties defines your true wealth, then just pause and ponder a bit. Once you are out of the party scene and all your party 'friends' have moved on, is there anyone still by your side? If you always have that special someone with you, who you can bank under any circumstances, that person is your true wealth. He could be anyone; someone from your family, a friend, a companion, or someone you love.

3.7.8 Not those latest movies you can watch in a multiplex, but the healthy mind and senses that allow you to enjoy it is a true wealth

If you feel catching all the latest movies in a multiplex on the weekends is what defines the riches of your life, you think twice. Having a stable mind and body is the biggest asset and a huge chunk of wealth anyone can have in today's rat-raced world. A healthy mind and awareness of your senses are your true wealth. The ability to enjoy a movie with your loved ones, leaving behind all the tensions of life, is a real asset. Appreciate these basic gifts you have for many who can't see, hear, or speak and yet know how to smile better than most of us who crib at things at the drop of a hat.

3.7.9 Not those great exotic vacations, but the memories any holiday builds are a true wealth

Going on exotic vacations, uploading photos on social media to boast about it, and counting those 'likes' is good; you may feel wealthy since you can afford that. Holidays will come and go, but you would have priceless memories if you had your loved ones by your side, and that is what you will have in your older age. Cherish those priceless memories; these experience assets are your true wealth.

3.7.10 Not the branded watch on your wrist, but having control over your time is a true wealth

Being able to afford an expensive diamond-studded branded wristwatch is nice, but well, it shows the same time as any other low-priced watch in the world. A watch is a status symbol that probably matters to an extent, but are you truly in charge of your own time or do you allow others to dictate your time schedule? Let alone be in charge of your own time; do you have time for yourself? If yes, you are probably among the wealthiest people, even if you wear a low-priced, unbranded watch.

3.7.11 Not your financial assets, but contribution assets are a true wealth

Accumulating financial wealth may be fine, but contribution assets matter the most. People like Dr. A. P. J. Abdul Kalam or Mother Teresa had no financial assets, but they had abundant contribution assets.

Even MasterCard agrees that there are some things money can't buy. One must earn money and grow it too, but at what cost is what matters. Being able to control your own time and have time for yourself or your loved ones is priceless. Life slips by too fast to get a hold of it. Hence, maintain a well-proportioned mix of all elements of true wealth.

3.8 THE MODERN-DAY TRAP OF THE FIVE ELEMENTS OF TRUE WEALTH

Be aware of a major trap related to the five elements of true wealth. Many people fall into this trap and never come out of it. Be wary of jobs that lure you in with the promise of extraordinary financial wealth and social wealth (status) but rob you of physical wealth and time wealth (freedom of time). This is one of the main challenges of the modern world. You can easily fall into this trap if you don't actively pursue what is meaningful and wise on this journey of life.

A jar filled with stones looks full, but it can accommodate pebbles of smaller sizes. Even after adding pebbles, it can take sand. Though the jar filled with sand looks full, it can still accommodate water. However, if the above filling sequence is reversed and the jar is first filled with sand, it can't accommodate stones and pebbles. Our life is like a jar. The stones are the important things in your life, like your health, taking your partner out for dancing, and playing with your children. Take care of the stones first, the things that really matter most. If everything else was lost and only these things were left with you, your life would still be beautiful. The pebbles are other things that matter, like your job, house, or car. The sand is trivial and small stuff. Set your priority right; don't fill the jar of your life with sand first. If you do so, you will have no space for vital things in life and it is vital things that matter for overall success. Building wealth is desirable, but if you build your wealth at the cost of your health and relationships with your family and friends; you are paying a great price.

Most people madly chase money and status at the cost of health and freedom. In the short term, this works somewhat in favour of the individual, but in the long run, it produces nasty consequences. You may achieve financial wealth and social wealth, thinking that you are on a proper path, but if you don't take care of other elements of true wealth, you are unconsciously travelling a road to the destination of a personal disaster. What good is it if you have all the money and status in the world but don't even have the physical vitality to feel good during the process or the time to enjoy yourself? The answer is that it is no good for that tradeoff. And it is a tradeoff, although it is often chosen unconsciously as opposed to consciously.

Get a deeper understanding of the current stage of your life. Examine whether you are trapped in your life. Are you seeing a value in focusing on your health, time and spiritual well-being, or are you over-focusing on your finances and social status? Does this reflect in your day-to-day actions? If you are weak in any of the five types of wealth, examine how this can be improved. If you are strong in any of the five types of wealth, examine how this can be consolidated.

Contrary to the common belief, it is possible to work on all the above elements simultaneously. We all have the ability to achieve holistic success with a judicious balance between all elements of true wealth. This is the place where we all want to be. Each type of wealth requires years of dedication, practice, humility, learning, understanding, and networking for their acquisition and decades to master them. On this journey, there is no destination.

We can only be happy if we recognise the importance of balancing all five elements of true wealth. True wealth is not necessarily the worth of money you have or the things your money can buy; it comprises the things money can't buy.

3.9 RELATIVE WEIGHTAGE OF CORE ELEMENTS OF TRUE WEALTH

True wealth is basically a function of the five core elements, viz. physical, social, time, spiritual and monetary wealth. However, this doesn't mean all people in the world will assign an equal weightage of twenty percent to each element. Over or under weightage depends on factors like country or community culture, religious beliefs and value systems. People give different weightages to these components depending on how they rank each type of wealth in the overall scheme of their lives. Thus, someone may give slightly more weightage to monetary wealth than social wealth in their personal lives or vice versa. Weightage also depends upon your age. For example, though you may assign lower weightage to spiritual wealth when you are young, you need to assign more weightage to spiritual wealth as you grow old.

However, the trifecta of life is:
- Early in life, we have ample time and excellent health but little money
- Midlife, we have decent health and sufficient money but little time
- Later in life, we have ample money and time but little health.

Our biological and career clocks are in complete contradiction with each other. When our children need our time, our career demands 24X7 attention from us. Also, the irony is we keep trading one for another.

A well-proportioned and dynamically balanced mix of these elements covers most of what can make anyone truly wealthy.

3.10 EVENTUAL GOALS: ACHIEVING FREEDOM

When can we say we have mastered all elements of true wealth? Mastery is achieved when we judiciously balance all five elements of true wealth and secure all five types of freedom, viz. physical, social, time, spiritual and financial.

Freedom	Definitions and examples	Action required
Physical freedom	Physical or health-related freedom means freedom to perform your daily activities with tremendous zeal and vigour with no physical restrictions, even as you grow old.	Balanced nutritional diet, exercise, yoga, rest, relaxation, sound sleep etc.
Social freedom	Social freedom means the ability to present yourself to the external world with no artificial masks of hypocrisy or pomp. It means not getting stuck in a self-created cage of fame, prestige or honour. It means remaining dignified yet not getting suffocated by dignity. The wise person can handle honour or fame with a sense of maturity and he is not unduly concerned, even if it falls apart.	Focus on core values like integrity, trust worthiness, humility, benevolence, kindness, gratitude, and love.
Freedom of time	Freedom of time means the ability to spend time on non-business activities of your choice to pursue your passion.	Organising, segregating vitals from trivials, setting priorities, eliminating non-essentials, delegating, outsourcing etc.

Spiritual freedom	Spiritual or emotional freedom is all about liberating yourself from negative emotions and creating a positive life. It means the ability to handle both success and failure with maturity. It is to feel free and not feel like a victim who is controlled by their emotions. You are the master of your emotions when you achieve emotional freedom. For example, emotional freedom is feeling utterly calm even when handling an emergency. It means remaining calm even if someone provokes you to lose your temper. How about enjoying a sense of belonging in a place of loneliness? This is what it feels like when you have achieved emotional freedom.	Positivity, optimism, feeling good, gratitude, mindfulness, detachment, meditation, embracing silence, etc.
Financial freedom	Financial freedom means the ability to live your life with no financial worries, even if you choose to stop working from tomorrow onwards.	Differentiating needs from wants, avoiding debts, disciplined saving, prudent investing and compounding, etc.

Remember, the ability to have freedom and actually exercising that freedom are two different things. To achieve mastery, you must have freedom, though you may not exercise the freedom available to you, or it may not be prudent to exercise that freedom. For example, financial freedom lies in the ability to retire early if you so desire, though you may choose not to.

4

THE SCIENCE BEHIND LIVING A LIFE OF EXCELLENCE

4.1 THE CONCEPT OF TIME: THE BANK ACCOUNT ANALOGY

We all have twenty-four hours a day, i.e. 1440 minutes or 86,400 seconds. To appreciate the concept of time, we often use the analogy of a bank account. We deposit salaries or business incomes in our bank accounts and withdraw the same as and when required. Similarly, in our life's account, 86,400 seconds are deposited each midnight and made available for withdrawal and use the way we like. While, in our normal bank accounts balances are carried forward, in life's account time can't be carried forward. When the day ends, all 86,400 seconds vanish whether or not we use it or whether we use it wisely or otherwise. Each day starts with nil carried forward balance, making unused seconds of the previous day irretrievable.

We all have a great attachment to money. We will not waste a single dollar if 86,400 dollars are deposited in our account. However, when it comes to time, unfortunately, our level of attachment is not the same, although time is relatively more important than money on several counts. We can get more money, but we can never get more time. We know how much money we have, but we don't know how much time we have. We can borrow money, but not time. We can own or store money, but not time; we can only use it. We can't keep it; we can only spend it. We can transfer money, but not time. Thus, the real currency of life is time rather than money. Time is more precious than money. Hence, we must reconsider our thinking about money and time and learn to subordinate money to time.

Also, time is like a flowing river. You can't touch its water twice. The water that has passed will never pass again. Time is a car that has no brake and no reverse gear. Time has no holidays. Life has no pause button. Remember, time waits for no one. Our indecisions or complaints will not halt time. Our excuses will not slow down the time. Our regrets will not turn back time. Time will not turn around and cry along with us. In short, time is highly perishable, irretrievable and non-renewable.

4.2 THE PRESENT MOMENT: A PRICELESS PRESENT

Most of the time, we either regret our past or worry about our future. This prevents us from enjoying the beauty of the present moment. We must remind ourselves that we can never get back to the present moment once lost. Yesterday is history. We can't retrieve our yesterday. It is gone forever. It is buried forever. It exists only in memory. Yesterday has no significance except that the memories we hold add or take away joy from our lives. If we hold on to the negative memories of yesterday, we spoil our present, too. Remember, we can't live in the past; we can't live in the future. All we have is today. Our only time is now. We live only in the present using the seconds and minutes available to us. Also, the present moment is our only opportunity to make choices, as we can't make choices retrospectively in our past. When it is inevitable that we can live only in the present, should we spend our present moment in anger, hate, jealousy, fear, etc.? Don't ruminate on the past. Don't waste even a moment mourning yesterday's misfortunes, defeats, or aches of the heart. Also, stop worrying about the future; instead, plan for the future.

Another thing that prevents us from enjoying the beauty of the present moment is the 'I-will-do-it-afterward' tendency. This human tendency is at the core of depriving us of the joy inherent in the present moment. We often give procrastination excuses like; I will think about it afterward, say it afterward, do it afterward, or pay a visit afterward. We leave everything for the future as if the future is ours. But we fail to appreciate that:

Afterward, the coffee gets cold.
Afterward, priorities change.
Afterward, health deteriorates.
Afterward, the kids grow up.

Afterward, the day becomes night.
Afterward, the charm goes.
Afterward, parents get old.
Afterward, life ends.

And then, it is often too late. So, leave nothing for the future. The day is today. The moment is now. Act now. If we procrastinate, we may lose the best moments, experiences and relationships. Remember, we will never pass this way again and hence make it count. We can do this irrespective of our past. The past doesn't decide our future. If you can't be happy here and now, you will never be happy at any time. The present moment is a priceless present. Each present moment is precious; enjoy it fully. Live it fully. Garland the present moment. Go with the flow. Dance with the moment. Let us love ourselves passionately and treasure life moment by moment. Tomorrow will come, but first, enjoy today. Let us spend our time with the right thoughts, with the right emotions, with the right purpose, with the right deeds and with the right people.

4.3 THE ZERO-BASED TIME PLANNING APPROACH

Old habits die hard. We often continue doing something just because we have been habitually doing this for several years. We don't even realise that our needs have changed over time and some of these activities might have become redundant. Hence, we must periodically review and align our time-use habits with our changing needs. We can do this either by an incremental approach or a zero-based approach.

The analogy of a cabinet reshuffle undertaken by a Prime Minister is often used to explain the above two approaches. If the Prime Minister wants to adopt an incremental approach, he would add a few new ministers to his cabinet, remove a few existing ministers, or reshuffle their portfolios. However, he would adopt a zero-based approach if he wanted to revamp the entire cabinet and needed a free hand. So he would obtain the resignations of all his ministers and reconstitute a new cabinet afresh.

Similar is the case with the exercise of planning time. In an incremental approach, you discontinue some existing time-use habits and adopt new ones. However, this is an ad hoc approach as against a systematic approach of zero-based time planning. In the zero-based approach, you start with a clean slate from ground zero. You discard everything and then redesign your time-use strategy afresh in line with the changing needs. This results in the automatic elimination of time-use habits that are inconsistent with your current strategy.

Repeat such zero-based time planning every year.

4.4 THE HIDDEN EXTRA HOUR

We often wish we had an extra hour! Though such an extra hour is very much embedded in our daily schedules, we don't know how to unearth this. We can easily unearth hidden extra hours if we question our time-use habits critically and identify time-use habits that do not contribute to our core values, objectives and goals. For this purpose, list core values, objectives and goals for the coming year on the left side of a piece of paper and the current activities on the right. Current activities may be categorised into the following four sections:

1) Urgent problems and crisis
2) Planning and prevention
3) Routine activities
4) Unimportant activities

Critically examine each activity listed on the right side and link it with the left side if it contributes to core values, objectives and goals. The orphan items on the right side that have remained unlinked to the left are prime candidates for elimination. Eliminate all such non-contributing items and get that much-needed extra hour. Utilise this newly gained extra hour for meditation, exercise, reading inspirational materials, or creative thinking.

4.5 THE HEART ATTACK APPROACH

A healthy person can easily work for eight to ten hours per day. However, if someone suddenly gets a heart attack, his working hours will be restricted to only three to four hours a day on medical grounds. This will compel him to delegate many of the current tasks and eliminate some altogether.

This happened to U.S. President Dwight D. Eisenhower. After he had a heart attack, he critically reviewed his workload and classified it into essentials and non-essentials:

ESSENTIALS	NON-ESSENTIALS
Leadership to Armed Forces	Routine jobs and correspondence
Preside over National Security Council	Travel
Watch and direct major foreign policies	Meetings and appointments
Supervise key economic matters	Entertaining diplomatic guests

When working beyond four hours a day was prohibited, he focused only on essentials and delegated all non-essentials to his deputies. He liked this approach so much that he continued this practice even after complete recovery and thus turned a crisis into an opportunity.

The heart attack approach is quite dramatic, but it can bring much-needed awareness to question the current non-essential things we are doing. Should we not learn from the experience of others to focus only on essentials without going through a heart attack trauma ourselves?

4.6 FLY TO THE U.S.A. APPROACH

One day, when you reach the office at 9-30 a.m., your boss tells you that you have to fly to the U.S.A. by today's midnight flight for an important business meeting. Your first immediate reaction would be that this is impossible. Perhaps, on second thought, you may say that you will try. You come back to your desk and list down things 'TO DO' that will include:

1) Ticketing
2) Foreign Exchange
3) Purchase of medicines and other items required during travel
4) Luggage packing
5) Arrangement for airport drop
6) Today's urgent work
7) Meeting preparation

Once you prepare the list, the thinking process starts. You delegate items 1) & 2) to the Travel and Finance Departments, respectively, by having a ten-minute brief with them. You phone your kid to purchase medicines and other items and your spouse to pack your luggage. You call your friend and schedule an airport drop by him. You delegate item 6) to your deputy and then settle down to work on meeting preparation. Your mind is now free to concentrate on this vital item, as you have already attended to the other six items.

Thus, by listing down 'TO DO' items and delegating, you accomplished what was otherwise almost impossible and could catch the midnight flight without any hassles. You have successfully done work of perhaps fifteen days in fifteen hours.

If we could do this one day, why not every day? Why don't we fly to the U.S.A. every day?

4.7 THE CONCEPT OF THE TIME WINDOW

We often find that if we reach our destination belatedly or miss an opportunity to complete a task in time, we end up with additional consequential delays of a larger magnitude. Take an example of a railway level crossing on the commuting route to your office that closes daily at 9-15 a.m. for fifteen minutes. If you are delayed by five minutes and reach the level crossing at 9-20 a.m., you will be forced to wait until 9-30 a.m.; consequently, you are delayed by twenty minutes and not five minutes.

Similarly, suppose a meeting with your boss is required to complete a report, which you scheduled for Wednesday. However, on Monday, you come to know that your boss is travelling from Wednesday to Friday. If you hasten and grab the opportunity to meet him on Tuesday, you can jump through the time window and complete the report early, failing which the time window is closed for you until Saturday.

Several such time windows open and close in front of us every day, which a little hastening can grab.

4.8 UNLOCKING ENERGY RESERVES

Energy is the first fundamental of life excellence. Without an abundance of energy, you are like a rocket without fuel. If you eat as per your body's rhythm and the body's natural cycle, your energy level will be at its peak and you will get the best out of your time. Following are the three sections of the natural cycle occurring in the body:

1) The Welcoming Cycle (Noon to 8 p.m.)

   During this cycle, foods are taken and digested.

2) The Absorption Cycle (8 p.m. to 4 a.m.)

   During this cycle, foods are absorbed. Hence, avoid taking food after 8 p.m.

3) The Removal Cycle (4 a.m. to noon)

   During this cycle, toxins and other wastes are eliminated from the body. Hence, eat only fruits or their fresh juices during this cycle to avoid disturbing this elimination process.

Recognise and respect the above cycles and allow each cycle to be most effective. This way, you will unleash tremendous energy reserves, bringing more vibrant health and improved productivity.

4.9 THE SCIENCE OF OUTPUT ANALYSIS

You can increase the output by using the scientific approach to the management of time. The output is a function of concentration plus intensity. If your mind wanders, the output will reduce substantially. Output also relates directly to energy levels. Factors like laziness, tiredness, or illness will decrease the output. On the other hand, streamlining all activities and eliminating wasteful activities and wasted motions will increase the output.

4.10 THE FOUR GENERATIONS OF TIME MANAGEMENT

The science of time management has evolved over a long period. This evolution can best be appreciated by understanding the characteristics of each of the four generations of time management.

The first generation of time management could be characterised by 'Notes' and 'To Do' lists - an effort to give some semblance of recognition and inclusiveness to the many demands placed on our time. However, these checklists only give us a place to capture things that penetrate our awareness and avoid forgetting them. We merely get a temporary sense of accomplishment every time we cross something off. The first generation of time management does not recognise the modern-day concept of priorities. As a result, there is no correlation between activities on the list and our core values, objectives, and goals in life. Hence, the time of first-generation managers is spent predominantly on non-priority trivial items. Also, first-generation managers don't feel it necessary to reinforce their future production capabilities.

The second generation could be characterised by calendars and appointment books that record future commitments and help achieve goals. Though second-generation managers assume some more control, even their activities or schedules have no priority or recognised correlation to their core values, objectives, and goals. The benefits they achieve are limited to schedule optimisation.

The third generation adds to the preceding generations the important idea of prioritisation, clarifying values and comparing the relative worth of activities based on their relationship to those values. The third generation provides a vast array of planners and materials, which helps assign priorities and plan routine activities. It also focuses on setting specific goals for different time horizons and their realisation through daily planning. Thus, third-generation managers take a significant step forward in managing their time.

The fourth generation advocates putting first things first. It provides us with a priceless compass to set the right direction for our lives. It brings about a paradigm shift in approach to time management and its implementation will empower us to move into Quadrant II - the heart of effective personal management. Activities like writing a PMS, long-range planning, building and nurturing relationships, or preventive health care are not urgent but important. Though we know we need to do the above things, we seldom get around doing such things because they appear relatively less urgent and other petty and trivial things that are urgent continuously keep popping up, infringing on our time.

THE TIME MANAGEMENT MATRIX

	Urgent	Not urgent
Important	I Crisis Strikes Pressing problems Deadlines	II Planning Prevention of crisis Relationship building Employee training
Not important	III Interruption Calls Mail, reports Meetings Complaints	IV Trivia Unimportant mail Casual phone calls Time wasters Pleasant activities

The essence of the fourth generation of time management is summarised in the above Time Management Matrix, popularly known as the 'The Four Quadrants of Time Management':

The four permutations as regards urgency and importance are given below, together with the respective strategies to deal with them:

Quadrant	Permutation	Strategy
I	Urgent and important	Do it now.
II	Not urgent, but important	Schedule a definite time to do it. Don't procrastinate.
III	Urgent but not important	Delegate it.
IV	Neither urgent nor important	Eliminate it.

The paradox of the above matrix is that what is important is seldom urgent and what is urgent is seldom important.

The Quadrant II approach emphasises maintaining a judicious balance between increasing our current production and upgrading our future capabilities. Hence, don't ignore Quadrant II activities. It is Quadrant II activities that will take your life to new heights. The executives who become proficient in Quadrant II philosophy can significantly improve their personal and organisational leadership.

This matrix is not merely a Time Management matrix; it is, indeed, a life management matrix. Time mastering is life mastering. Guard your time. It is the most valuable commodity. It is the most prized possession of humankind.

4.11 EFFECTIVE ROLE MODELING

As a youngster, you probably tried to emulate your parents or a teacher who embodied the characteristics you wanted to possess. This approach can be extended to select role models in your profession. Many successful people worldwide have reached the top in their professional fields and performed remarkably well in their social and community lives. Identify such successful people and study their lives. Then emulate good practices successfully followed by them. Think and act like your role model. Aim for a fusion between your and his thinking. This way, you can become as successful as your role model.

When you select the right role model and mentor, develop the right habits, nurture the right values and combine this with hard work in a disciplined manner, you are bound to achieve outstanding success.

4.12 THE PARETO PRINCIPLE

The Pareto principle, named after an Italian economist, states that the significant items of any group are relatively small in numbers. He discovered the universal truth that roughly 80% of the effect comes from 20% of causes. For example, 80% of the income tax is collected from 20% of the assesses, 80% of bank deposits are from 20% of the customers, or 80% of the value of inventory in a store is contributed by 20% of items..

We can identify vital items by arranging the items in descending order of value in a tabular form and working out the cumulative totals for each row. When the cumulative total reaches the threshold level of approximately 80% of the total value, items in terms of numbers are around 20%.

This principle applies to the management of time as well. In any 'TO DO' list, 20% of items are vital, bringing 80% of results. In a basket of several items, not all items are vital and not all items deserve equal attention. High-value items must be paid more attention than low-value items. However, in the absence of segregation of vital items, our attention is dissipated more on minor items as they are large in number. Since life is all about priorities, the Pareto Principle can be effectively used to segregate top priority 20% vital items. We must manage at least that 20% well as a priority.

We can also use the Pareto Principle for delegation. For example, if a Materials Manager is issuing around 100 Purchase Orders every month, out of which, typically, 80 Purchase Orders are valued at less than $10,000; he can delegate all

Purchase Orders valued at less than $10,000 to his deputy. He can then focus on Purchase Orders above $10,000. This gives him more quality time for high-value Purchase Orders, which are vital.

4.13 THE CONCEPT OF THE CIRCLE OF INFLUENCE

When we focus on the things that we can do something about, we achieve satisfaction. However, when we worry and fret over the things that are not in our control, we add to the stress in our lives. Hence, we must learn to segregate things over which we have control from those beyond our control. We can do this using the concept of Circles of Concern and Influence. A Circle of Concern encompasses a wide range of concerns we may have, such as our health, career, the well-being of our children, excessive Government borrowings, and the threat of nuclear war. However, we don't have control over many of these concerns. Here comes the concept of the Circle of Influence. A Circle of Influence carves out only a part of those concerns we can do something about and eliminates the rest of the concerns we have no control over. Focusing on the Circle of Concern depletes our energy, results in frustration and adds to feelings of stress and helplessness. If we continue to focus on the Circle of Concern as a habit, we tend to neglect the Circle of Influence and gradually, it will get smaller and smaller. However, we can reduce stress levels and increase our happiness by consciously and proactively focusing only on the Circle of Influence. This is because these things are in our control and we can initiate and influence a change. When we do this as a habit, the Circle of Influence gradually gets bigger and bigger.

Consider an employee working for an organisation that is going through a merger. If he complains about the merger or stages a protest against the merger, he will sink into an unproductive and negative spiral of helplessness, which becomes uncontrollable once triggered. Instead, he can upgrade his knowledge and skills to provide value to the merged organisation. This will proactively direct his actions towards things he can influence, triggering a spiral of positivity.

Learn to gracefully accept what can't be changed or just overlook it. If a situation is beyond even acceptance, remove yourself from it or rise above it. The secret to a stress-free, successful life lies in focusing on the Circle of Influence and expanding it.

4.14 THE CONCEPT OF THE CIRCLE OF COMPETENCE

"One of the greatest pieces of economic wisdom is to know what you don't know."

- John Kenneth Galbraith

Since we can't be good at everything, we must concentrate only on our Circle of Competence. This means focusing on what we know and understand well and ignoring everything else. The secrets of maximising your odds of success is to choose the right field of competence. The Goldilocks Rule states that humans experience peak motivation when working on tasks that are right on the edge of their abilities.

For example, if you are investing in the stock market, you should invest in companies whose business you fully understand. Thus, first, you need to segregate the business you understand and eliminate the rest. Your first list should not contain more than fifty stocks. Next, inside your Circle of Competence, draw one inner circle (Circle A) covering companies whose business has strong fundamentals (a durable economic moat, little debt and excellent return on equity). Next, draw a second inner intersecting circle (Circle B) covering companies that adhere to corporate governance norms (running the business for the benefit of shareholders with strong ethics and character). Now draw a third inner circle (Circle C) covering companies with an attractive market price in relation to their intrinsic value. The intersecting portion of the three inner circles should comprise business houses with strong fundamentals, sound corporate governance and attractive prices. These are the stocks in which you should invest.

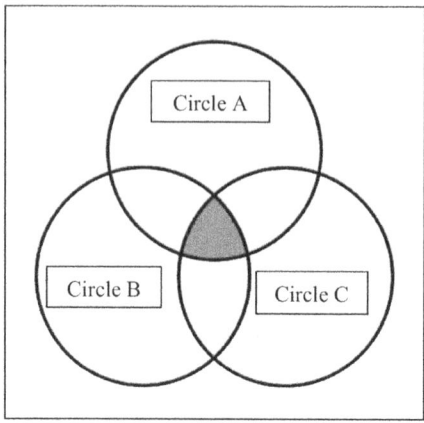

Intelligent people do a few things well. They focus on their Circle of Competence. They don't fall prey to each and everything under the sun.

4.15 THE SCIENCE BEHIND POSITIVE RESTLESSNESS: THE DXVXF>R FORMULA

In a constantly changing world, individuals and organisations must continuously reinvent themselves if they want to stay relevant and competitive. However, human nature is risk/change-averse. Also, human behaviour follows the law of least effort. We will naturally gravitate toward the option that requires the least amount of work. Whether referred to as the status quo or a comfort zone, people resist changes. Resistance to change is, therefore, a natural response. Individuals or organisations change only when there is a compulsion. Also, such changes can take place only after the inertia or resistance to change is overcome. However, the million-dollar question is, how do we generate force that is strong enough to overcome the resistance to change?

Coined by Beckhard-Harris, the $D \times V \times F > R$ formula works wonderfully well for this purpose. It offers a simplified analysis of the conditions governing the potential success or failure of a given change initiative. According to this formula, a change initiative will be successful only if:

1) the dissatisfaction level with the current situation is high enough for employees to acknowledge the need for change, making them restless, of course, in a positive manner.
2) employees should share a reasonably clear vision of a future situation that is both better and achievable.
3) the first step is taken immediately upon finalisation of the action plan, or else the enthusiasm may fizzle out.
4) the combined strength of the three factors viz. D (dissatisfaction), V (vision) and F (first step) are greater than R (resistance to change).

Since the formula is a multiplication, if one of the three variables is absent or equals zero, the product is also equal to zero. Hence, all factors must be activated with full force if resistance to change is to be overcome. This formula can help steer big transformation projects by generating a force that is greater than resistance to change and can be used by individuals as well as organisations.

4.16 TIME: THE ESSENCE OF DECISION-MAKING

Speed is the essence of decision-making. An executive or a leader is a man of action. He must act and accomplish goals. His prerogative and duty are to cut across indecision with the decision. He should galvanise indifference into enthusiastic performance. He should take steps to stop his everlasting disposition to keep thinking, keep listening and keep procrastinating. Learn to make timely decisions and shoulder the responsibility of the outcome. Most of the time, doing something is better than doing nothing. Except for a project of paramount importance, the speed is just as important as the accuracy, if not more. So don't wait around indefinitely, fluctuating between right and wrong. Stop dilly-dallying and decide faster. Your decision might be right; it might be wrong, but take chances and do something. Don't wait for the right time or perfect conditions. The time will never be right, and conditions will never be perfect. Don't procrastinate. Take action. Indecision is more harmful than bad decisions. This is because you can always correct bad decisions but can't retrieve time lost in indecision.

For decisions that are expensive to fix, you are perhaps justified in taking reasonable time. However, don't spend an unduly long time on inexpensive decisions. Here, the criteria for expensiveness may also include time, human resources, or prestige. Also, learn to decide based on available data even if the data is not cent percent accurate. Beyond a certain limit, improving the data accuracy takes disproportionately more time and the incremental benefits go on diminishing. Wise leaders use their judgment to make crucial decisions in a limited time, even with imperfect data and this decisiveness grows with each decision.

4.17 THE 37% RULE TO MAKE BETTER DECISIONS

The 37% rule comes from the optimal theory in mathematics. This rule determines the optimal time to stop seeking more options and pull the trigger. According to mathematicians, the optimal point is right after seeing or exploring the first 37% of your options. After this threshold level of 37%, the benefits of further exploration go on diminishing. Hence, decide your total universe first and then calculate the 37% threshold level. Alternatively, you can also set a time-based deadline.

This rule can be applied to decisions like buying a car, choosing a vacation spot, or selecting a scrip for trading. Of course, this rule doesn't account for feelings, gut instincts or instant chemistry. This rule gets you into action and maximises your probability of success rather than unnecessarily getting mired in information gathering and data analysis. We must avoid analysis paralysis. If, for example, you're buying a second-hand car of a particular brand and decide that you'd like to see ten cars before making a decision, you may plan to see the first three or four cars without serious intention of buying them. When you complete your exploration of those four cars, your exploratory period reaches a point of diminishing returns. Now, the fifth car you see is the keeper if it is better than those initial cars. If you continue exploring endlessly, you may get so frustrated at some point that you may end up with a sub-optimal decision.

4.18 THE LONG AND SHORT OF EMOTIONS

"The obsession with instant gratification blinds us from our long-term potential."

— **Mike Dooley**

We live almost in instant gratification mode. We focus on the instant satisfaction of our desires, thinking that such instant gratification will make us happy. The human brain evolved to prioritise immediate rewards over delayed rewards. We are so impatient that we often ignore the long-term effects of those short-term decisions.

For example, we get instant pleasure when we eat a big pizza or gulp another chocolate cake. Similarly, snoozing our alarm and sleeping one more hour in the cozy morning is quite gratifying. Of course, for a moment, a thought of getting up and walking in the garden also comes to our mind, but instant gratification finally wins. In the instant moment, the above decisions appear quite appealing and tempting.

Why do we often get enslaved by instant gratification? Why do we make decisions based only on our short-term emotions? Why do we overlook the bigger picture, though it leads us to a better future? We do so because our present emotions are clear, sharp and precise, while future emotions are not yet well defined. The future feels blurry and fuzzier because probabilities are involved. Our present emotions are always in the spotlight and significantly influence our decisions.

In such situations, the 10/10/10 Rule comes to our rescue. Coined by Suzy Welch, this rule empowers us to make smarter choices. A fast and powerful, this 10/10/10 Rule empowers us to equalise the impact of short-term thinking on our emotions. Rather than deciding solely based on short-term emotions, the rule suggests we also consider probable medium and long-term implications. We should thoughtfully consider the potential positive and negative consequences across three time frames, i.e. in ten minutes, ten months, and ten years for each major decision. This rule provides a level-playing field for our emotions across all time frames. It forces us to imagine a moment ten months or ten years into the future with the same freshness we feel in the present. This shift helps us look at the instant and future emotions with equal clarity and thus improves the quality of our decisions. This rule doesn't mean we just ignore the immediate short-term feeling. It only recommends that we consider both sets of emotions and then decide on the best course of action.

Often, clever salespersons exploit this human tendency to sell more products or services. They cleverly craft promotional messages to trigger instant emotions. Influenced by this attack, we unconsciously make an arbitrary decision to buy a product (known as impulse buying). Of course, later, we regret making such decisions. Consider a case of a video gaming application offering two subscription options, viz. quarterly and annually. To encash our current emotions, the video gaming company offers a 50% discount on an annual subscription. Our present emotions will tempt us to grab this huge discount. But if we think from the 10/10/10 perspective and consider the future outcome, we soon realise that taking a one-year plan is likely to make us more addicted to video game playing. Although we are saving money currently, in the future, we could enslave ourselves into an unhealthy habit. Having realised this possibility, we are now better positioned to make the most optimal decision.

4.19 THE RULE OF TWENTY-ONE

If you do anything for twenty-one days in a row, you will have an excellent chance of making it into a habit. This applies to any good practice. For example, getting up before sunrise for twenty-one days in a row will develop into a powerful habit. Whether trying to control wasteful expenditure or get rid of your worry habit, persevere for twenty-one days in a row. Perseverance and determination are omnipotent. There is power in persistence. Persistence induces faith. Great successes are accomplished not necessarily by strength but by perseverance.

4.20 THE LAW OF WASTED EFFORTS

Do you know lions succeed only in a quarter of their hunting attempts? They fail in 75% of their attempts. Despite this small percentage of success most predators share, they don't despair in their hunting attempts. This is not because of hunger, as some might think, but the understanding of nature's law of wasted efforts that have been instinctively built into animals. Similarly, half of the eggs of fishes are eaten, half of the baby bears die before puberty, most of the seeds of trees are eaten by birds and most of the world's rain falls in oceans. Scientists have found that animals, trees and other creations of nature are more receptive to the law of wasted efforts. Only humans think that the lack of success in a few attempts is a failure, though the truth is that we only fail when we stop trying.

Achieving excellence in life is no different. Success doesn't mean zero failure. Let us not aim for a life free of pitfalls and falls. Let us walk over our failures and go beyond every stage of wasted efforts, looking forward to the next attempt. Start all over again if you encounter failure. Be inspired. Never give up.

4.21 THE LESSER OF THE TWO EVILS PRINCIPLE

Normally, it is easy to choose if choices are to be made between good and better. However, choices in life are not always that simple. Many times, we face a situation wherein no good choice is available. The 'Lesser of the Two Evils' principle states that when you are faced with a situation wherein all the options available for selection are unpleasant, select the least unpleasant option. For example, voting for the mildly unpopular candidate is desirable in elections between only two candidates, where one is mildly unpopular and the other highly unpopular.

In personal and business situations, whenever we face such dilemmas, this principle helps us select the lesser of the two evils rather than endlessly remaining undecided.

4.22 THE SCIENCE OF INFINITE POSSIBILITIES

The universe is full of infinite possibilities and so is the human mind. However, we rarely exploit the full capacity of our minds.

Once, a mother said to her daughter, "Bring two apples from the fridge-one each for you and your brother." The daughter brought two apples, but instead of giving one apple to her brother, she took bites from both apples. This made the mother and the brother angry and they were about to scold her. However, before they could scold her, she gave one apple to her brother and said, "You eat this apple-it is sweeter." Both mother and brother realised how wrong they were in hurriedly jumping to a conclusion and cursed themselves for not thinking about this possibility. This simple example reveals how grossly we underutilise the thinking capacities of our minds. Often, we tend to pre-judge people and hastily jump to certain conclusions without thinking about all possibilities. However, if we train our minds to think about infinite possibilities, the tendency to hastily pre-judge people will reduce.

The mind is like a parachute; it works only when open. So, we must make conscious efforts to open up our minds. A mind open to everything means being peaceful, radiating love, practising forgiveness, being generous, respecting all lives and visualising ourselves as capable of doing anything we can conceive with our open mind and heart. Deep within all of us dwell those slumbering powers that would astonish us, abilities that we never dreamed of possessing, forces that would revolutionise our lives if aroused and put into action. Nothing on earth is greater than the human mind in potential power. This philosophy for successful living is called Possibility Thinking. However, we often log on to limitations of our body, mind and emotions. Remember, our capabilities are beyond any limitations. Make your limitations ineffective by logging on to your vast capabilities. Don't restrict your achievements based on some limiting beliefs. For example, don't rule out your promotion, thinking your IQ is lower than your peers. List down all such imaginary beliefs and overcome them. Release your limits. Stretch yourself. Once your mind opens up, the sky is the limit for your achievements. Limitations about what you can achieve are only those you create and place on yourself.

Whereas a closed mind seals off any creative expansion, the ability to participate in miracles happens once you open your mind to its inherent limitless potential. The daily practice of silence, spending time with picturesque nature, meditation, remaining detached and non-judgmental will open your mind to infinite possibilities. This will help you feel your thoughts. Remember, thinking is one level of understanding, feeling is another level of understanding and being is yet another level of understanding. So go beyond mere thinking; feel your thoughts and get into being.

In short, the human mind can perform miracles if properly conditioned and used for excellence. So powerful is the human mind that it can develop the qualities you desire, the friendship you need, the position you covert and produce the wealth you desire. And yet, unfortunately, most human minds remain unexplored, uncultivated and underutilised.

4.23 THE SCIENCE OF MIND CONTROL THROUGH THOUGHT CONTROL

Our thoughts are a form of energy and the source of virtually everything in our life. Our life is primarily determined by thoughts that habitually occupy our minds rather than external conditions or circumstances. Conditions are created by thoughts far more powerfully than conditions that develop thoughts. Everything that we feel and experience results from our thoughts. We become what we think about all day long. A man's life is what his thoughts make of it. Man moulds himself by his thoughts as a sculptor moulds clay.

The factory of the human mind processes nearly 60,000 thoughts in a day, out of which over 50% are negative thoughts and 85% of these negative thoughts are repetitive. Anger, hate, jealousy, fear etc., are negative thoughts that attract more of the same and weaken us. Our mind is an emotional carrier carrying the weight of our thoughts. If our thoughts are fewer and lighter, the mind remains light. Waste thoughts are a major leakage of our energy. An elevated stage can be achieved only if we are light. Hence, be like an angel who is free from gravity, is detached and carries positive thoughts. Kindness, gratitude, love, harmony, peace, etc., are high-frequency thoughts that attract more of the same. These are the most empowering thoughts we can have as they create happy molecules. If we want to give away such gifts, first we should create its inventory with us, as we can't give away what we don't have. The day we start transmitting such high-frequency thoughts, our world will change.

You can use thoughts to direct your actions to areas of your choice. If you focus your thoughts on what you want to attract in your life and maintain that thought with the passion of an absolute intention, you will eventually act on that intention. If you strongly believe you can do a certain thing, you shall surely become capable, even if you may not be capable initially. However, if you keep telling yourself that you can't do a certain thing, you may eventually become incapable of doing it even if you have those abilities. Hence, don't lower your goals to the level of your abilities. Instead, raise your abilities to the height of your goals. Since your thoughts are the servants of your will, it is in your hands to keep yourself empowered or weakened by consciously choosing your thoughts. You can make yourself ill with your thoughts; by the same token, you can also make yourself well by using a different and healing type of thought. Similarly, you can think your way to failure or unhappiness, but you can also think about success and happiness. You will be successful if you think about success hard enough, steady enough, long enough and passionately enough. Thinking is arduous and tiring work. When a tough situation confronts you, you should not give up easily just after looking at it superficially. Instead, think hard. Think till it hurts. Think until it seems there can't be another aspect that has not been considered. Thus, mobilise the positive power of thoughts and use it to realise your goals. This process would include igniting a burning desire in you, setting a challenging goal, committing your goals on paper (thereby setting up a red flag in your mind and assigning more importance to this single thought than the rest of the thoughts swirling around your mental factory) and pursuing the goal with a strong conviction and an intense single-mindedness of purpose. If you follow this process, you are bound to realise your goals. You are what your deep driving desire is. As you desire, so is your will. As your will is, so is your destiny. Our thoughts, words and deeds are the threads of the net we throw around ourselves to build our destiny. Hence, make a conscious decision to be in charge of your thinking. Be vigilant about your thoughts. Notice when your thoughts drift into negativity. At the very moment, replace disempowering or weakening thoughts with thoughts of higher spiritual frequency. Thus, you can change your life by changing the texture of your thoughts.

Thoughts also create words, for words are the vehicles of ideas. But words also affect thoughts and help to condition, if not develop attitudes. Therefore, choose your words wisely. Your mind is at peace if your conversation contains peaceful expressions. A peaceful mind generates peaceful ideas. Thoughts are also influenced by many other factors like the picture a man hangs on his walls, the books he keeps in his library, the movies he watches, the words he speaks, the prayers he makes, the sort of things he inscribes on flashy tablets of his heart, the conversations he holds in his dreams, the station in life to which he inspires, the sort of friends he gathers about his fireside. These factors collectively control his thought world in his subconscious mind, which in turn, dictates his accomplishments.

Even relationships are first conceived and developed in thoughts. The only way you can experience another person is through your thoughts. If your relationship is bitter, it is because you think of it that way. If you look for what is wrong in them and store a negative image in your mind, then that's where your relationships exist. Change your thoughts to what you love rather than what you think is wrong. This alters your entire relationship. If you process others based on what you think they should be, you have sent the love and other higher energies away. This pollutes your mind, resulting in bitterness in the relationship. However, filling your mind with high-energy thoughts allows the world to be as it is. Once you accept the world as it is, you will be in a state of pure bliss and develop a great reverence for all lives. This transformation, being paradigm in nature, will elevate all your relationships to the next level and bring a quantum jump in the quality of your life.

4.24 THE ASTONISHING POWER OF AUTO-SUGGESTIONS

Words have profoundly suggestive power. Each word has a frequency and energy. This energy sends impulses to the brain and we produce the corresponding chemicals. This changes the alchemy of our body and we feel happy or sad, disturbed or panicked. There is healing in the very saying of some words. You speak peaceful, quiet words and your mind will react peacefully. Tranquillity is one of the most beautiful and melodic of all English words and the mere saying of it tends to induce a tranquil state. Another healing word is serenity. Visualise serenity as you say it. Repeat it loudly and in the mood for which the word is a symbol. Such words have a healing potency when used in this manner. On the contrary, if you utter a series of panicky words, your mind will immediately go into a state of nervousness. You might feel a sinking in the pit of your stomach that will affect your entire physical mechanism. Similarly, if your mind suggests you are intelligent and confident, that is how you will appear and your body language will show it, but if your mind suggests you are ugly and dull, that is how you will be.

Recognise and cultivate the power of auto-suggestions. It is a medium for influencing and reprogramming your subconscious mind. Repeat some positive words audibly and activate the tremendous power of suggestive articulation. Energy flows where attention does. Harness the power of auto-suggestions by continually making positive affirmations. Affirmations are positive self-talk. These are powerful and easy-to-use sentences that we constantly repeat in our minds and hearts until they get embedded in our subconscious minds. The auto-suggestion technique is immensely powerful and can be effectively used in maintaining good health, healing, improving self-image, etc. It works and is an essential tool in maintaining peak performance.

However, ensure the power of auto-suggestions is used only for positive things, not negative ones. Repeated use of phrases like 'I am tired' will eventually make you feel tired.

4.25 THE STUNNING POWER OF SILENCE

Silence is a journey in itself - a quiet journey that eventually ends up in finding our soul. In the chaos of life, we usually forget the real purpose of our lives. Our mind gets confused because we hear different voices coming from different directions and these voices control our mind so much that we lose the ability to think on our own. We become a puppet of someone else's mind. When life brings you into such a chaotic phase, there is a message it wants to give. It wants you to slow down and rethink your life and priorities through silence. It is the time to reconsider the very purpose of your life and to reconcile with your inner needs. It allows you to connect with your inner self to find solutions. Silence isn't empty; it is full of creative answers.

To practice silence, spend quiet time with yourself. Go alone into the most peaceful place and sit and practice the art of silence for at least fifteen minutes every day. Sit quietly and enjoy the power of silence. Learn to be still. Don't talk to anyone. Don't write. Don't read. Be with yourself. Be inwardly silent. Be with your breath. Connect with your true self within. Think as little as possible. Throw your mind into natural surroundings. Whatever thoughts are coming, let them come. Don't try to control your mind. Don't resist thoughts, as resistance creates disharmony. Wherever your mind goes, let it go with a deep sense of wonder. With a sense of wonderment, look at your mind. Conceive your mind as inactive, as still as the surface of a body of water without a single ripple. When you have attained a quiescent state, you listen to the deeper sounds of harmony and beauty of the almighty God that is to be found in the essence of silence. Thoughts or ideas alone can't do anything unless you listen, reflect, develop a deep sense of awareness and meditate in silence. Only then will thoughts transform into wisdom, giving you the purifying effect of understanding. This enlightenment brings in certain synergy and with this synergy comes true transformation.

4.26 THE PRODIGIOUS POWER OF PRAYERS

Prayer has been human's natural response to cope with difficult situations in life, such as poverty, petulance, sickness, death, or disaster. Traditionally, we pray to a higher power or the almighty God for things of need and want. Prayer cultivates an attitude of humility and acceptance and establishes our relationship with the ultimate source in the right manner. It creates a feeling akin to a baby cradled in his mother's arms. To remain perpetually connected with the almighty God in a state of humility and surrender is to have entered a state of prayerfulness. This prayerfulness resolves in deep meditation, where we transcend relationships and move toward infinite closeness and even oneness. It can take us beyond words, deep into the realm of sacredness. So, make the almighty God your partner in all your endeavours.

The air you breathe, the water you drink, the food you eat - all are energy. We are a bundle of energy and have the power to create good and bad energy. If done with a clean heart and bona fide intentions, prayer helps generate good energy or convert bad energy into good energy. Thus, by exploiting the prodigious power of prayers, we can create good energy and channelise the same for healing. Let medicines do their work, but through prayers, we can achieve astonishing results beyond medicines. Prayer in any form, if done with faith and belief, counts. We don't have to be hard-core religious persons, nor do we need to visit a sacred place to pray. The only requirement is that it should be done with a pure heart. It is not to be offered by rote memorisation without deep feeling or understanding. It should be intense enough to melt the heart.

Prayer is an inner expression of immense gratitude. Its intensity can also affect us at a genetic level. They can awaken emotions in our system that can turn on and off certain genes. Our lifestyles have a huge role to play here. While clean lifestyle habits can turn on genes that can heal you, unhealthy lifestyle habits can turn on genes that can bring about sickness and diseases. This is called epigenetics, where 'epi' stands for the environment and how it can control the functionality of a certain gene. For example, watching a clip from a funny video, a movie or a good laugh with friends can turn on over 700 genes and activate our immune system. But a drag of an anxious and angry lifestyle can also turn off those same 700 genes and dampen your immunity.

It is natural to share our sorrows during prayer, but let us also share our joy in the same manner. Let us offer gratitude and count our blessings. Instead of asking for something, the prayers should be full of gratitude for what the almighty God has given us. Convey your gratitude by saying, "Thank you for your blessings. Thank you for the air we breathe, the water we drink, and the food we eat." Also, we should include the entire universe in our prayers rather than limiting to ourselves.

We go wrong when spirituality is practised as a fad. This adds more complexity to it. Prayers are not any other To-Do list activity in our day. Prayers and their teachings must slip into our daily lives. The three essentials when it comes to prayers are faith, belief, and surrendering. Is it in order if we pray fervently almost daily and visit different religious places but are still anxious and worried about the very problems we prayed for? Let us pray with the utmost faith and belief and just surrender the outcome. Above all, we should keep practising our prayers until we build enough faith that there is no room for fear. Also, we should not take the power of prayer for granted because it is free or because the results of prayers aren't immediate. The power of this simple act is astonishing. Sometimes, when life hits us through some emotional, physical or financial challenge, all we need to do is step back, pray, and ask for help. Also, cultivate the habit of prayers in our children.

4.27 THE ASTOUNDING POWER OF ASSOCIATION

You are an average of five or six people you spend the most time with. Long associations tend to create similarities. Both positivity and negativity are highly contagious-more so is negativity. Hence, exploit the positive power of association by selecting and associating with people who cause you to perform better. Keep company with those who are thinking and acting at an extraordinary level. The greatest value of having good people around you is not what you get from them but the better person you become because of them.

Avoid the company of negative people. Also, don't surround yourself with yes-men.

4.28 WHAT IS MY BIOLOGICAL AGE?

Two persons having the same chronological age may have different biological ages. Everyone doesn't age at the same pace. Some people seem to age very rapidly, while others experience ageing at a much slower pace. For example, if I am a thirty-year-old male who doesn't exercise, only eat junk foods, and have been smoking five cigarettes per day for the last ten years, it's likely that my biological age would be greater than thirty years. Similarly, if I pursue resentments, don't forgive anyone, and always keep searching for occasions from even the smallest day-to-day situations to get angry or offended, my biological age would be much higher than my chronological age. Even the converse is also true. If a person is spiritually enlightened and emotionally stable and has healthy food habits, a balanced lifestyle and a philanthropically sensitive heart, not only his biological age will be lesser than his chronological age, but also he will have fewer age-related ailments.

The concept of biological age uses bio-physiological measures to determine an individual's age-related risk of adverse outcomes. It is the inner age, the age which internal biomarkers are clocking. While chronological age refers to the number of years a person has lived on Mother Earth since birth, biological age refers to epigenetic alteration and DNA methylation, which expresses how able and functioning he is and whether he has diseases related to old age. If we talk about longevity and living those years healthier with a quality life, the biological age matters the most - not the chronological age. Some people believe that biological age depends on hereditary factors. This is only partially true. We can very much control our ageing speed because the biological age, to a very large extent, depends upon our food habits, lifestyles and spiritual enlightenment. The imprints created on our minds affect our biological ageing process. Sattvic or naturopathic food, healthy lifestyle, detachment, philanthropic sensitivity, etc., create good imprints on our minds, reducing the pace of ageing.

What is my biological age? What steps am I taking to reduce my biological age in relation to my chronological age? These are the crucial introspection-provoking questions one must pose to oneself. While this is best done in the early stage of life, no stage of life is too late to start implementing biological age reduction measures. The scope of these steps must encompass both body and mind with a threefold aim to live younger from within, live longer and live a disease-free life with serenity and peace of mind.

In the Hindu religion, our life span is believed to be pre-decided. Even if we believe in this philosophy, we should not refrain from pursuing biological age reduction measures because such measures will reduce our age-related ailments and improve the quality of our lives. Another school of thought states that chronological age is a function of a predetermined number of breaths. That is why pranayama (the art of controlling breathing) prolongs longevity.

Besides biological age, we sometimes also refer to appearance and mental age in terms of spirit and IQ. For example, a sixty-year-old gentleman may appear younger than many fifty-year-old gentlemen, or a fifty-year-old gentleman may be young at heart with a spirit that may envy even a thirty-year young youth or a twelve-year-young boy may have mental age equivalent to that of a fifteen-year boy.

5

THE ART OF LIVING A LIFE OF EXCELLENCE: LAUDABLE PHILOSOPHIES AND AVOIDABLE SYNDROMES

5.1 THE ALTRUISTIC PHILOSOPHY

Altruistic philosophy is a philosophy of unselfishness. It is a philosophy of generosity and magnamity. It calls for living for the sake of others. Life is all about living for one another. To find yourself, lose yourself in the service of others. Your greatness lies in your ability to transcend the service of that which has greater value than yourself. At best, a selfish or self-centered person can achieve limited success or limited wealth. He can't live a life of excellence. He can open doors to abundant wealth only when he shifts his focus away from himself and his self-interest.

Self-centered philosophy is a philosophy of scarcity. Altruistic philosophy is the philosophy of abundance. Self-centered philosophy is a philosophy of zero leverage. Altruistic philosophy is the philosophy of mind-boggling leverage. Self-centered philosophy is me-oriented. Altruistic philosophy is we-oriented. Self-centered philosophy is a philosophy of loneliness leading to unhappiness. Altruistic philosophy is the philosophy of connectedness leading to happiness. Only altruistic intentions drive great success. We can't reach the top by pulling down others. We can uplift ourselves to the top only if we lift others. Bending down to lift someone else up is the best social exercise. Hence, we must embed the altruistic philosophy in our DNA and keep the same in focus while establishing the predominant purpose of our life and designing PMS.

5.2 THE UBUNTU PHILOSOPHY

One anthropologist studying the customs of a poor African tribe bought some delicious candies from the nearest town and put them all in a decorated basket at the foot of a tree. Then he called the children and suggested they play the game. The children had to run to the tree upon getting a green signal. The first one to get there could have all the candies to himself. So the children lined up, waiting for the signal. Immediaitely on receiving the signal, all the children took each other by hand and ran together towards the tree. They all arrived simultaneously, picked up the basket together, sat down, shared the candies equally and began to munch away happily. The anthropologist was expecting that, being extremely poor, the children would push each other to grab the basket. He asked, "Why did you run together when any of you could have had all the candies?" The children responded: "Ubuntu. How could any of us be happy if all the others were sad?"

Ubuntu, a philosophy of some African tribes, is the essence of being human. It is about humanity towards others. Ubuntu highlights the fact that we can't exist as human beings in isolation. We can't be human all by ourselves. It speaks about our interconnection. We think of ourselves far too frequently as just individuals, separated from one another, although we are connected and what we do affects the entire world. When we do well, it spreads out; it is for the whole of humanity. Ubuntu also signifies generosity. Sustainable success can be achieved only by altruistic efforts, spreading happiness, and generously sharing our wealth and resources.

Altruistic and Ubuntu philosophies must also be inculcated in our children from childhood.

5.3 ARE WE RECIPIENTS OR GIVERS?

Prepare a list of those who have helped you. The help need not necessarily be financial but could be in any form, like sharing knowledge, advice, wisdom, hope, love, or time. Remain grateful to them forever. Praise them in public. Reciprocate their help whenever possible.

Prepare a second list of those you have helped selflessly and unconditionally. If the second list is bigger than the first (both in terms of numbers and the magnitude of the help), you have lived a life of excellence. This is probably the best index for measuring life's success because helping others gives you a sense of fulfilment and makes you feel happy inside. When you help others, do so privately and delete it from your memory.

5.4 SHOULD MONEY BE THE CENTER OF LIFE?

If you start your business simply with the idea of getting rich, it is unlikely to succeed. However, when you turn your thoughts (and hence activities) to serving others, those things you used to chase after will follow you. In business, as in life, you are rewarded for your intense passion for serving others. You can't prosper without bringing prosperity to others. Hence, becoming rich shouldn't be your goal. Instead, let money come as a by-product to you. You must have a larger aspiration beyond self-interest or beyond becoming rich. The aspiration should include serving others, resolving some burning issue, or contributing valuably to the world. Of course, for this to happen, you must also create impeccable goodwill ahead of earning income and anchor the superstructure of your career or business on a strong foundation of sound core values and principles. Once you do this, you can write your price tag.

5.5 THE NET APPROACH V/S GARDEN APPROACH TO EARNING MONEY

If we want to catch or attract butterflies, we can either use a butterfly-catching net or develop a garden. Since money is as tricky and transient as butterflies, we often use the analogy of butterflies to explain the distinction between two strategies that can be deployed for earning money. While the first strategy for earning money uses a direct approach similar to the butterfly-catching net to attract customers, the second strategy indirectly attracts customers by first developing a garden.

5.5.1 The net approach to earning money

You can catch butterflies by building a net. You can gradually catch more butterflies by using a bigger net or sharpening butterfly-catching skills. However, this approach has a fundamental flaw because even after many years of hard work, you still need to wake up every day and go out to catch butterflies. Also, you need to hold on to the butterflies you have caught, or they will fly away just as quickly. You are constantly in a state of fear that the butterflies will disappear. When the butterflies disappear, you're left with nothing.

We observe that many highly educated people who have learned well about sales, marketing, customer service and finance have to struggle a lot to earn even survival income. They carefully follow the strategies they learned but remain baffled as to why they do not attract the same opportunities, resources, and sheer luck as their role models. They are erring in as much as they are trying to make money without first building a sound foundation of true wealth.

5.5.2 The garden approach to earning money

"I brought a sparrow. She left me. Then I brought a squirrel. She also ran away. I planted a tree. Sparrow and squirrel both came to me on their own."

– Dr. A. P. J. Abdul Kalam

Wise wealth creators don't focus on building a butterfly-catching net. They know that if they do so, they will struggle every day to earn even a survival income. Instead, first, they grow a beautiful, inspiring garden around their passions. Once they build a garden, opportunities or customers come to them on their own. As the garden grows, more and more butterflies come. In fact, the butterflies, birds, and bees end up proliferating your garden for you. You don't have to worry about catching butterflies daily nor fear that they will leave, as they always come on their own and stay with you.

Every successful wealth creator is focused essentially on building a sound foundation ahead of their money-making activities. This garden could be in the form of a knowledge base, a resource base, a reputation, an enviable goodwill, a powerful network, a popular brand, an economic moat, or an impeccable track record. They build this garden not around their skill or expertise but their passions. Once the garden is created on sound principles, it soon attains a self-proliferating status. They wake up to their passion every day, unlike daily income earners who start the day with an empty net. Thus, by using a garden approach, you can create wealth on a sustainable basis and that too effortlessly.

In a speech to a group of students, Warren once said, "I may have more money than you, but money doesn't make the difference. If there is any difference between you and me, it may simply be that I get up every day and have a chance to pursue my passions and do what I love to do. This is the best advice I can give you."

Apart from Warren, there are several examples where the garden approach to wealth creation has worked effectively. Richard Branson attracts the right businesses that suit Virgin. Jack Welch, CEO of GE and one of America's best-known leaders attracted the right people who suited his leadership style. Mukesh Ambani is able to attract investors because of the garden of goodwill created by his late father, Dhirubhai Ambani. Thus, each wealth profile has a unique value that creates this attraction–a different garden they are tending to.

5.6 FORGIVENESS: A VIRTUE OF BRAVERY

क्षमा वीरस्य भूषणम्.

Forgiveness is a virtue of bravery. It is essential to maintain a peaceful mind. Life is too short to waste time hating anyone. Hate the sin; not the sinner. On the contrary, love the sinner. Forgive all. Forgive freely. Forgive unconditionally. The ability to forgive is not a sign of weakness; it is a sign of the biggest personal strength. Whereas tolerance represents the highest degree of our strength, the desire to take revenge is the first sign of weakness. Wise people are powerful; they are not powerless. They can forgive others because they are not powerless. Powerful people forgive. Powerless people pursue resentment. Wise people overlook. Weak people take revenge.

Practice forgiveness for two reasons. One is to let others know that you no longer wish to be in a state of hostility with that person and the second is to free yourself from the self-defeating energy of resentment. You don't have to make others wrong or retaliate when you have been wronged. Send love in some form to those you feel have wronged you and notice how much better and more peaceful you feel. When you respond with hatred to hate directed at you, you become part of the problem that is hatred rather than the solution, which is love. Love is without resentment and readily offers forgiveness. Love and forgiveness will inspire you to work at what you are for rather than what you are against. Be a part of the solution rather than a victim of a problem. Focus your energy on a solution rather than justifying a problem.

Dr. Wayne Dyer, describes ten principles for living successfully with serenity and peace of mind. The fifth principle says, 'There are no justified resentments.' Whatever the severity or magnitude of our pain, we are not justified in pursuing resentment. Often, we are hurt by others severely. Many times, we keep pursuing resentment for decades after the event. Every day, we think about that old event as if it happened yesterday. This does not allow us to forget that event. By remembering that event every day, we are, in effect, giving the Power of Attorney (with a lifelong validity) to the other person to degrade us perpetually. We must learn to depersonalise the event and respond with kindness. We must treat this as a comment on our actions, not on us.

Visualise yourself as a competent person in your own right. Learn to avoid craving for external validation. Don't pursue revenge. Once you forgive, your mind is free from the old baggage and you are able to move ahead in life. Dr. Dyer goes on to say further, "Still, in your wisdom, if you wish to pursue resentment, better dig two graves." This is a priceless message. Your resentment can destroy you. Resentment is a bundle of low energies. Forgiveness is a bundle of high energies. Pursuing resentment changes the entire alchemy of the body. It internally damages our body beyond repair, especially when we pursue resentment for extended periods. It is scientifically proven that whereas pursuing resentment releases harmful and toxic chemicals in our bodies, forgiving releases many beneficial hormones. We may have to change our outlook and treat those who have hurt us as Purifying Agents sent by the almighty God.

Also, if someone has admitted his mistake, forgive him gracefully and close this chapter permanently. Don't keep on harping or reminding him about this for the rest of his life. And if you are so compassionate, why don't you help him correct them? Otherwise, leave it to nature; she has her own ways of setting it right. Similarly, provide room for a graceful exit. Allowing others to exit gracefully from an unpleasant incident is an art. Articulate graceful exit with extra care. Allow him a face-saving opportunity. Skilfully cover up the incident so that his self-respect is maintained in the eyes of the public. Not only will he remain grateful to you forever, but he will also learn from this incident and correct himself on his own. However, if you don't facilitate a graceful exit, his self-respect will receive a permanent blow, adversely affecting his morale.

5.7 OUR JOURNEY IS TOO SHORT

Once, a young lady was travelling on a bus. At the next stop, an elderly, obese lady gets onto the bus and sits beside the young lady. She pushes the young lady and makes herself comfortable, occupying much more space than her share. She had also brought big carry bags with her, which she kept encroaching on the area of the young lady. Disturbed by this, one young boy sitting next to the young lady said, "Why are you not saying anything to this lady? She is causing a lot of inconvenience to you." The young lady smiled and replied, "There is no need to react to something so insignificant. Our journey together is too short.

I am getting down at the next stop." This reaction deserves to be inscribed in golden letters. What a beautiful message the young lady has conveyed by her conduct and reply! We must keep reminding ourselves that our journey is too short. Let us not spend our time and energy on useless things. Is it worth spending $100 emotion on a five-cent irritation? While the journey on the bus is limited to a few hours, life's journey spans over a few decades. Though the unit of time in a life's journey is larger than that of a bus journey, it is still limited. It is finite. We have very little time in our life.

When our life span is limited, should we spend our time picking up unnecessary fights, arguing with others, maintaining a non-adjusting nature, blaming or cursing others? Is this a wise use of our time and energy? If someone insults or hurts you, ignore it and remain calm. Our journey is too short. If someone has betrayed or cheated on you, intimidated or harmed you, relax and don't stress. Let it pass because our journey is too short. If I have hurt you knowingly or unknowingly, forgive me. If you have hurt me, I have already forgiven you long back. Hurt no one. Hurt no one even by thoughts in your mind or your words. Let us forgive others. Let us appreciate others. Let us be kind to each other. In return, you will be filled with gratitude and joy.

5.8 OVER-FORTY MINDSET

When you are young, you feel no urgency. You think there is plenty of time. You believe there is always tomorrow, more days and more years. You behave with a carefree attitude as if you have infinite time at your disposal. You don't eliminate or offload irrelevant tasks. You surrender control of your time to others. You allow others to dictate the activities that fill your days and weeks; in the process, you tend to postpone activities that pursue your personal interests or passion.

However, all of that changes once you hit forty. You find that time is racing by very fast. You feel the day barely has started and it is already six in the evening. Barely arrived on Monday and it is already Friday. Months and years fly before you realise what is happening to your life. Suddenly, you start realising that you are mortal. Incidents like the death of parents, relatives, or friends shake you completely. You regret not spending quality time with them. You realise it is too late to go back. While more than half of your life is over, you still have a long bucket list of unfulfilled items. The over-forty mindset is sparked by the realisation that the balance period of life is limited. This realisation makes you more self-centered and me-oriented. You now regret what you have been neglecting for years. This makes you a little selfish about your time. You start concentrating more on your bucket list and what is good for you and less on what everybody else demands from you. You also realise that you don't have to please other people all the time.

Should we consume an inordinate amount of time from our limited life span merely to learn that our interests and passion deserve the topmost priority? Should we not learn from the experience of others to have an over-forty mindset without growing old ourselves? If you can adapt to an over-forty mindset even when you are under forty, you can start pursuing your personal interest right from the early stage of your life,

When you are spending another day doing what somebody else has dictated or something which is not part of your life's passion or when you have lost a sense of purpose in your life, remind yourself that you have a finite time to get on with for what you showed up here in the first place. Stop being that perfect person for someone; live life on yourself. Take yourself under your control and make it perfect for yourself. Tap into your inspiration and channelise your inner muse. Listen to your inner music and ignore what everyone else around you thinks about what you should be doing. Get that music out. Let it play. Sing the song you came to sing. Don't leave this unsung. Don't spend your life stringing or unstringing your instrument. You become alive, motivated and energised when you sing your song. Love your work. Your work brings meaning and fulfilment. It is a wonderful feeling. Live your life fully. Don't just live; celebrate life. Embrace every breath you are taking. Be grateful. Be alive and live every moment. Keep looking for activities that you like. Put some vibrant colours in your grey. Smile at the little things in life that put balm in your heart. Dance, even if you are too bad at it. Pose stupidly for photos. Take funny selfies. Don't die with your music still in you. Similarly, don't die with guilt. Instead, develop a coping mechanism. Don't die before your death. Death is not the greatest loss of life. Great loss is when life dies inside you while you are alive. Though we do not have control over the timing of our death, we have complete control over the time between our birth and death. So, despite everything, follow your passion and try to enjoy the remaining time of your life with serenity and peace of mind.

5.9 THE MAGNIFICIENT MUSE OF MIRROR PHILOSOPHY

Once, I went to a small village in Gujarat. In villages, the relationships between mother-in-law and daughter-in-law are usually quite strained. I saw the old lady of the house making a statement in the morning, "I am going to have a terrible day today; I have seen the wretched face of my daughter-in-law early in the morning." The next day, she makes the same statement. So, I went to that lady and asked her whether I could suggest something. When she replied affirmatively, I said, "I suggest you fix a big mirror in front of your bed." She implemented the suggestion without understanding its deep implications. The next day, the whole family was surprised, though I wasn't, that she didn't make her usual morning statement. After a few days, she started saying, "I am going to have a wonderful day today." When she sees her face in the mirror first thing in the morning, can she make any other statement? Incidentally, once your mind decides that you will have a wonderful day, you will definitely have a wonderful day. The seeds of a wonderful day are first sawn in the mind.

This simple example describes the essence of a mirror philosophy. The mirror is a muse of many, be it authors, poets, or philosophers, though we usually look in the mirror only for cosmetic purposes. Mirrors have great utility beyond cosmetic objectives if we introspect in front of the mirror. Before finding fault with others, we must look in the mirror. Before criticising others, we must look in the mirror. If we have tried hard to improve all people around us and failed, it is time to look in the mirror for self-improvement by applying the same yardsticks we have been applying to others. If we have been searching for one person who can transform our lives, our search ends when we look in the mirror. Thus, the mirror is a powerful tool that forces us to deal with ourselves at a deeper level. We must develop the habit of looking in the mirror if we want to live a life of excellence. We must make this habit a part of our personality. Once we do so, we don't need a physical mirror.

5.10 ONE PLUS ONE FREE PHILOSOPHY

We all love shopping, especially when we get one plus one free, even if it is a marketing gimmick. This scheme applies to our life as well. We get acidity free with anger. Ulcer comes free when we get pink. We get high blood pressure as a free gift when we stress ourselves. We get headache free when we become jealous.

On the other side of this philosophy, good health comes free with exercise. Sound sleep comes as a free gift with a positive attitude towards life. Peace of mind comes free with forgiveness. Trust in relationships brings enrichment in relationships as a free gift.

Which of the above two schemes do we want to grab?

5.11 THE ART OF MANAGING EXPECTATIONS

Expectations are a part of our life. Expectations are natural. These are just our imaginations about how things might be in the future. However, most of us do not even realise that having too many expectations could be a reason for not being naturally happy. It prevents the mind from being in harmony with what is happening at the present moment and reduces the joy inherent in the present moment. Expectations are not something we can or should avoid. Like all other thoughts, they arise and pass away on their own. We must learn the art of managing expectations. Simply remaining detached and observing them with an awareness that they reduce joy in life is enough to avoid getting caught up in it. While expectations, especially unfulfilled expectations, reduce joy; surprises give us more joy.

5.11.1 Not the situation, but your response to the situation dictates your happiness

Have we observed that different people respond to the same situations differently? Remember, your response to a situation (which, in turn, is based on your expectations) is far more important than the situation itself. It is not the situation but your response to that situation that dictates whether you become happy or sad, as illustrated by the following simple example:

Suppose you are attending a group meditation session and someone's phone rings. While some members may ignore this, others get irritated. Those who are mature enough to manage their expectations are not disturbed by the phone ringing. But those who feel that the phone owners lack discipline and are inconsiderate are unable to accept this disturbance. Consequently, their mind will simmer with irritation and anger, jeopardising the very purpose of meditation. The underlying situation is the same for both categories of people, but responses are different. The second category of people gets disturbed because they believe people should behave as they expect them to behave. Thus, their expectations are at the core of their disturbance. The problem is not with the situation. Loud noise can also be created by dogs barking, rain, thunder, or traffic. However, they would not be annoyed about these noises because they would accept them as part of nature, as spontaneous happenings. You have a choice to change your state of mind or break your head in trying to change situations. Once you choose to change the inner state of your mind, you will look at every situation in your life with a positive frame of mind. This positivity will help you interpret the situation harmoniously. It is the inner state of your mind that will determine the quality of your life. While a negative inner state is your enemy, a positive inner state is your friend.

5.11.2 Expectations pertaining to day-to-day situations

While some people get irritated even by ordinary situations of life (like a traffic jam, scolding by the boss, a spouse picking up a quarrel or an insult by someone), others maintain an enviable composure even under the most unpleasant situations. The root cause of this irritation is our expectations from others about their behaviour. Also, instead of treating this as a one-time event, we tend to generalise this situation. This tendency can trigger a chain of negative thoughts if we do not control our inner state. One insult reminds us of many of our past insults. We don't even realise it when we log on to our hurt-bank account and open a treasure of perpetual unhappiness.

5.11.3 Expectations pertaining to materialistic possessions

We expect to possess many things in our lives, but not all expectations are fulfilled. Unfulfilled expectations, especially those pertaining to materialistic possessions, are the predominant source of unhappiness. While an excessive desire for materialistic possessions can lead to perpetual unhappiness, a contented mind is a continual feast. However, we observe that most people are madly running after material possessions and contentment is practised only by a few people. We must learn to differentiate between need and want. If we don't draw a line, the fulfilment of one desire gives rise to the next desire and happiness will keep eluding us. Since man is a wanting animal by nature, seeking happiness through materialistic possessions is a never-ending phenomenon. There is always enough for the needy but never for the greedy.

Also, if a person is deeply bound to material things, he becomes unhappy when they are taken away. By all means, enjoy worldly objects, but don't become bound or get wedded to them. Don't make your happiness dependent on material possessions. We must realise that true happiness doesn't come from worldly possessions. If we look within ourselves and source our happiness from the inside, we will always be happy and external factors will not be able to destroy our happiness. We need a deep understanding of our minds and life before we 'let go' of our expectations. When you grow in wisdom, you see these impressions drop off and give way to something bigger and more beautiful. We can achieve lasting happiness, serenity and peace of mind if we curb greed and material desires and strengthen our willpower. Those who live a contended life without undue attachment to worldly possessions and strive for spirituality at the core are likely to live a happier life.

5.11.4 Expectations pertaining to fame, prestige or honour

Expectations pertaining to fame, prestige, or honour are yet another source of unhappiness. Many desire and crave fame, but little do they know they are looking for a cage. Most people are stuck in their self-created cage of fame, prestige and honour. They can't even smile or behave normally. They are constantly worried about keeping up their fame. It becomes more important than their own lives. Is being good or looking good to keep the fame so important for you to stop living your natural life? Mad pursuit to keep up fame can bring more misery into life than financial poverty.

5.11.5 Expectations pertaining to relationships

In relationships, you often find people don't live up to your expectations. This leads to unhappiness if you are spiritually unenlightened. A spiritually enlightened person never gets upset for two reasons: firstly, he has very few expectations from relationships and secondly, even if his expectations from relationships are not fulfilled, he remains compassionate and lets it pass. When you expect others to do something for you, don't become miserable if they don't do it. Remember, people's behaviour is the outcome of their upbringing, education and exposure. They are probably not fortunate enough to have an upbringing like you. Don't get frustrated and blame or curse them. You can overcome frustration arising from unfulfilled expectations from relationships by forgiving those who broke your heart. Whereas cursing those who hurt you generates negative energy, blessing them, even when your expectations are not met, generates positive energy. Dropping off expectations and accepting others as they are is the master key to enriching relationships.

5.11.6 Misinterpretation of the philosophy of managing expectations

The philosophy about expectations needs to be understood in its proper perspective. Expectations reduce joy in life, but that doesn't mean you should have no expectations or fewer expectations, nor does it mean that you should not have goals in your life or aim low. Goals are very much needed in life and goals should be challenging. They say missing a goal can be pardoned, but not setting a low goal. An aimless or low-aiming life will be quite boring and may lead to depression. So, set some challenging goals and keep moving in that direction. Well-structured goals will move your life in the right direction and you will get satisfaction upon achievement. However, don't link your happiness to success. Learn to remain detached from the outcome.

5.11.7 Managing expectations through meditation

Meditation helps to uproot the disturbance or disappointment arising from unfulfilled expectations. When you meditate with no attempt to control your mind, you will sooner or later arrive at the conviction that thoughts, feelings and body sensations are arising and disappearing all by themselves with no volition on your part. This awareness brings more calmness, allowing the mind to rest more and more in the present moment. Meditation will give you a dose of joy, peace, and contentment. It'll also create new pathways in your brain, making it easier for you to feel joy. The mind gains the spontaneous ability to accept people and situations as they are. Consequently, regular meditation will result in fewer expectations. This leads to the elimination of disturbances and disappointments arising from unfulfilled expectations.

5.11.8 Managing expectations through dilution from demand to preference

You can reduce likely pain arising from unfulfilled expectations if you change your outlook towards expectations. The stronger the attachment to the expectations, the more is the pain when expectations are not fulfilled. So, the secret of reducing pain lies in diluting attachment towards expectations from demands to preferences. Have expectations but not as absolute non-negotiable demands or your birthright. Dilute your expectations. Let it be in the form of preferences. This will reduce pain in life because preferences are not so taxing. For example, don't expect pin-drop silence as an absolute or non-negotiable demand. Expect silence as a preference rather than a demand so that you will still be in harmony with the situation even if silence is not maintained.

5.12 THE ART OF ARTICULATED RESPONSES

Many people get offended even by ordinary situations in life. They always look for an occasion to be offended. A news report, an economic downturn, a traffic jam, a rude stranger, someone cursing, a sneeze, a black cloud, or any cloud-just about anything will do to offend them. This happens because of a low level of awareness. We can eliminate the tendency to get offended by uplifting our level of awareness. Remember, we have the freedom to choose our response and we can make a conscious choice and refuse to get offended. Be a person who refuses to be offended by anyone, anything, or any set of circumstances. Not being offended is a way of saying, 'I have control over how I am going to feel and I choose to feel peaceful regardless of what I observe going on.' When we feel offended, we are practising judgment. We judge someone else to be stupid, insensitive, rude, arrogant, or inconsiderate. We become upset and offended by their conduct. We wear the hat of a judge and give our verdict. When we judge someone, we don't define them; we define ourselves. This shows our craving to judge others. A wise man will never judge others. He would merely observe or rather coach others. When we stop judging others and become observers, we will appreciate the value of inner peace and find ourselves free of the negative energy of resentment, leading to a life of contentment. A bonus is that we will find others much more attracted to us, leading to enriching relationships.

Also, we don't have to be upset with any person or situation because both are powerless without our reaction. If someone calls me a donkey, I don't become a donkey, but if I get worked up and roll up my sleeves and fight with him, I become one, as I have accepted his comment. When we react to negative things, we accept and invite those negatives into our lives. Thus, we must learn to control our reactions. Establish awareness in defenselessness. Unless I attain a deep level of awareness, I am merely adding years to my life - growing older but not becoming wiser.

"Between (external) stimulus and (our) response, there is a space. In that space is our power to choose our response. In our response lies our growth and freedom."

— **Viktor E Frankl**

Humans have evolved from animals over millions of years. Animals have a primitive brain known as the reptilian brain or lizard brain. Animals live in a jungle and they are under continuous threat of getting killed by other animals. Every stimulus is treated by their reptilian brain as if it is a threat to their existence. Hence, the instinctive tendency of the reptilian brain is to respond violently to any stimulus in order to save its life. Whereas animals have only reptilian brains, humans have two more brains: the paleomammalian or emotional brain (limbic system) and the neomammalian or rational brain (neocortex). The electronic signal of stimulus takes a quarter of a second to travel from the reptilian brain to the paleomammalian brain. If we respond to a stimulus instantly, our response will be animal-like. If we allow a quarter second to pass, our paleomammalian brain takes over control of the situation. Once the paleomammalian brain is activated, our response will be human-like. So, we should never translate our thoughts into action in anger. Handle this space by taking a deep breath, counting from one to ten, chanting some mantra etc. and allowing time for the paleomammalian brain to take control of the situation. Thus, how we handle the space between external stimulus and our response decides the quality of our life.

The situation is an external reality. Our reaction or response to that situation generated in our mind is the internal reality. Our internal dialogue, likes and dislikes, temperament, judgment and preconceived notions constitute our internal reality. We should purify internal reality with enlightenment to view external reality in its unpolluted form and interpret it in its proper perspective. We don't have control over the situation coming to us, nor can we control the behaviour of others; but we have full control over our response. Our greatest inner strength is the power to be silent, the power to be calm. Our belief that life is full of infinite possibilities is our internal strength. This belief gives us ample scope for creative solutions. Our inner strength is a commitment to be a part of the solution.

Getting worked up is a movement of thought. When there is a movement of thought, we see the object, not the subject. Don't go to the object; go to the subject - our thought space where there is silence. When we log on to the subject of thought - the silence, the thought disappears slowly. However, if we log on to the object of the thought, we add our internal chaos to it. We should learn to log on to our inner strength, the silence, the way a tennis player logs on to the ball and not his opponent. Like Hanuman, we should log on to our inner strength and draw energy from there.

5.13 DETACHMENT TO RESULTS: THE BHAGAVAD GITA PHILOSOPHY

कर्मण्येवाधिकारस्ते मा फलेषु कदाचन।

मा कर्मफलहेतुर्भूर्मा ते सङ्गोऽस्त्वकर्मणि॥ २-४७

You have the right to work only but never to its fruits. Let not the fruits of action be your motive, nor let your attachment be to inaction. This quote from the Bhagavad Gita is worth its weight in gold.

While efforts are in your hands, the results are not always in your hands. The results are a function of your efforts and external factors beyond your control. These two variables can generate four permutations as follows:

Scenario	Permutation	Result	Remarks
I	Cent percent of self-efforts + favourable external factors	Excellent result	
II	Cent percent of self-efforts + Unfavourable external factors	Poor result	Gita teaches us not to get disheartened in such situations.
III	Lack of self-efforts + favourable external factors	Poor result	Because you were disheartened by Scenario II, you missed the opportunity to convert Scenario III into Scenario I.
IV	Lack of self-efforts + Unfavourable external factors	Poor result	

Many people define success wrongly and as a result, they define failure also wrongly. Success is not in the results or achievements. Success is not what you get at the end. Success is in your endeavours, your intentions, the noble thing you are trying to do, your efforts and the character that goes behind it. Once you have invested in all these things, it is already a success, whatever may be the result. If you measure success by a pre-determined specific outcome, the thought of failure will dominate your mind throughout your journey. The goal of life is not to be the best. Hence, keep performing your duty to the best of your abilities. Give your cent percent and leave the rest to the almighty God. This philosophy will eliminate your undue craving for a specific successful outcome and help you avoid a demoralising effect on your mind if you fail to achieve goals despite giving your cent percent. When you fail, it is important that you don't give up. If you fail, start all over again with even more vigour.

5.14 THE SPIRITUAL LAW OF DETACHMENT

The law of detachment states that for the truly meaningful acquisition of anything in this physical universe, you have to relinquish your attachment to it. While attachment is based on fear and insecurity arising out of ignorance, detachment is based on the unquestioning belief in the power of your true self. In detachment lies the wisdom of uncertainty and in the wisdom of uncertainty lies the freedom from the prison of our past. When we are willing to come out of this prison and step into the unknown, the field of infinite possibilities, we are, in effect, surrendering to our creative mind that orchestrates the dance of the universe. Forcing solutions to problems is an attachment. Limiting your thinking to past benchmarks is an attachment. Opening your mind to infinite possibilities and allowing the solution to get evolved creatively is detachment. Attachment, at best, can fetch you some incremental success with respect to the past. However, detachments can fetch you limitless success to the next level. The source of wealth, or abundance of anything in this physical world, is the self, the consciousness, that knows how to fulfil every need. Everything else is a symbol. Things like cars, bungalows, and currency notes are symbols. Symbols are transitory; they come and go. Chasing symbols is like settling for a map instead of territory. It creates anxiety, emptiness and hollowness because you exchange yourself for symbols of yourself. Whereas attachment to symbols represents poverty consciousness, detachment represents abundance because you have the freedom to create without benchmarking to the past. Every attachment is an impediment to living at a higher level of consciousness. If we don't practice detachment, we continue to remain prisoners of helplessness, hopelessness, mundane needs, and trivial concerns.

Detachment means neither overrejoicing in success nor weeping in failure. Your failure should not confine your happiness and your happiness should not be defined by success, either. Don't entrap your happiness by your success or failure. Don't let your life depend on success or failure. This law doesn't mean you give up your desire or intention; you only give up your attachment to the outcome. Relinquish your rigid attachment to a specific outcome. Allow uncertainty to play out. When you keep yourself detached from the outcome, you are in a state of inner peace with whatever is to happen, be it good or bad. However, being detached doesn't mean being unconcerned. It is possible to have a burning desire yet not have attachments. This can be done by visualising what you want to manifest and still detaching yourself from the outcome. If Thomas Edison had a strong attachment to some pre-conceived outcome, he would have given up after the first few attempts. But since he detached himself from the outcome, he kept trying incessantly till he successfully invented the light bulb. Similarly, the Wright brothers could invent a new mode of transport only because they detached themselves from the past mode of transport (i.e. surface transport).

Realise that your attachments are the biggest source of all your problems. We usually refer to attachment only in the context of the need to possess something or someone. This definition needs to be widened. The broader definition of attachment includes the need to be always right, win arguments, craving to be viewed by others as superior, and so on. The open mind resists these attachments and consequently, you experience inner peace and tranquillity. But if you are attached to being right or need something to be at peace, you will always strive but never arrive. Detachment is the only vehicle that can take you from striving to arriving. Detachment is one of life's greatest lessons for those on the path to enlightenment.

5.15 CELEBRATE BEST EFFORTS

Learn to celebrate your best efforts rather than getting disheartened over failures. Most people don't celebrate their best efforts because we are only taught to celebrate if we are a winner. It is a great feeling to win, but if you don't win after putting in your best efforts, it doesn't make you a loser, either. Most of us wait for that one perfect moment to feel like a winner. We see a true accomplishment only when we showcase we are the best. We don't realise that we can never be the best in everything.

Give your best in everything you do. Learn to crave for excellence, though you don't have to be perfect. Remember, perfection is not the same thing as excellence. Hence, don't aim for perfection. Be progressive. Perfection is a consequence. Progressiveness is a journey. Give your cent percent but remain detached from the outcome. Don't worry about intermittent failures. Celebrate your best efforts and see how you can do even better next time. Keep trying. Never give up. Keep growing and maturing. Remember, success is not measured by the heights you may scale in the future; it is measured by how happy you are in the present moment with what you have achieved. Don't link happiness to your future success. If you do so, you will always be striving but never arriving.

5.16 THE TENDENCY TO JUSTIFY THE STATUS QUO USING EXTERNAL REASONS

Human beings usually prefer the status quo. The status quo bias is one type of cognitive bias that involves people preferring that things stay as they are. It refers to the human tendency to follow the line of least resistance and avoid making extra efforts which are required to change one's environment or a situation for the better. People don't change when you give them an option; they change only when there is no other option.

If we want to change the status quo, we need strong motivation. Also, we need to overcome the inertia. However, our desire to maintain the status quo is so strong that we even find some external reason to justify our status quo. Once this happens, we stick to it with even more force; consequently; it becomes almost impossible to change the status quo.

Suppose a person is currently living in poor financial condition. If he links his current poor status to some external reasons, like his parents not giving him adequate capital to start a business or his business partner betraying him, he will justify his poverty by taking the help of such external reasons and he will keep on doing so for the rest of his life. Since he has managed to get some external reason, he doesn't feel it necessary to make extra efforts on his part to change his status quo. He wanted to avoid making extra efforts in any case, and now that he has got some external reason beyond his control to justify his status quo, he will not make any efforts to change the status quo. Thus, external reason provides him with a very convenient way to follow the line of the least resistance. He convinces himself that changing his poor status is not in his hands.

Unless we avoid blaming others and take responsibility to carve our lives into ourselves, we can't succeed. We must make extra efforts to improve our lives instead of taking the help of external reasons to justify the status quo. The habit of giving excuses shouldn't be in our genes.

5.17 THE ART OF MANAGING PHYSICAL PAIN

Have we observed that some people mentally collapse even with minor physical pain, whereas others face physical pain of the highest severity with a smiling face? What is the reason for such two exactly opposite behaviour?

We know that the root of physical pain is in the body and mental pain is in the mind. It is possible that physical pain may induce mental pain and vice versa. For example, cancer in the body results in physical pain, but if our mind is full of worries about its outcome, we are adding mental pain to this physical pain. Similarly, mental pain can also induce physical pain. For example, if we habitually worry about even small things in life, we may eventually get an ulcer in our stomach.

Psychologists have established with evidence that the connection between physical pain and mental pain is not absolute; it is dismantleable. The wise people dismantle this connection. They don't allow physical pain to attend a status of mental pain. They restrict physical pain at the level of pure physical pain only. If we allow mental pain to combine with physical pain, even a minor physical pain attains the status of severe pain because the mind has the power to exaggerate physical pain manifold. Our ignorance and absence of spiritual enlightenment make this connection stronger.

Whenever something is internally wrong in the body, the body raises the alarm through physical pain so that we take action to eliminate that disorder. This is nature's way of warning. How else do we know that something is wrong internally inside our bodies? Physical pain is an inbuilt natural relief mechanism that communicates something wrong inside the body. For example, a fever by itself is not a disease, but it indicates something wrong in the body- the level of infection in the body might have increased beyond acceptable limits. A wise and enlightened person knows that worrying about physical pain or adding mental pain to physical pain will not help reduce physical pain; on the contrary, this deadly combination of physical pain and mental pain makes it even more difficult to get rid of physical pain.

5.18 I-AM-OK-YOU-AREN'T-OK SYNDROME

Many people suffer from the 'I'm-OK-you-aren't-OK' syndrome. This syndrome is an aggressive philosophy focused on self-superiority, represented by one of the four quadrants of the transactional analysis matrix. 'I'm-OK-you-aren't-OK' thinking develops when people think only they are worthy and others are not. They suffer from a superiority complex. They self-certify themselves as OK and label the rest of the world as not OK. They believe that the fault always lies with the rest of the world. If something is wrong, it is with others, not with me. This is exactly the opposite of a mirror philosophy. This aggressive philosophy can result in arrogance or disrespect for authority. They may also develop a perfectionism streak to prove their self-proclaimed superiority.

Managers or leaders suffering from the 'I'm-OK-you-aren't-OK' syndrome may overpower the employee whose box is south of their box on the organisation chart, mistaking positional or hierarchical power for having a greater societal worth. They don't respect others' viewpoints and are insensitive to others' feelings. They dictate or force their views on others and expect others to change their viewpoints, actions and behaviour. If we assume another person is OK, wants to do the right thing, or has good intentions, honest mistakes are accepted. However, when we hold an aggressive view that others are not OK, we regard their human errors as the result of their inferiority or an act of malice. Managers with such an aggressive philosophy are more likely to domineer, sharply criticise and cut short feedback from others. This undermines workplace communication and creates an atmosphere of fear. This is the opposite of a collaborative workplace, where the entire team works toward common goals, even if it means challenging a boss' incorrect assumptions or opinions.

Even parents who continuously nag their children inadvertently fall into this aggressive syndrome. Such parents see themselves as OK or valuable while devaluing their own children. The children who are victims of this syndrome devalue themselves and this inferiority complex may continue even when they grow up, keeping them permanently suppressed.

However, we must remember that humility is the most important quality of a gentleman. Life is all about accommodating others. We can live a happy and peaceful life if we accommodate others, respect others, accept others as they are, forgive others, pursue patience and learn to overlook many things. Hence, get rid of the 'I'm-OK-you-aren't-OK' syndrome. The day we realise that the other person is not wrong, only his thinking differs from our thinking (or rather, our thinking differs from his thinking), all our miseries will go away.

5.19 MY-WAY-OR-HIGHWAY SYNDROME

My way or the highway is an ultimatum that means either fulfill my requirements or do not participate. Some people think that only their viewpoint is right or only their way of doing things is right. Such people don't respect others' views. They insist people adopt only their way of doing things and not any other way. They are not sensitive to others' feelings. They suffer from a superiority complex. This is called 'My-way-or-highway' syndrome. It is highly autocratic approach.

As a leader, we should be more interested in results and we should allow our team members to use their own methods to achieve the desired results. However, a leader suffering from the above syndrome insists his team members use his methods to achieve the desired results or do not participate. Because of such a threatening ultimatum, people have no option but to obey their leader. This not only kills the motivation of team members but also dampens creativity.

5.20 WHY-SHOULD-I-BEND SYNDROME

Often, we are on an ego trip. We refuse to bend even a little. Why should I phone him first? Why can't he phone me? Why should I go to his place? Why can't he come to my place? Why should I say sorry to him? Why should I adjust every time? These posers are symptoms of a big cancerous disease at a spiritual level.

A wise or enlightened person will not get such petty posers in his mind and even if such posers are generated in his mind during some weak moments, he knows how to address these posers appropriately.

If you are estranged from your loved ones, patch up the differences. Think of the pain you can eliminate on both sides. Think of the joy that could be yours. Who makes the first move for patch-up is not important. If required, take the help of a neutral person known to both in patch up. If your ego prevents you from patching up, tame, eliminate, or dissolve your ego. Ego is not being natural, not feeling at home, and not having a sense of belongingness. The ego creates tension and problems within you. It makes you stiff. The ego is like a wall. It blocks the flow of divine love. Ego is separateness – the sense of wanting to prove and possess. While an egoistic person demands that the world and all people be as he thinks they should be, an enlightened person refuses to be anything but peaceful and sees the world as it is.

If I am in such a situation, I should decide the righteous way to respond to such a situation. I will do it because I want serenity and peace of mind. I want good health. I want a good relationship. I will phone him first because I am powerful. I am blessed with that divine power to forgive others. Everybody is not blessed with such power. I always win because I have many weapons, like saying sorry, letting it go, smiling and silence. I will not sit at a long table; I will build bridges.

Life is a combination of adjustments and compromises. Adjust when someone wants to be with you; compromise when you want to be with someone. The test of love is sacrifice. How much are you prepared to sacrifice for the sake of those whom you love? Sacrifice is bigger than love. Character is bigger than beauty. Humanity is bigger than wealth. But nothing is bigger than keeping relations alive; for that, be prepared to do whatever it takes.

5.21 I-AM-INDISPENSABLE SYNDROME

We are not the only ones who can do our work. And if we think we are, it would be wise to reconsider and change this thinking. Delegate the job and give responsibilities. When given responsibilities, most people will rise to the occasion.

We often think that we are indispensable and don't even take vacations. We apprehend that the organisation will not run in our absence. In fact, if it is indeed so, it reflects poorly on us. One of the essential qualities of a successful leader is that he trains and develops enough deputies to step into his shoes and run the show equally well in his absence.

5.22 I-TOLD-YOU SYNDROME

Many of us suffer from I-told-you syndrome. If something untoward happens, we retrospectively say, "I told you this would happen, but you never listened to me." There are a couple of variants of this syndrome. In its simplest form, one category of people makes the above statement and gets satisfaction merely by uttering it. Other categories of people are so egoistic that they even go to the extent of sabotaging merely to prove that what they told was right. In yet another variant, people say, 'I told you' even when they have never told you so. This satisfies their ego. They want to show that they have a sixth sense and they can predict the future.

While we should avoid this syndrome, we should be aware of people suffering from this syndrome with an appropriate strategy to deal with it.

6

KNOW THYSELF AND FOCUS MORE ON SELF-IMPROVEMENT

*B*efore you attain a frame of mind conducive to living a life of excellence, you must master yourself first. Before you face the world with a desire to launch a serving or helping mission or produce your signature job, you must face yourself first. If you want to manage a family, you must learn to manage yourself first. Learn to lead yourself first if you want to lead a team, corporation, and professional or community fraternity. If you want to control others, first learn to control yourself. Self-mastery is the DNA of life mastery. Self-mastery is a two-step process. Firstly, you should know yourself and secondly, you should continually improve yourself. Hence, conduct an honest self-appraisal. Also, talk to your friends, colleagues, peers, and boss for their honest opinions about yourself and have a 360-degree appraisal done. Know thyself. Discover yourself. Know your strengths and weaknesses. Know your passion, dreams, objectives and goals in life. What kind of person are you? What are your core values? Your answers to these questions will determine your ability to live a life of excellence and create and compound true wealth.

Unless we know ourselves and learn to manage ourselves, no extent of knowledge, abilities, skills, or talent will make us effective. Self-appraisal is also essential for effectively managing our time and other resources like money. This is because we are often unaware or unconscious of our habitual behaviour that wastes valuable time or money.

6.1 COUNT YOUR BLESSINGS

Count your blessings. When upon life's billows, you are tempest-tossed, or when you are discouraged, thinking all is lost, count your many blessings. Are you ever burdened with a load of care? Does the cross seem heavy you are called to bear? Count your many blessings and every doubt will fly. Count your many blessings; money can't buy. So, amid the conflict, whether big or small, don't be discouraged; almighty God is continually showering blessings on you. Focus on your blessings, not on your misfortunes. Focus on what you already have, not on what is missing. Focus on your strengths, not on your weaknesses. Have a humble and positive mindset, whatever situations you are facing. Count your blessings and you will realise how beautiful your life is.

Count your blessings by preparing your gratitude list. Itemise your assets. List all that you have in your life. Name them one by one. Start with health, family, and friends – the things you often take for granted. The list is endless. Write randomly first and then select the top twenty-five items. You will be surprised to know what the almighty God has given you. Just count your blessings when you are sad, down, or depressed. Before long, you will feel uplifted and happy. The moment you act like life is a beautiful blessing; it manifests like one. Counting your blessings will give you more blessings to count.

Some people look at life with no purpose other than finding out what is missing. This hymn urges us to move beyond such a narrow outlook. It encourages us to rise above envy's corrosive effects and realise how blessed we are. This hymn is a reminder to be grateful. It is a hymn about gratitude. It is a call to rise above discouragement, doubt, envy, and self-pity to reach a new appreciation for the blessings the almighty God has been continually showering upon us. Surrender to almighty God with your troubles and have a faith in him because he is present everywhere, taking care of us. Fill your cup with gratitude and it will overflow with blessings.

The wonderful message conveyed through the 'Count your blessings' hymn is often misunderstood. This hymn does not ask you to deny the existence of problems. It does not mean you cheer up and act like everything is fine. It doesn't mean that you need not take any action on your part to eliminate your problems. This is not the message. The hymn encourages us to bring our concerns into our prayers. The central idea of this hymn is to remove negativity from our minds about any of our misfortunes. It advocates focusing on what we have without getting overwhelmed or discouraged by what is missing. If misfortunes overwhelm you, you will not be able to take any action to remove those misfortunes and consequently; misfortunes will become a permanent part of your life. However, when you count your blessings, your entire focus shifts to what you already have. This positive frame of mind helps you multiply your good fortunes and diminishes the effect of misfortunes.

If you have food in your fridge, clothes to wear, a roof over your head and a place to sleep, you're richer than 75% of the world's population. Life is not about complaining. Life is about thousands of other reasons to be grateful and happy.

6.2 DISCOVER YOUR PASSION

One of the most common regrets of life that we generally hear is, 'I wish I had pursued my passion.' Often, a person passionate about photography becomes a clerk in a bank, or a person who loves painting becomes a shopkeeper. Let this not happen to you. Discover your passion before it is too late. Identifying your passion is not difficult. You can find your passion in what inspires you the most. What stirs your soul is your passion. What resonates with you is your passion. If you are passionate about something, you lose track of time when you are engrossed in it. A cause for which you can wager yourself with confidence and dive in wholeheartedly is your passion. A cause for which you feel you can even give your life is your passion. What makes you feel you are totally in harmony with why you showed up here in the first place is your passion.

Marry your work with your life's passion. Let your work attain fusion with your passion. Reach the stage of enlightenment wherein you do what you love to do.

This requires courage, but once you do what you love to do, you get tremendous fulfilment in the process. When you enjoy your work as a play, you experience a divine feeling in your work. It is a myth that you can't earn a living following your passion. The reality is that you can earn your living following your passion and also provide service to others. If you don't dare to do what you love to do, you will have no option but to love what you do.

6.3 TRANSFORM YOUR LIFE THE BUTTERFLY WAY

> *"To achieve something that you have never achieved before, you must become someone you have never been before."*
>
> **– Les Brown**

Elegant butterflies and their fascinating colours attract us all. However, we may not know that once they were ugly caterpillars lying somewhere in a dirty corner doing nothing except eating insects and sleeping. To transform into a beautiful butterfly, the caterpillar has to undergo an extremely painful metamorphosis process. Incidentally, the caterpillar is the only known living entity in the universe that can completely change its DNA.

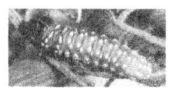 

We spend most of our life only thinking of our immediate needs like a caterpillar struggling to survive. To be reborn like the beautiful butterfly emerging from its burial shroud-like cocoon, our souls need to break free from the illusory veil of the egoistic mind and free ourselves from attachment to the physical body and the material world. Unless we endure the pain of this metamorphosis, we will remain as caterpillars. When we break free of this mental cocoon, we can spread our wings like a butterfly gliding above the ground and enjoying the world's true beauty. Butterfly symbolism represents the ephemerality of time, change, renewal, hope, endurance and courage needed to embrace a radical transformation to improve our lives. Butterflies show us how we can go within ourselves to dissolve old sores and morph, rebuilding and evolving ourselves as part of the essential process of growth and renewal.

6.4 ARE WE WILLING TO COME OUT OF OUR COMFORT ZONE?

If we were to name one thing that separates the few who achieve excellence from the masses who wallow in mediocrity, it is the willingness to step out of our comfort zone and go beyond our self-assumed limitations.

We can maintain the status quo of the comfort zone effortlessly. We don't need extra effort for this. This is our safe haven. It is the zone of least resistance. Our bad habits, day-to-day ruts, and tendency to operate within the zone of predictability and familiarity will all maintain the status quo. However, our life's greatness cannot be won within the circle of mediocrity. If we want to excel in any endeavour in life, we must make choices that lie beyond mediocrity. We must stretch ourselves. A life of excellence lies only beyond this comfort zone. The zone which can help achieve excellence is undoubtedly uncomfortable. The discomfort could be in physical, mental, or spiritual forms. It may involve unpleasant things like leaving the cozy comfort of a woollen blanket and getting up at 5 a.m. every morning for walking or exercise, giving up those cigarettes, and choosing an apple over ice cream. It involves overcoming procrastination and starting that business we've always dreamed of. It involves learning to control those deadly attacks of anger. It involves the painstaking nurturing of relationships. It involves a willingness to sacrifice, forgive, and compromise. It requires a preparedness to keep pouring unconditional love.

Every moment, we have the option to operate within or outside our comfort zones. Our current situation is the direct result of choices we have made in the past. It is the by-product of the zone we have been operating in. This inter alia also means that by choosing to operate outside our comfort zone from now on, we can articulate a life of excellence for the future. When we make choices outside our comfort zone, something interesting happens. We get a broader and new perspective on what our capabilities are. We find that limitations, which were once considered unsurmountable, are no longer unsurmountable. This opens the door for the next round of excellence, and the cycle repeats itself. Remember that this is a lifelong process.

6.5 GOING THE EXTRA MILE

Be known as the person who goes that extra mile. This is the start of the uncrowded extra mile where you have only love to give away. You will find no one engaging in any absurdities along the extra mile. Along the extra mile, you will meet only those who have grasped this philosophy fully. The others who haven't made it to this are back with the crowd, wondering why they went home with nothing and blaming others for this emptiness.

Go far beyond the normal call of duty. Travel that extra mile. Be the person who works longer than others - not necessarily only in terms of the number of hours, but also in terms of quality, speed, or scope of the work. Take initiatives. Render more and better service than what you are paid for. Once you do this, it is a matter of time until you will be paid for more than your work.

6.6 PUTTING FIRST THINGS FIRST

All of us are confronted with multi-faceted demands on our time. We all feel challenged by the day-to-day and moment-by-moment decisions we make regarding the best use of our time. Our struggle to put first things first is characterised by the contrast between current pressing demands and future planning needs. What we stand for shapes our lives. Our heart and conscience work as a compass pointing towards long-term life goals. But there are day-to-day pressing demands in the name of urgency. The struggle starts when our current time use habits don't contribute to what is most important to our lives and there is a misalignment between the two.

Some of us feel empty. We defined happiness solely in terms of professional or financial achievement, but we were disappointed to find that our success did not bring us the happiness we thought it would. We painstakingly climbed the ladder of success rung by rung-the schooling, the diplomas, the degrees, and the promotions-only to discover that the ladder is leaning against the wrong wall. In our race up the ladder, we deteriorated our health and ignored our family and friends. Instead of looking for a deep chronic cause, we periodically kept applying Band-Aid kind of solution to treat the acute pain. We did not do what really mattered most until some catastrophic mishaps, like a road accident, took place. In the absence of such wake-up calls, many of us never really confront the critical issues of life. Should we not learn to put the first things first without going through the trauma of catastrophic events ourselves?

Apart from time, this principle also applies to other facets of life. Meeting day-to-day expenses and saving for future events like children's education or marriage is a big challenge for middle-class families who have limited resources but many needs. They have to prioritise between buying an air-conditioner or a fridge. Of course, a housewife sets her priorities right and manages these challenges successfully.

6.7 THE PERSONAL MISSION STATEMENT

Stephen R. Covey, the author of the best-selling book 'The Seven Habits of Highly Effective People' starts his book with the chapter titled 'Begin with the End in Mind.' He beautifully describes how we should plan to live our lives. Just imagine we are dead and a prayer meeting is going on. Usually, on this occasion, at least four people will speak about us - someone from our family, someone from our office, some of our friends and someone from our community. In this eulogy, they will speak about our character, achievements, and contributions to the welfare of our near and dear ones and society. Now, think about what we want them to speak in the prayer meeting after our death. Would we like to be remembered as the richest person in our country, the honest business person, the happiest person, or the best social worker? Depending on how we wish to be remembered, we can design our personal, professional, social and community lives. Though quite dramatic, this approach can be used in deciding the overall direction of our lives.

Stephen refers to what people will speak about us after death. However, people do not always wait until our death to give their opinions. People also speak about us as we live our life and this spread of words could influence our personal, professional, social and community lives. For example, if we are doing our business with the highest standards of ethics and our friends and associates speak about this publically, word will spread around, increasing our business manifold. What others speak about us carries a lot of weight. Third-party opinions are extremely powerful. We may blow our trumpet, but third-party opinions matter the most in our personal and professional lives.

Also, even if we don't want to attach much importance to what others say about us, remember that our entire life will flash in front of our eyes one day. Would we not like to make sure that it is worth watching? When we look in the mirror, would we be happy to see a tarnished image of ourselves? If we were to die today, would we be pleased with how we have lived so far? Besides this, planning our life is also essential for providing a direction to our life, as without a concrete life plan and precisely defined goals, we are like a ship drifting aimlessly in the sea. We will go wherever the tide takes us. Such a lifestyle is not only highly unproductive but is also incapable of providing true happiness and fulfilment. Thus, from whichever angle we look at, we need to proactively decide how we want to live our life and design it accordingly and the best drawing-board tool we can use for this purpose is a PMS. Make firm blue prints. If we want to construct a bridge, we don't go to the bank of the river and commence construction. We first go to a drawing board and plan the bridge, its foundation, piers and superstructure in minute detail. If we do this for even a bridge costing only a few million dollars, can we afford to start living our life (which is priceless) without a plan in place? While iterations post the drawing-board stage in the case of a bridge may cost only a few million dollars, it will cost us a fortune in our lives.

What are you passionate about? What are our objectives in life? What do we want to achieve in life? Where will we want to be after five years and ten years from now? These are the questions one must ask oneself and our PMS should answer these questions. We must visualise a bigger picture of our life in an integrated manner instead of seeing several discrete fragments of our life. A PMS, vital for real self-mastery, is a capsule statement of our life's predominant purpose. It must accurately represent our ideas, desires and dreams and inspire us to realise them. The PMS should include the aspirations we want to pursue, the habits we want to develop, the core values we believe in and the personal character we want to build. It must come from our deepest core and reflect the fundamental principles which drive us. It lays down the basic core values and principles around which we want to build the foundation of our successful life. The way a multi-storied sky-scrapper can't be built without a sound foundation anchored to the ground, a successful life can't be built without a sound foundation of core values and guiding principles that govern life. The principles provide an anchor to our life - the sounder is the anchor; the sounder is the superstructure of our life. The taller the edifice, the stronger the foundation needs to be. These principles can guide us at every step of our lives through good times and bad times. In our life, we may face many crossroads. One path may give fulfilling and long-lasting success, but it will be long and difficult. Alternate shortcut and easier paths may give overnight success. In a mad pursuit to achieve quick or overnight success, we are often tempted to adopt a shortcut that does not conform to our core values and principles. In such situations, the PMS works as a lighthouse that keeps us continuously focused on our goals. If honesty and integrity are the core principles of our life, we would prefer a loss rather than a dishonest gain. Similarly, if someone asks us to spend time on something that is not aligned with our overall mission, we can refuse to oblige him.

Give a considered thought before drafting the PMS. Don't rush through this exercise. Take adequate time. Deeply think about what meaning you want to attach to your life and what legacy you want to leave behind. Take one quiet hour every day for a fortnight to draft the statement.

Let your spouse write her PMS separately and then exchange the notes. Take initiative and align your PMS with that of your spouse. Consider removing those items that are contradictory and strengthen common items. Refine the draft and prepare the final statement. Make it concise. Present it as an 'I-oriented' statement, signifying that you are committing to yourself or taking a pledge. The final statement should ideally contain three or four paragraphs. A typical brief PMS might read:

> "My mission is to become a person of good character and impeccable integrity. I shall pay due attention to the health of my body and mind. I shall take a properly balanced nutritional diet. Exercise, yoga and meditation shall be integral to my daily routine.
>
> I shall have a superb family and a fulfilling professional life. While building monetary wealth, I shall not lose sight of true wealth.
>
> I shall live my life with tremendous zest and joy. I shall be courteous and kind to all. I shall contribute to the welfare of my near and dear ones and society."

Alternatively, the top twenty-five to thirty items of your personal mission can be presented as bullet points. For a Typical PMS in bullet form, refer to APPENDIX I.

Frame the PMS in a nice frame and display it prominently in your office and home.

Once you establish your life mission, fuse it with all your personal, professional, social and community activities to unleash your full potential and find fulfilment in your journey. Also, with the finalisation of your PMS, your life's purpose and the course of your life's path are set. However, this doesn't mean you can't modify your mission as you progress. Reviewing and updating your mission statement every year is a good practice.

A PMS is somewhat like a bucket list, but the two differ significantly. Whereas the bucket list is reactive and represents the regrets of our life, the PMS is proactive and helps us design our future life as per our desires and dreams. A well-conceived PMS will make us feel proud about how we lived our life when we look back at our life at a subsequent stage, as there are no regrets and hardly any unfulfilled items on our bucket list.

6.8 LONG, MEDIUM AND SHORT-TERM PLANNING AND GOAL SETTING

Once a PMS is prepared, the next step is to plan and set precise and specific goals for the future. Convert your PMS into an Action Plan by dividing the same into long, medium and short-term goals. The goals should be quantifiable and capable of dividing into annual, monthly and daily units. The acronym SMART describes the characteristics of goals - Specific, Measurable, Achievable (yet challenging), Relevant and Time-bound. Setting goals converts vague inspirations into tangible and attainable forms. You can facilitate realising these goals by preparing look-ahead plans for different time horizons. The benefits you can derive from look-ahead plans depend upon the plan's time horizon. A one-week look-ahead plan can help you get as much as ten percent more done and a one-month plan can increase your output by fifteen percent. While a six-month plan makes you a dynamic manager, a five-year plan can help you take charge of your career and life.

6.9 KNOW YOUR EMOTIONAL QUOTIENT

Emotions are another, even deeper aspect that requires you to know yourself. The contribution from IQ in achieving success is only about seven percent; the rest 93 percent contribution comes from EQ, i.e. Emotional Quotient. EQ is important for all facets of life across all stages of life. Hence, you must know yourself before making decisions like selecting the career that is just right for you, selecting your life partner, inculcating prudent saving habits or making the investment and other decisions. Only after such know-yourself exercise do you have the ability to make an intelligent move in your life. While making these decisions, you need to consider your nature, temperament, passion, emotions, optimism, pessimism, etc. You have to know and do what feels right and safe for you, what empowers you, what helps you grow and what works for you emotionally and mentally.

Even investment decisions require an understanding of your emotions first. Different people seem programmed to suffer different stress and anxiety levels when subjected to volatility in their investment portfolios. If, for example, a fifty percent loss in your capital scares you to death and gives you sleepless nights, investing in equity may not be the right option for you. We must never forget that human life is the most important thing in this world. After all, you are at the center of your life. Without you in your world, nothing else would exist. Your investment objective is to make you more secure and not give you sleepless nights. The secret to your financial success is inside you. You might have extensive knowledge of finance, accounting and stock market lore, but you can't be a successful investor unless you control your emotions. Also, while IQ is a hereditary gift that you can improve only marginally until age fourteen, you can improve EQ at any stage of life.

6.10 KNOW YOUR PERSONAL STYLE OF MANAGEMENT

Understanding your management style will help you plan your time and achieve maximum personal effectiveness. Know whether you have a diffusion style or a focused style. Diffusion style means having several irons in the fire simultaneously. You get stimulated by starting new projects even when few others are in midstream. People with a diffusion style lose effectiveness if forced to work on a single project. They become bored and stifled. If you are a diffusion-style manager, start new projects but delegate existing projects to your team members and check the progress periodically.

A focused style means zeroing down on one project at a time. People with a focused style derive much satisfaction when they pay their full attention to one project. If you are a focused-style manager, choose one top-priority project to get the best return on your time investment.

6.11 PLOT YOUR EFFICIENCY CHART

Our efficiency does not remain constant throughout eight or ten working hours of the day. At some point in the day, the efficiency is at its peak and then the efficiency starts dropping as the day progresses and tiredness develops.

Prepare your efficiency chart or energy curve to pinpoint the most productive hours during a typical day and then shape your day around these prime hours to suit your bio-rhythm. If your efficiency reaches a peak level at 10 a.m. and remains elevated until noon, schedule tasks requiring deep concentration or Quadrant II activities like creative thinking during this peak efficiency slot. Make special efforts to plan and productively utilise this prime-hour slot for an important task, or else this time slot is likely to get consumed by so-called urgent or pressing tasks that keep popping up, demanding your attention. Be firm and don't get carried away by the pressure of urgency such tasks create on you. Anything less than a conscious commitment to the important is an unconscious commitment to the unimportant.

6.12 IMPROVE YOUR CONCENTRATION SPAN

Most people require a minimum of ten minutes to become intensely focused on a task and can sustain such intense focus for a mere twenty minutes at a time. Then they need a break. Thus, within a time span of forty minutes, only half of the time is spent on the concentrated work and the remaining time is spent on warm-up and cool–down.

Practice and improve your concentration span. If you could learn to concentrate for forty-five minutes at a stretch, you would have increased your output by as much as twenty-five percent.

6.13 DAILY TIME LOG

Do you know where exactly your hours and minutes are going? If your reply is affirmative, it needs reconsideration. The best way to get a handle on your current time use is to watch it like a hawk for a couple of weeks and prepare a white paper.

Prepare a Time Log showing how you spend a typical day, critically analyse the same and use this input for a serious time-reform programme. Eliminate all redundant activities and replace them with new activities that contribute to your core values, objectives and goals. If your allocation of time is frivolous, consider reallocation. You may be spending an hour daily on routine correspondence, which can be delegated to your secretary or assistant, making this time available for Quadrant II activities.

Motivate your staff to log their time. However, don't shove it down their throat. Tactfully involve them by showing your time logs and admitting how unwisely you have been spending time on some redundant activities for the last several years, which would not have surfaced even now but for the time log. Your success story should inspire them to realise the importance of a time log.

6.14 VIDEO RECORDING

A time log records how we spend our day but it doesn't capture many habits that may have become so integral to our personality that they are taken for granted. Hence, set up a video camera and record yourself working for one full day as usual without being conscious about recording.

When I watched the tape of my video recording, I was surprised to see myself daydreaming, yawning, biting a nail, sitting idle, staring into space, making unnecessary movements, picking up papers and files and keeping back without working on them. I was frequently checking social media messages on my mobile phone, chatting with colleagues, making prolonged personal calls, surfing the internet for breaking news and doing all sorts of unproductive time-wasting activities. This video was an eye-opener for me. It motivated me to eliminate many time-wasting habits and saved over ten percent of my time.

6.15 PRICE YOUR TIME

A few things in life may be free, but many people erroneously consider even time as one of those gifts. Time is free, but it is priceless. Though our time as an executive is quite dear, we seldom appreciate its value as we never try to quantify what each hour of our time costs us.

A conservative estimate of the hourly cost of a typical middle-level Corporate Executive is given below:

Own salary per year	= $48,000
Perquisites per year	= $24,000
Overheads per year	= $48,000
Supporting staff salary	= $24,000

Total cost per year	= $144,000

Taking 2400 working hours per year, the hourly cost works out to $60.

Before spending half an hour on any task, we need to ascertain whether that task deserves our time investment worth $30. When we pick up a paper and put it down without working on it, a few dollars are down the drain. Awareness of the hourly cost can help eliminate many such time-wasting habits and improve productivity.

6.16 BUDGET YOUR TIME

We all meticulously budget our expenses to preserve cash for the future and keep us financially sound. We can buy a luxury car or a new house by budgeting expenses and saving regularly. Similarly, we must budget our time. In fact, budgeting time is more important than money as time is priceless. While budgeting our time, we must always keep in mind the hourly cost of our time in dollar terms. We can get an extra hour a day to expand our creativity by trimming and cutting wasted minutes.

6.17 BEING PROACTIVE

There are two categories of people - reactive and proactive. Reactive people are like spectators. Sitting on the sidelines, they merely watch what is happening in their lives and react after the event. In contrast, proactive people act in advance and make things happen.

Proactive people don't spend time on the Circle of Concern; they spend time on the Circle of Influence. They spend more time on Quadrant II activities. They proactively design and shape their lives and enhance their future production capabilities. Being proactive means you shape your circumstances rather than allowing circumstances to shape you. It means you no longer link your failures or lack of achievements to your family background or the treatment you got from your family, friends, boss, or the entire world. Proactive people don't blame others for what they are today. They realise that they must act to change their situation. They take charge of their careers and lives in their hands. Being proactive means you no longer cry over spilt milk; they move ahead. It means living a blissful existence and seeing the good in all events unfolding in this beautiful canopy of life. Proactive people are Possibility Thinkers or Wow! Thinkers. Proactive people, being possibility thinkers, view even the most negative events positively. In fact, there is no such thing as an unpleasant experience. Every experience can improve some element of your character or present a challenge to you, which may lift you to a higher level physically, mentally and spiritually. Difficult or bad times bring the best out of you. If you have never undergone a failure, you are to be pitied, for you have missed one of nature's greatest processes of true education. All highly successful people are proactive. They view setbacks and failures as lessons and stepping stones. They treat pain as a teacher.

Reactive people are Impossibility Thinkers. They feel changing their current situation is not in their hands. They fold their hands and sit down in despair. Also, they blame others for their present situation. For a simple thing like a headache or some depressed feeling, you will do something to get rid of it if you feel you are responsible for it. However, if you think someone else is responsible, you have to wait until they change for you to get better, which is unlikely.

Proactiveness can be acquired through self-control. And self-control, like all essential mastery qualities, can be developed through patience, perseverance and regular conditioning. Once you are determined to be proactive and choose to run these muscles every day, you will take charge of your life in your hands and unleash the true potential that slumbers deep within you.

6.18 DEVELOPING A POSITIVE ATTITUDE

A positive attitude is a state of mind that envisions success and accomplishments rather than setbacks or failures. It is a mental outlook of optimism. With a positive attitude, you see the bright side of life. Positivity brings enlightenment, hope and enthusiasm to life, reducing worries and other negative feelings. A positive mindset makes you believe in yourself and your abilities. It helps you see and recognise infinite opportunities. People with a positive outlook view life challenges and situations with confidence and a mindset to find solutions. While they firmly believe that everything will turn out right, they also mentally prepare themselves to accept that whatever happens is for the good. They would not be stuck in low-energy thoughts of fear, lack of self-esteem, or passivity. They dump negative thoughts which perpetuate adverse situations. They don't dwell on the problems and difficulties of the past. They would rather learn from past mistakes and move on without giving up. Thus, they learn to cope with the daily affairs of life with high confidence. A positive attitude also helps you see the good in people.

While a positive attitude favourably affects your life in all areas with a solution-finding mindset, negative thoughts visualise and expect failures instead of solutions, progress and success. Negative thoughts, if not eliminated, can have cancerous effects. Slowly, our negative thinking starts governing our actions, unconsciously leading us to make bad choices. Hence, take a close look at your life. Examine your daily routine and its effects on your life and your attitude. Start your day with positive thoughts. Develop a routine that promotes enough energy to maintain a positive attitude throughout the day. Don't allow negative thoughts to dominate you. Listen to your internal dialogue. Be aware of your state of mind and change to positive thoughts the moment it drifts towards negativity. Cultivate positive relationships. Interact with people who positively reinforce you. Go places that have special meanings and positive memories or associations. Get pleasure out of the simple things in life. Permit yourself to be loved. Everyone deserves to be loved. Everyone likes to be loved. Be proud of your accomplishments and the hard work you have done. Of course, a positive attitude by itself is not enough. We should have positive feelings and also take positive actions. Also, remember adopting a positive attitude does not necessarily mean everything will always move smoothly or without hurdles. There may be setbacks and failures, but a positive attitude will ensure that such setbacks will not stop you or change the state of your mind and that you will move on, try again, and do your best despite any setback.

6.19 DEVELOPING A WINNING MINDSET

Developing a winning mindset is the fundamental prerequisite for being successful. Even if I am highly talented or have many top-level connections, I may not go far if I don't have the right mindset. While people with a winning mindset become successful despite adversity, those with a losing mindset give up when the going gets tough. The right mindset separates the best from the rest.

Your mindset will give you an advantage over the rest of the population. Rewards are great if you succeed, but rewards are also great because only a few with winning mindsets succeed. So, focus on building a strong, winning mindset that puts you on the brink of greatness. A winner's mindset needs to be earned painstakingly; it is never received on a silver platter. Also, winning and losing mindsets are mutually exclusive. You will have either a winner's or a loser's mindset. A winning mindset can be developed by believing in yourself, feeding your mind with positive thoughts, having patience, developing a routine conducive o winning, maintaining a laser-like focus on goals, coming out of your comfort zone, forcing yourself to do even uncomfortable things and willingness to do whatever it takes. Regardless of age, keep pushing yourself to reach your full potential and always remember that you can do much more than what you think is possible.

The key to success lies in continual growth. If we want to live our lives fully, we must grow every day. When we stop growing, we give up on life. The day we stop growing is the day we die.

6.20 DEVELOPING A CHAMPION'S MINDSET: OPENING UP MAGNETIC CENTER

Have you observed Olympic Champions? How do they break records after records? They focus on accumulating physical, emotional, intellectual and spiritual energies and aligning them. They create synergy by aligning all components of positive energy and renouncing negative energy. This synergy opens up the magnetic center. A magnetic center is much more powerful than a mechanical center. An athlete will never win if he uses only a mechanical center. He can succeed only if he harmonises all his energies, avoids their leakage and opens up the magnetic center. That is why performances like hitting six sixes in a competitive cricket match or the last-ball win by a six in a World Cup match occur only once in several decades.

6.21 OUR CHOICES DECIDE THE TRAJECTORY OF OUR LIFE

Tony Robbins once rightly said, "It is in the moments of decision that our destiny is shaped." Also, Stephen signified the importance of making good decisions when he said, "I am not a product of my circumstances. I am a product of my decisions."

What we are today is the product of endless choices we have made in the past. This also means that what choices we make from now onward will dictate our future. Though what situation comes to us is not in our control, how we choose to respond to that situation is definitely in our control and the choices we make will decide our future destiny. In that sense, man is the maker of his destiny. Our choices decide the trajectory of our life. Destiny is not created by the shoes we wear but by the steps we take. Similarly, building character is not a function of a station in life, parentage, ancestral wealth, privilege, or status; it is the result of choices we have been making in our lives.

6.22 DEVELOPING GOOD ATOMIC HABITS

Achieving success or failure in our lives depends on our personality, background, attitudes, habits, stress tolerance level, etc. Positive personal traits like self-confidence, optimism, and single-mindedness of purpose dictate our success. On the other hand, negative personal traits like poor self-image, lack of confidence, pessimism, and fear lead to failure.

They say to change your life, change your habits. When we start our path to findings, there will be changes that have to be made. Fortunately, we can change. We can change by developing good atomic habits. Atomic habits are tiny, incremental everyday routines that compound into incredible positive changes if we stick to them for years and keep looking for improvements. Thus, even tiny changes can fetch remarkable results if you pursue continual improvements as a lifelong process. Also, when you bring several small changes in your life, such small things don't simply add up; they compound. That is the power of atomic habits.

Use the following five-step action plan to develop good atomic habits and break bad ones:

1) Identify a top-priority new practice that, upon implementation, can bring a quantum jump in your effectiveness.
2) Display the new behaviour at the first opportune time. Don't procrastinate.

3) Take along some like-minded persons with you on this mission. Join a culture where your desired behaviour is the normal behaviour
4) Broadcast the new practice publicly to your family, friends, colleagues, boss and others. This is an excellent way to get leverage and motivation. When the going gets tough, this public awareness will prevent you from drifting. For example, suppose I have publicly broadcast that I will reduce my weight by ten kilograms in the next three months. In that case, the pressure of this public awareness will keep motivating me to exercise and control my diet. Surely, I would not like to be seen in public as someone who has failed to achieve even such a simple goal.
5) Paint a picture of success in your mind. Visualise yourself succeeding. Until established, never slip from the new behaviour.

So, develop good atomic habits and become their slave. The new habit must be mixed with the hemoglobin of the blood. Since evolution is easier when we are young, we should adopt these changes gradually from a young age. Don't rush them because these changes should be allowed to work their way into your existence. Remember, at first, the chains of habits are too light to be felt and then later too heavy to be broken. Hence, keep practising new traits till these become part of your personality and habits in doing. Read and learn every day. Activate your mind by playing what-if games and engaging in mathematical games of probability and skill like a bridge. The collective effect of a series of good habits can lead us to the top when these habits become an integral part of our life.

6.23 ACTIVATE WINGS OF SELF-EFFORT

Many people believe in fate or luck. That may be fine, but many people also believe they will automatically get what is in their fate with no effort. If so, this needs reconsideration. Also, when we are less successful than others, we often take this philosophy's help to justify our lack of achievements.

When all of us enter this world, we do so with two wings. One wing is the wing of grace. This wing is flapping by our side, supporting us twenty-four hours a day, all 365 days. The other wing that we have to activate consciously is the wing of self-effort. This wing has to flap equally hard as the wing of grace. The wings of grace by themselves can't do anything. When the wing of grace works in tandem with the wing of self-effort, we will have a flight that will introduce us to a world of unlimited possibilities. We all are born with a divine fire in us. We have the potential to fill the world with a glow. We have a supreme urge to realise our full potential. Within us, we have what it takes to create what we deserve. However, we unleash our full potential only when we activate the wings of self-effort. We may have plenty of knowledge, but knowing is not enough. We also need the skill to apply our knowledge. Even knowledge and skill by themselves are not enough. We need willingness on our part. Even willingness is not enough. We must act. Thus, self-effort is the key to success; without self-effort, we can't achieve what we deserve or what is in our fate.

6.24 THE ART OF HANDLING SUCCESS AND FAILURES

- Say hello to success and farewell to failure, but remain non-addictive towards both.
- Accept the challenges, make your journey to success exciting and treasure the exhilaration of victory.
- Develop soberness and humility in success. Handle success or good times with maturity and humility, without ego or arrogance.
- Don't achieve success at the expense of others. Don't belittle or exploit others for climbing the corporate ladder.
- Share the credit for success with your team and celebrate with them. Find a cause to celebrate and take time out to do just that.
- Failure is an illusion. Failure is a judgment - just an opinion. It comes from your fear, which can be eliminated by love for yourself, others and the planet. When you are passionate about what you do and when you

Know Thyself And Focus More On Self-Improvement

have love within you, fear can't survive. You don't worry about someone's disapproval if you are fearless.

- Failures are necessary before you achieve worthwhile success. No one has ever travelled the road of success without crossing the streets of failure. Hence, do not let losses or obstacles stop you from heading towards your goals. Your past or current sufferings need not make your life uglier. You can pick yourself up from what has happened to you and become a better person. There is a great lesson from every failure. After an accident, a person may choose to get completely demoralised or look at it as a God-sent opportunity to transform his life. You can turn your scars into stars and proudly wear them as a badge of honour. Every spiritual advance you make is most likely to be preceded by some kind of fall or seeming disaster. Every next level of your life will demand a new you and sometimes it takes being broken to get that version of yourself. Those dark times, accidents, illnesses, tough episodes and abuses happened for your good. Tough times bring the best out of you and make you strong. Easy times create weak men and weak men invite tough times. If, in good times, you voluntarily do what you are forced to do in tough times, you will not have tough times. So embrace failures from that perspective, understand them, accept them, honour them and finally retire or transform them.

- Accept blame for failures yourself. Take personal accountability for what didn't work instead of passing blame. 'Buck stops here' is a good policy. No man can become a power in his professional or community life or achieve enduring success until he becomes big enough to admit mistakes and failures. Finger-pointing and assigning blame to others breeds discontent and alienation. It destroys team spirit. Those who stop bucks at themselves are more likely to be elevated than those who pass them.

- Back up your staff. Always be available to support each team member, especially when they encounter failure. This is the time when they need your support the most. Realise that past experiences, failures, or trouble spots have nothing to do with the potential that exists within people.

6.25 FOCUS MORE ON SELF-IMPROVEMENT

Once you have conducted a thorough self-appraisal, the next logical step is self-improvement. Remember, improving ourselves is within our Circle of Influence. Changing others is outside our Circle of Influence. Self-improvement means that we are willing to grow. It means that we are not merely preaching to others to eliminate their imperfections but mastering our imperfections first and leading by example. Hence, focus more on self-improvement than on trying to change others.

Consider the tips given below for large-scale self-improvement:

- Character is the most powerful signature a person can have. Your knowledge may give you power, but your character will get you respect. Character is not a hereditary trait. It needs to be painstakingly built piece by piece. They say what we do when everyone is looking at us is our behaviour, but what we do even when no one is observing us is our character. Character is built up by the influence of the endless chain of decisions we are called upon to make during our life. When you sow an action, you reap a habit. When you sow a habit, you reap a character. When you sow a character, you reap a destiny.
- The character cannot be hidden, nor can it be faked. You can tell from thousands of miles away if someone is the type of person you want to associate with. Warren stressed the need to develop a good character. What good is being a value investor if you are not a value manager yourself? If you are asked to select a classmate to whom you would want to hand over ten percent of your earnings for investing, you are likely to choose a classmate with the right mentors, habits, values and principles. He need not be the most intelligent or best-looking. Integrity stands for the most. Warren recommends looking at three character traits in the people surrounding him: integrity, energy and intelligence. The last two traits will kill you if you don't have the first one. Integrity is oxygen; nothing else matters if you don't have it. Like the air we breathe, you don't notice it until it is gone.

Know Thyself And Focus More On Self-Improvement

- Be careful about your reputation. A good reputation can take you to the highest of highs. Building a reputation is a painstaking process requiring years and decades. However, tarnishing can happen in a few minutes and can't be regained easily.
- Carefully cultivate your image as a highly competent, strong, disciplined, calm and decent individual. Once you walk in, thoughts of power and authority should come.
- Take special efforts and pay attention to how you implant your impressions on others so that you can make them do what you want them to do in less time. For example, your image as an honest and business-like person will help you to close a business deal faster.
- Don't give yourself airs and graces. Don't madly run after status. Avoid insisting on reserved parking places, special quality stationery, a separate dining hall, unique office furniture, etc.
- Recognise capability gaps. Learn new skills and ask for help. Continually upgrade your intellectual capacity. Investment in yourself is the best investment you can make.
- List traits and habits you admire in people close to you or your role models. If you start soon enough, these traits can be part of your makeup and mindset. Also, make another list of the character traits that you don't admire or respect in others. By relentless perseverance, you can avoid these undesirable qualities. Don't neglect the beam in your own eyes. Don't be oblivious to your shortcomings. If you could see yourself through the eyes of the people you work for, you would be astonished. Make an honest appraisal of yourself. Make a list of your weaknesses. A truly confident and enlightened person will be mindful of his shortcomings and seek to eliminate them methodically.
- Cultivate the quality of being interesting so that people will want to be with you and get something stimulating from you. Be a comfortable person - an old-shoe, old-hat kind of individual, so there is no strain in being with you. Be homey.
- Be as soft as a flower when it comes to kindness but as tough as a rock when it comes to principles.

- Be shrewd when you should become tough and courageous. Realise that to be truly successful, you must foster worldly wisdom together with shrewdness. Whereas you should not take undue advantage of others, don't make yourself so vulnerable that others take undue advantage of you. Here, your shrewdness comes into play. Be shrewd enough to realise if something is cooking against you or if someone is trying to take undue advantage of you and proactively stop it. Be aware of the surrounding politics. While you should stay above petty gossiping and office politics, be aware of its existence. Remain alert to know what goes behind your back.
- Be street smart. Street smartness is the ability to effectively use your instincts and insights while dealing with people. Street smartness gives you a slight psychological edge over others or helps get you most from others.
- Develop the sixth sense. It is the door to the temple of wisdom.
- Never complain. Someone who complains habitually is cynical and always looks for the negative in everything.
- See no evil. Speak no evil. Hear no evil. Never speak ill of others and let all know you will not malign them behind their back. Malicious tattle prevents good work. What you say about others also says a lot about you.
- Don't spread rumours.
- Live life fully. Go with the flow. If you go with the flow, life is easier. If you go against the flow or current, you toil a lot.
- Present your best to the public. Always put your best foot forward.

6.26 IN SEARCH OF HAPPINESS...

"Happiness cannot be travelled to, owned, earned, worn or consumed. Happiness is the spiritual experience of living every moment with love, grace and gratitude."

– Denis Waitley

From time immemorial, men have been desperately searching for happiness. This mad pursuit of searching for happiness continues till death, though objects of happiness keep changing constantly. A child finds happiness in toys. When he grows up, playing with friends makes him happy. In college, having coffee with a boyfriend or girlfriend brings happiness. In adulthood, money brings happiness. Can we really achieve happiness this way? We spend decades of our lives searching for happiness, only to realise that our search was not directed where it should have been directed. Our search for happiness ends only when we control our insatiable desire to seek more and more happiness.

The following points must be kept in mind when we run in search of happiness:

- Happiness has nothing much to do with money or worldly possessions. Worldly possessions are incapable of providing lasting happiness. Happiness is a choice. While unhappiness comes automatically, happiness is not experienced automatically. Happiness doesn't fall from the sky. Happiness is an inside job. It is a state of mind. It is an attitude synthetically manufactured by our minds. We have to painstakingly manufacture happiness by controlling our thoughts and also prevent unhappiness from getting manufactured in our minds. Happy people build their inner world; unhappy people blame their outer world.
- Happiness is priceless, yet free. It is about treasuring pleasure in the present moment and achieving satisfaction in pursuing your goals and enjoying the journey. Take time to be happy.
- While it is good to be ambitious and achieve more and more success, if we can't achieve success for any reason, should we become unhappy? Should we make our success a prerequisite for our happiness? If so, then it is the surest way to remain perpetually unhappy. Hence, let us not make our success a prerequisite for our happiness. To achieve lasting happiness, we must learn to delink our happiness from our success. As far as happiness is concerned, let us be content and happy with what we have today at the present moment. For inspirational purposes, we may compare ourselves with our role models at the top, but for happiness, let us count our blessings and compare ourselves with those below us. However, this should not be construed as advocating mediocrity or encouraging a lack of effort. You must work hard, make

sincere efforts and excel in whatever you do, but do so without making your happiness dependent on the specific outcome of your efforts.
- Happiness lies in liking what we have rather than having what we like. Happiness is a delicate and judicious balance between what I want in future and what I have at present. In pursuit of happiness, we expect so many things in our lives, but life has no obligation to give us what we expect. Happiness starts when expectations are over.
- We can be happy only if we remove ignorance and delusion.
- No one is in charge of your happiness except you. The happiness we are searching for is right within us. We become happy when we eventually experience God as divine light. He continually showers his blessings. Patience is the keyword here. After sustained diligent efforts, the soul is able to discover and acquire that immutable, permanent source of hidden power slumbering within us. The search and quest for man's lasting happiness in the outside world end here. The source and origin of sorrow, grief, anguish, and disappointment are due to wandering aimlessly in this transient world. The real source of perpetual bliss is found within oneself. Immense joy is found in pursuing and eventually discovering that divine light and wisdom are within us and never in chasing trifle things. That which is immortal, never changing, everlasting, incorruptible and intangible; that which resides in us as pure light is constant. It gives us unadulterated happiness, joy, accomplishments and pure bliss. Those who desire the ultimate and lasting peace of mind go after it instead of going after illusive worldly possessions.
- The most difficult task is to change others. The simplest task is to be happy with everyone. This is the master key to happiness.
- The more we are connected with each other, the happier we are. Loneliness is the biggest driver of unhappiness.
- The most predominant cause of unhappiness is self-centric activities. Open the doors to happiness by shifting your focus away from yourself.
- Live a simple life. A simple life is a happy life; no regrets, just lessons; no worries, just acceptance; no expectations, just gratitude; no conditions, just unconditional love.

7

THE ART OF PEOPLE MANAGEMENT

*M*an, being a social animal, it is natural and intrinsic to interact with others. Man always needs friends and the warmth of fellowship. We can't live in a vacuum. In our personal, professional, social and community lives, we continuously interact with our family, friends, colleagues, boss, customers, vendors and others. The time efficiency and spiritual maturity with which we conduct these interactions affect the quality of our lives.

When individuals feel kindly towards one another, there is a natural tendency to cooperate. Also, other things being equal, people definitely prefer to deal with the people they like. Even if other things are not equal, people still prefer to deal with the people they like rather than those they dislike. Hence, try to make it easy for others to like you or at least avoid giving them reasons to dislike you. Longer is the list of people who like you, shorter is the list of people who dislike you; happier is your life. Relationships built along these lines are always enriching. Rich relationships are the DNA of a fulfilling life. Remember, every personal or business situation eventually boils down to a people situation.

Self-centered people are unlikely to achieve great success even if they possess a high IQ. However, people with a high Selflessness Quotient and a high Social Quotient achieve broad-based, long-lasting success. They establish goodwill first and painstakingly build and nurture a network of friends and associates. Since their success is based on the sound foundation of enriching relationships, their friends and associates become their brand ambassadors. This triggers a positive virtuous cycle and they achieve more and more success effortlessly. Thus, people with a finely tuned people-savvy sense will have the edge over others.

However, the million-dollar question is how to develop such enriching relationships. For this, we need to go beyond simple, quick fixes of behavioural engineering and dive deep into the fundamentals of human behaviour. Certain principles of human psychology apply equally well in all human interactions. If we develop a deep understanding of human psychology, we can appreciate why people behave as they do. Developing enriching interpersonal relationships becomes much easier if our interactions are based on a sound understanding of human psychology.

Consider implementing the following people-management tips:

7.1 DEVELOPING ENRICHING RELATIONSHIPS

- Cultivate a people-focused culture.
- Forge and foster great friendships. Friendships are the backbone of an enriching and fulfilling life. A man's friendships are one of the best measures of his worth. Of all possessions, a friend is the most precious. Friendships are important both in personal and professional lives. If you want to walk fast, walk alone. But if you want to walk far, walk together. 'Don't worry; I am there' is a magical phrase that can rejuvenate a broken person. Such assurance by itself can work as a tonic, whether encashed or not.
- Keep all your relationships cordial. Relationships need curiosity to grow, candour to deepen, and integrity to continue.
- Celebrate in others their finest qualities. Treat them all in an 'as if' manner. Treating others in an 'as if' manner means visualising as if the qualities you are looking for already exist in them. You can do this merely by changing your thoughts. Once you change your thoughts about relationships, you will respond according to your highest expectations. And gradually, you will see the rightness of your thoughts manifesting everywhere you go.

- In relationships, learn to see. Don't merely look. When you look through lenses of anger, hate, jealousy, and fear, you look more but see less. See more by removing all those negative lenses. Overlook the weakness of others. Your mind is likely to be irritated if you think about the imperfections of others. Leave the imperfections of others to them. Let them handle it. If you look for flaws, you will surely find them. Don't search for flaws using a magnifying glass. Instead, use a magnifying glass to search for as many good qualities in others as you can. Be mature enough to ignore the petty feelings of others.
- Having too many expectations from our relationships is often at the core of strained relationships.
- Realise that relationships function as a mirror and are governed by the Law of Reciprocity. Treat people the way you want to be treated. Don't treat people the way you would not like to be treated. If someone does not treat you well, you are probably not treating him well. Hence, the only course of action is to change your behaviour.
- The relationship is not finding gold or silver among the rocks of life; it is accepting each other as coal until diamonds are formed.
- Start each day by asking, "How do I want others to feel?" Then, act accordingly.
- Eliminate 'I v/s you' or 'Us v/s them' mentality.
- Remember, you don't meet people by accident. Every person you meet will have a role in your life, big or small. Some will inspire you to do better, some will help you grow and some may hurt you. Similarly, you are also playing some role in their lives. Know that paths cross for a reason and hence be kind to everyone.
- Remember, everyone has a story. Everyone has a past. People's behaviour depends on what they have gone through in the past or something they are still going through. Behaviour doesn't happen in a vacuum. Everyone has inner battles and issues. Some are a source of pride, and others are best left behind. But whatever their past, people do change and grow. Withhold your judgment about others. Instead of judging people by their history, stand by them, help them build their future and offer the same consideration you would like to receive. Never look down on someone unless you are helping

them up. We think of life as a meritocracy, so we tend to look down on someone who isn't as successful, accomplished, or well-educated as we are. But you may not know how far that person has already climbed in some other field or where he will end up in the future. Time could easily reverse your positions, so treat everyone with dignity.

- Don't try to make yourself great by making someone else look small. The moment you think you have the right to belittle others because you feel you are better than they are, at that very moment, you become powerless.
- Create barriers to entry. Don't make yourself too accessible to everyone. Remain slightly aloof. Stars remain far above the earth. So keep a distance from all but your closest relations. Don't let everyone know everything about you. Cultivate a mystique. Judiciously balance working on the image you project to the rest of the world and your inner character. Familiarity breeds contempt. Once people see everything about a leader, he loses his aura and also the authority and mystique he may have created. However, avoid arrogance.
- Don't meet a man whom you don't like. Don't get this wrong. Beyond its literal meaning, it emphasises the need to start liking every person you meet. That is the way you should feel about people. Can you strike a successful business deal with someone whom you don't like? And even if the deal is stuck, will it be executed successfully? Expand your circle and like every person whom you meet. This will enrich your life. Practice liking people until you learn to do so as a habit. People open up to you like a flower to the sun when you like them.
- Stay connected. Meet like-minded people regularly.
- Treat everyone you meet with honour and respect. Do so even if they disrespect you. If anyone is rude, don't stoop to their level but remain graceful and poised. Should you allow others to make you quit your good manners? Learn to respect all staff (including juniors), customers, vendors and competitors. Respect is an investment that comes back to you with compounding returns. Respect should be visible even in small gestures. Open the door for the

persons coming behind you, including juniors. You don't become small by treating others well.

- Be kind whenever possible. And know that it is always possible. Treat everyone with kindness, not because they are kindhearted, but because you are. Kindness to others is one of the most valuable qualities. Kindness is the language that even a deaf can hear and a blind can see. Expressing kindness may need a few words and communicating the same may need a few minutes, but their echoes are truly endless. Be kind to even those who are unkind to you. They need it more. Your greatest test is how you handle people who have mishandled you.

- Add a flavour of the human touch to all your interactions. Demonstrate sincerity, courtesy, kindness and consideration to all your staff rather than a non-humane, mechanical and selfish approach to get your work done by any means. Respect them as people and respect their contribution, irrespective of what their role is. They appreciate courtesy from the boss and are quick to notice the lack of it, too. You can buy a man's time, physical presence, and a measured number of muscular motions per hour, but you can't buy enthusiasm, initiative, loyalty, and devotion of heart, mind and soul; you have to earn it. If you treat your men like machines, they will respond like machines, which means they will do just so much and no more. Conversely, if you show concern for them as human beings, they will feel obliged to help you and the organisation. Make them feel they are mattered; they are belonged. Make them count and let the evidence be visible to them. Avoid lip service. Demonstrate by your actions and behaviour that you mean what you say. Don't say you will do something unless you will indeed do it. Say only what you can do and do what you say.

- Show a personal interest in the lives of your employees. Look after their welfare. Enquire about the welfare of their families. Remember their birthday and wedding anniversary dates, wish them and present gifts. If someone takes leave for his wife's illness, enquire about his wife's health when he returns. If someone walks with a limp, enquire how it happened. Allow him to tell his story and exaggerate as much as he pleases. If someone has a personal

- problem affecting his mood or performance, be considerate and go out of the way to help him. If we have a caring heart, people see that and perform better.
- Never miss an opportunity to congratulate anyone's achievement or, more importantly, express sympathy in sorrow or grief.
- Be courteous and polite at all times. However, never be pushed around. Ensure that you are always treated with respect.
- Don't laugh at others' dreams. Instead, encourage and inspire them to develop their vision. Help them reach a level higher than they ever would have imagined on their own. However, don't spoon-feed them. Instead, guide them to the source of their power. Offer them support and motivation. Every person is born with a special ability. Just help him bring that to the world.
- Read people and influence the reading of yourself by others and customise both for any personal or business situation. Don't get carried away by the first impressions. Take a second look at the first impressions. We have an outward appearance - how we look, the clothes we wear, the car we drive, the house we live in and the money we have. However, what really matters is our character. So dress up your body, but don't forget to decorate your soul. The exterior or outward forms of an individual are an illusion. The reality lies in that which is the esoteric - the inner part.
- Be close to your enemy and yet create a distance from him. If you notice a change in him, ensure it is not superficial.
- Life is not easy. It has to be made easy by patiently waiting, accepting whatever comes our way, bearing many things, and ignoring and overlooking many things. Life could be unfair to you at times. However, life's unfairness doesn't give you a license to walk the wrong path. Treat all people with love and compassion. Appreciate those who have supported you, forgive those who have hurt you, and help those who need you.

7.2 TRUST: THE CORNERSTONE OF RELATIONSHIPS

- A commitment builds hope, but when you keep it, you build trust.

- Trust means giving someone the power to break your heart but faith that he will not do so.
- Trust is the glue that holds relationships together. Trust is built from love and respect and is a cornerstone for our future success. Trust is the foundation of all relationships – personal, business and social. Trust is the soul of relationships. Relationships that are based on a sound foundation of trust live long, weathering out storms of misunderstandings. With trust, every silence is understood. But without trust, every word could be misunderstood.
- Don't spy on any relationship. It shows a lack of trust and breeds dishonour. When you don't trust someone, can you expect him to act honourably? Trust a man and he will trust you. Trust begets trust.
- Default to trust. Don't pre-judge someone guilty unless proven. Even the judiciary can't do this. When you demonstrate unwavering trust in your team, they give you their best.
- Earn trust from others by demonstrating your honesty, integrity and sincerity. There is no such thing as a minor lapse of integrity. Integrity has to be cent percent. Show zero tolerance for those who compromise their integrity. Of course, before doing that, you have to lead by example and maintain your integrity at a cent-percent level. Therefore, make it a habit to have integrity in your life that will stand up to any close scrutiny.

7.3 REMAINING DETACHED IN RELATIONSHIPS

- Be aware that this moment is as it should be. Don't struggle against the entire universe by struggling against this moment.
- Be enlightened. Don't cloud your intellect with ignorance. Don't live your life in delusion. Instead, eliminate your sorrow by removing the underlying cause - a delusion.
- Attachments cause feverish breath, which takes away your peace of mind, making you fall prey to misery. In all your relationships, if you can love someone enough to allow them to be exactly what they choose to be with no expectations or attachment from you, you will get true peace in your lifetime.

True love means you love someone for what he is, not for what you think he should be. Changing people to fit into the moulds you think are right in your perception is outside your Circle of Influence. Stop expecting that those who are different will become what you think they should be. It is unlikely to happen.

- Let it all come and go as it will. Enjoy it all, but never make your happiness dependent on an attachment to anything, any place and more particularly, any person.
- Practice the spiritual law of detachment. Begin your day with a statement, "Today I shall judge nothing that occurs nor anyone whom I come across. I shall allow myself and those around me the freedom to be as they are. I shall not rigidly impose my idea of how people or things should be. I shall participate in everything with such detached involvement."

7.4 LAUGHTER: A TONIC OF HEALTHY LIFE

- Smile freely. It increases your face value. We are never fully dressed unless we wear a beautiful smile on our faces. Your smile is a signature of the almighty God on your face. Don't allow it to be washed away by your tears or erased by your anger.
- Share your smiles with others. It is free and has an amazing and lasting positive impact on others. Don't be a miser in smiling. For some people, smiling means giving income tax to the Government. They don't even smile.
- Smiling tends to create smile lines around the corners of the mouth. Laughter creates laugh lines around the corners of the eyes. If you want to lift your spirit, lift the corners of your mouth while smiling. Laughter is one of the most powerful mood enhancers. It changes your brain's chemistry and you feel happier even if there are no other changes to your situation or environment. Laughter therapy has been regularly used to heal persons with varied ailments and is a wonderful tonic for life's ills. It's hard to be negative when you're smiling or laughing. Those who smile also seem more approachable and contribute to the happiness of others around them. Thus,

a bright, good-natured, gleaming smile combined with gentle words and a kind look benefit both - the giver and the recipient. It can create wonders and accomplish miracles.

- Frowning tends to create wrinkles between the eyes and at the edges of the mouth. Smiling is more beneficial than frowning. Smile more. Frown less.
- Try to make at least three people smile each day.
- The speed of the vehicles is specified in miles per hour, but that of life in smiles per hour. Accelerate your life. Increase your life's speed. Get extra mileage by increasing your smiles.
- Humour is the spice of life. Develop a good sense of humour. (A survey was conducted to ascertain which single most quality young girls look for in their life partners. "I love a good sense of humour" was the reply from 80% of the girls. This is a nice incentive for eligible young boys to develop a good sense of humour for this objective alone, if not for anything else!)
- Apart from making conversation much lighter, humour also helps to defuse tension.
- Be aware that some people are sensitive and can't take humour. Hence, be careful in directing humour at someone you don't know well.
- Don't mock others. Don't use laughter to discriminate, shame, or ridicule others. Use laughter constructively.
- Laugh loudly. Laugh for five minutes in front of a mirror each morning. Laugh till your stomach hurts. While a child laughs about 500 times a day, an adult is a miser in this matter and hardly laughs fifteen times a day. Laugh like a child; it will bring far more living into your life.
- Laugh at yourself. Laugh with your family, friends and colleagues.
- Laughter is the shortest distance between two people. Laughter is a sign of life. If you have not laughed today, you have not lived today. The most wasted day is the day in which you have not laughed. Find something to laugh about. If you have nothing particularly funny in your day, think about a memory that never fails to make you laugh.

7.5 EMPATHY: A PSYCHOLOGICAL HUG

- Empathise. Empathy is a psychological hug. Empathy is the ability to put oneself in someone else's shoes (after getting out of one's shoes) and understand the situations and emotions from their point of view. It is about finding echoes of others in yourself. It is a respectful understanding of what others are experiencing. Empathy is simply listening, holding space, withholding judgment, emotionally connecting and communicating the incredible message that you are not alone.
- Frequently use phrases like 'I understand.' or 'I appreciate.' This doesn't mean you agree; it only means you heard what he said and considered it while forming your opinion, which you may present subsequently. It means taking the feelings of other people into thoughtful consideration and then, with this input, making intelligent decisions in such a way that other people realise that you have taken their feelings into account.
- Empathising doesn't mean that you, as a leader, should adopt other people's emotions as your own, or you always have to strive to please everybody. The essence of the philosophy of empathy requires that you don't ignore other people's feelings or be indifferent to their feelings and, more importantly, avoid creating impressions that you don't care about their feelings.
- Empathy begets empathy

7.6 THE ART OF LISTENING

- Listening is the most useful skill you can have, as out of every ten minutes spent in communication, five minutes are spent on listening. How well you listen greatly impacts your personal and professional life and the quality of your relationships. However, in our fast-paced, ego-centric world, we are often too self-centered to spare our precious time to listen to others, even those whom we love the most.
- Learn to listen with curiosity, speak with candour and act with integrity. Listening with curiosity allows relationships to thrive. Telling your truth will enable people to be honest with themselves and with you and acting with

integrity keeps relationships on a high standard. Also, when you lend your ears to others, people enjoy your company even more.

- Learn, cultivate and master the art of active listening. Whereas hearing is a physiological process that our body innately does, listening is an active process that we must consciously accomplish by making special efforts. Work on all four elements of listening: hearing, interpretation, evaluation and response. Since the brain can think four times faster than a person can speak, use this gap to evaluate.

- Listening is a multi-level process. Listening from the ears is the first step in the process of listening. Listening from the mind is one level of understanding. Listening from your heart with feeling and devotion is another level of understanding. Listening from the very core of your being or the deepest part of your being is yet another level of understanding. So don't merely listen from the ears. Listen from the mind. Listen from the heart with feelings and don't even stop at feeling; get into being. Uplift the level of your listening. 'I hear what you say' is low-level listening.

- Open up your senses and listen earnestly. Listen attentively, keeping your eyes peeled, your ears open and your mouth shut. The words listen and silent use the same five letters. Listen with a laser-like focus when someone is talking. Don't work or look somewhere else when someone is talking to you. Make the speaker feel you are listening to him attentively. Discipline yourself to attentive listening techniques. Attentive listening means hearing what is said as well as comprehending and understanding what is being omitted. Listen not only by giving thoughtful attention but by opening your third inner ear to the leanings and feelings that lie like the music behind words. Listen between the lines and catch what is not said. Listen with eyes too, for so much communication is still non-verbal. Get clues from the tone, facial expressions, gestures, body language, etc.

- There are different levels of grasping. When a drop of water falls on a hot pan, it disappears instantly. If it falls on a lotus leaf, the lotus becomes more beautiful, though it will disappear with a bit of breeze. However, if it falls on an oyster, the same water drop converts into a pearl. Be like an oyster.

- Be genuinely interested in what the speaker has to say. Have an open mind about what is being said. Leave behind your prejudices.
- Don't be under the false impression that you are intelligent enough to understand everything every time. This is a myth. Don't feel shy to admit that you have not understood. Besides making a feedback-type physical response, a good listener also asks questions to clarify the information and test its validity. Repeat the message in your own words and confirm whether you have understood him correctly. Respond by using encouraging verbal utterances like yes, ok, or right. Respond by using encouraging non-verbal clues like nodding, leaning forward and smiling. Don't be a miser in nodding. Nod requently as if you have Parkinson's disease. Nodding doesn't necessarily mean you agree with the speaker. However, keep in view local practices regarding nodding. For example, in India's southern region, what a particular nodding means is the opposite of what it means in the northern part.
- Listen patiently. Don't interrupt the speaker. Wait until the person is done speaking to respond. Interrupting a speaker is one of the most common discourtesies.
- Don't frame counter-arguments while listening. Listen to understand, not to reply.
- Listen to complaints. Whether complaints are made for the first or the tenth time, listen patiently and attentively. Be an empathetic listener rather than merely a sympathetic leader. See the problem from their point of view or frame of reference. Even if a complaint is unreasonable, don't brush it off. Allow him to tell his side of the story. Nod your head, ask questions and clarifications. Don't interrupt. Don't directly contradict. Instead, use a well-conceived pointed question to highlight contradictions. This way, the person feels he was allowed to present his grievances and sometimes, all he wants is a patient hearing. He will go back satisfied, whether his complaint is resolved or not.
- Watch your listen-talk ratio. Listen twice as much as you speak. Knowledge speaks, but wisdom listens. When you talk, you state what you already know, but you may know something new when you listen. When you listen to those

you are surrounded by, you learn things you never knew before. Everyone you meet knows something you don't know. When you listen, you find that people who once appeared boring have valuable insights to offer. Be willing to learn from them. It is more profitable to be an attentive listener than a fluent speaker.

- Listen to your spouse attentively. Many marriages end up in divorce primarily because the husband doesn't attentively listen to the wife or vice versa.

7.7 THE ART OF COMMUNICATION

- For seven out of ten minutes of our non-sleeping time, we communicate. The quality of our life depends on the quality of our communication.
- Communication is the sister of leadership. Communication means imparting information to others to secure the desired effect. Don't be an impersonal transmitter. Feel what you say and your feeling should be one of caring. Feelings connect people. Also, communicate your inner thoughts, emotions and spirit. Emotions mean energy in motion. Impart energy. Build up energy and enthusiasm. Shake up. Stir up. Inspire while you inform.
- Open an emotional account with whom you are communicating. Engage him with the objective of developing a relationship beyond the current transaction. This will create a sense of belonging.
- Speak only when you are sure your words are better than silence. Sometimes, not saying anything is the answer. Though silence might be misunderstood as arrogance, it can never be misquoted. Measure your words wisely. Calibrate your words carefully. Practice writing poems and essays, as this will improve your word selection. Before you speak, your words should pass three tests. Is it necessary? Is it true? Is it kind and non-offensive? Test your words on yourself before using them for others. Words that come out of the mouth can't be taken back. Sometimes, words may hurt more than a slap on the face. The tongue has no bones but is strong enough to break a heart. The life span of spoken words is more than human life.

- Be soft-spoken. Make your conversation soft and palatable. The more knowledgeable the person, the softer he is in expressing his views. The more your communication is soft, the higher is the probability of getting your work done. A wise leader won't say, 'I want this task to be done right now'. The other person can give several reasons, validly justifying why he can't do that task right now. He would rather say, 'This task is urgent. I know you are too busy. Depending upon the urgency of other tasks you are preoccupied with, you may decide.' The most likely answer will be, 'I will do it right now, Sir.'
- Breathe your character through the sentences you speak.
- Talk at a slow speed to take care of any speech distortions.
- Never raise your voice. Practice a gradual decrease in your decibels. Low decibels bring divine serenity to your voice. Aim for whispering-level decibels. High decibels don't mean your statement is true. In fact, the converse is true.
- Avoid a monotone. Speak enthusiastically. Learn to make your tone pleasing.
- Prepare well. Be articulate and brief. Communicate using telegraphic language. Communicate like in commercial advertisements on television, where they convey a message with high impact in less than thirty seconds.
- Use simple language. It should be direct and obvious.
- Talk to people at their level using language they can relate to. Keep in view the perceptions, prejudices and values of the recipient. Never talk about your riches amid the poor or about your children amid the barren.
- Prefer positive to negative statements. Start your conversation positively by saying, 'You have completed 90% of the task' rather than 'You didn't complete the task.'
- Call people by their first names. Pronounce names correctly. A man's name is very dear to him. One's name is like music to one's ears. In whichever language you call his name, it is the sweetest sound for him! Remembering and using someone's name is an instant rapport builder and a solid foundation for great relationships.
- Talk face-to-face to assess the listener's comprehension through his facial expressions and body language. Maintain eye contact while talking. It is as

important as your speech and demonstrates truthfulness. Look into the eyes of others fearlessly. Remove your sunglasses if you are talking to anyone in the street. It is a sign of respect.

- Ask questions or seek opinions. This makes the other person feel important. Occasionally, ask questions, even if you know the answers.
- Communicate clearly and unambiguously. If anything can be misunderstood, it will be misunderstood. So devote a little more time and communicate correctly in the first place rather than correcting the repercussions of misunderstandings.
- How you are understood is what matters, not what is said or how it is said.
- 'I' is the most selfish single-letter word. Frequent use of 'I' reflects your ego and dampens the spirit of teamwork. 'I', 'me', 'mine' and 'myself' bring so much attachment, leading you to identify with something and imparting expression to the attachment. This makes your inner world much bigger than the external world, though the converse is reality. Hence, use 'We' more often than 'I'. Try to go through one full day without uttering 'I, me, mine or myself' in your communication and then make this a habit.
- Four hard-to-say but very effective phrases are:

    - I don't know.   - I was wrong.

    - I am sorry.   - I need help.

- Never order anyone. No one likes to receive orders -not even a two-year-young child. Don't even request. Because even if you prefix the order or instructions with 'please' or convert those into a question form, it is still as good as an order, though a little less offensive. Instead, why not use the passive voice and thereby smartly avoid the tone of an order or even request? For example, instead of saying:

    -'File these papers' or

    -'Please file these papers' or

    - 'Can you file these papers?' or

    - 'Can you please file these papers?'

say, 'These papers need to be filed.'

Your secretary will like this and she herself will say, "I will file it, Sir." Now, this is her own commitment and not your request or order. One's own commitment is more likely to be carried out than order, even if the order is from the boss, who derives hierarchical authority from the employer-employee relationship. The best way is to talk about what is required to be done and keep talking patiently. Your talk should inspire your staff to make a commitment on their own. Learn the art of getting people to do what you want them to do because they want to do it. Ignite the fire within them. Your Leadership Quotient can be considered high if you can extract the desired commitment from your followers without using your authority to issue orders. A wise boss never orders. He doesn't have hierarchical undertones. All he does is that he tells what is required to be done and his followers are more than willing to cooperate. He knows the secret of arousing his followers' willing and enthusiastic support. Generally, human beings are most willing to obey those they believe to be the best. In sickness, people most readily obey the doctor. They don't question doctors' prescriptions. Aboard a flight, people obey the pilot. Thus, professional or technical competence is essential for a leadership position. Be the best in your field and your followers will most readily obey you without you using your authority to order.

- Even in restaurants, don't order but request! Also, one more tip as a part of a good recipe for successful living is to mix a bit of a smile with the request.
- Make everyone feel that they are partners in the common enterprise. This is the index of the effectiveness of your communication.
- Anyone can hold the helm when the seas are calm. The critical test of the power of communication comes when the seas are rough and people feel disoriented and out of touch. Communicate hope when all around people are doubting the promise of the future.

7.8 IS WINNING ARGUMENTS MORE IMPORTANT THAN RELATIONSHIPS?

- Cultivate a habit of showing tolerance towards the feelings of others. We all are entitled to have our opinions and beliefs and hence respect different shades of opinions. You don't have to agree with everybody in this world and everybody doesn't have to agree with you, but that doesn't mean you are right or they are wrong. Be open to all points of view but remain detached.
- Relinquish the need to defend your viewpoint or convince others to accept your perspective.
- Eliminate the desire to be right and to win the argument. Focus on what is right rather than who is right. Is winning an argument worth it if you lose peace of mind? Value relationships more than winning an argument.
- Keep your personal feelings, prejudices and ego right out of the picture. This way, you will get along with others easily. Each time we kill our ego, we rise spiritually.
- Discussion is an exchange of thoughts and knowledge. Promote it. The argument is an exchange of ego and ignorance. Avoid it.
- Disagree tactfully. Start by requesting the other person to explain his views. Listen patiently and attentively. Don't interrupt him. After he has done speaking, first convey your agreement on whatever points you agree on. If you can't find even a few points of agreement, think hard. Still, if you can't find points of agreement, compromise and agree to some of his points. Remember, you can't always have your way and that too fully. Stress the points of agreement and keep repeating them. Even if you think he is absolutely wrong, don't flatly contradict him. Instead, say he is right in his thinking and he has reasons to do so. You show that you have an open mind, which will encourage him to keep his mind open. Once a background is created this way, the other person will have a proper frame of mind to digest your disagreement. Now, convey your disagreement gently without anger. Put across your views; soft paddle your opinion. Present your idea in the form of a question rather than a statement. Use phrases like: 'How about

this?' or 'What do you think about this?' or 'What if you were to be on the other side of the table? This way, people will be more willing to listen and less quick to bristle. Hence, never get into an argument. Your aggressiveness will make the other person dig in his heels and stick to his opinion with even more force. Of course, eventually, it is a game of power. Whosoever is more powerful will have his way, but the decisions are likely to be accepted without much bitterness if you adopt the above approach. You may win by not listening and dictating your views, but it will strain relationships and people will retaliate at the first opportunity.

7.9 ILLS OF ANGER

- Anger is a state of insanity. You get angry when, according to you, someone else's action is imperfect or not as per your expectations. Can you correct somebody's action by becoming upset or showing anger? In the first place, his actions may not be imperfect. It may be merely your personal perception, but now your mind has surely become imperfect by judging it. At least save your sanity. Others may have gone on the wrong path; why should you let your mind also dwell on the wrong path? When you permit another person to make you angry, you allow that person to dominate you and drag you down to his level. Getting angry means, 'I want the world to be the way I want it, not the way it is.'
- For every minute you are angry, you lose sixty seconds of happiness. Anger is a punishment you give yourself for someone else's mistake. The moment a thought comes to your mind to destroy someone with anger, you have already started destroying yourself, whether or not you will succeed in destroying others. Get rid of anger and make room for positive energy.
- The habit of striking back at those who anger you is a weakness bound to degrade you and cause detrimental negative energies, pushing away anything with a positive vibration.
- A well-balanced person is slow to anger and remains cool and calibrated in his procedure. He remains poised under all conditions. Once, someone

spitted on Lord Buddha. He was surprised when Buddha didn't become angry. Buddha replied, "Should I show even my anger when you tell me?"

7.10 PRACTISING GRATITUDE

- If we were to name the single most important psychological trait or state that can contribute to individual and interpersonal well-being, it would be gratitude. Interpersonal gratitude is a cognitive emotion. It refers to the thankful and joyful attitude that a certain individual expresses towards another's benefaction with kindness.
- Express your gratitude generously. It replenishes. Hence, don't be a miser in expressing gratitude.
- Make gratitude the religion of your home. Cultivate a habit of expressing generous gratitude in your children.
- Use 'Thank you' freely. Never forget the stimulus and morale-building inherent in these two little words.
- Send personalised handwritten 'Thank you' notes rather than typed notes or through email.
- Don't hesitate to thank even your juniors.
- Develop a habit of thanking when you receive some service. For example, thank a steward for serving you tea or a housekeeping boy for cleaning your room. This way, you will receive better service and help bring a smile to their faces. Also, they will feel important as you have valued their services.
- Always respond to greetings by leaving out pride, arrogance and boastfulness.
- Learn to replace 'Sorry' with 'Thank You'. For example, instead of saying, 'Sorry I am late', say, 'Thank you for waiting'.

7.11 PRAISE: A POWERFUL PEOPLE-BUILDER

- The human appetite for praise is prodigious. As humans, we love praise; we are neurologically wired that way. When praised, human beings react favourably regardless of gender, race, religion, or age. In fact, girls love praise much more than boys, especially when the subject of the praise is their beauty!

Something happens with the body's chemistry that even medical science can't explain, except that the brain releases hormones called dopamine. Still, the fact remains that human beings melt down when praised. Also, the praise and chemical release of dopamine is a continual cycle. Having experienced pleasure through dopamine release, people work harder to get more praise and more pleasure. So explore the joy of spreading immense pleasure through the abundance of sincere praise.

- Praise freely. Appreciate freely. Compliment freely. Inject a high dose of praise and appreciation in your routine talks. Praise in public. Use a loudspeaker. Praise at least three persons every day.
- Praise selflessly. However, make sure the praise or appreciation or compliments are sincere. Never praise sarcastically.
- Never ridicule a person in the presence of others in his organisation. Instead, make him look good in the eyes of others in his organisation.
- Get rid of the myth that employees or children become arrogant when praised.

7.12 CRITICISM: A DIRE NEED FOR A CAUTIOUS APPROACH

- Do unto others as you would have them do unto you. When you are about to discipline your staff, ask yourself, 'Would I like to be spoken to the way I am thinking of speaking to him?'
- Before you criticise, give a person a chance to criticise himself. If he is aware of his shortcomings, he might prefer to admit them himself rather than have you point them out. Invite him for a cup of coffee. Talk about other things for an extended duration. Give examples of your shortcomings. Leadership quality in you should lead him to open up and admit his shortcomings on his own. Self-criticism is far more effective than criticism by the boss.
- Be so busy improving yourself that you don't have time to criticise others and thereby avoid criticism. If unavoidable, constructively criticise only the performance. Never criticise the performer. Criticism as a performer demoralises him permanently. It affects his self-image, making him a poor

performer even if he was not one before your criticism. Criticising only the performance leaves the scope for him to become a star performer in the future. This way, you are treating this particular performance as a temporary one-time correctible event and since you are also delinking it from him as an individual, he continues to remain a capable performer.

- Never criticise in public. Criticise only in private on a one-to-one basis. When done in public, criticism is taken as an insult and is highly counterproductive. It puts people in a defensive mode and is likely to provoke retaliation in public either instantly or subsequently. Thus, what should have remained a private matter is now dragged into the public domain, defeating the very purpose of criticism. On the other hand, criticism done on a one-to-one basis is treated as a piece of advice and is more likely to be accepted.
- If criticism is unavoidable, don't do it in isolation. Instead, wait for the most opportune time and mix it with praise. Praise before you criticise. That way, criticism is a lot easier to swallow and more likely to be taken positively.
- If criticism is unavoidable, make it soft and palatable. Don't belittle others. Don't act superior. Talk as one sinner to another. Give examples of your mistakes and how your boss's advice helped you avoid their reoccurrence in the future.
- Don't be overly critical.
- Avoid criticism in writing. If unavoidable, don't target a single individual. Address this to two or more people. Speak personally to those for whom the criticism is not meant.
- Don't keep reminding others, for no one likes reminders. Prefixing reminders with words like gentle or humble makes them slightly less offensive, but still, they are reminders.
- Avoid reprimanding. If unavoidable, restrict the scope of reprimanding to cover only the present undesirable behaviour and nothing beyond that. Avoid the temptation to generalise his behaviour or character.
- Never reprimand in public. Don't shout. Explain in low decibels. Count one to ten when you want to let fly at someone. It is your safety valve. Cool off and think over things properly to avoid regretting later.

- Don't degrade the person and make him feel bad about his mistake. When a mistake happens, your primary aim should be to avoid its future occurrence rather than degrading the person. Don't say, "That was stupid." or "You should never do that again." or "I will not tolerate this anymore." Instead, politely say, "I think we can't let that happen again." Also, avoid a direct attack. Make your sentence soft and palatable.
- Humiliate no one. Embarrass no one. Take extra care to ensure no one is embarrassed, even unintentionally. Do everything possible to nurture the self-respect or self-esteem of a person and guard against even the slightest damage to his self-respect that could possibly happen unintentionally. The self-respect of an individual is a prized possession.
- When something is going wrong, investigate or ask, but don't accuse. Give the person a chance to tell his side of the story. This way, he will be far more willing to accept responsibility for his mistake. If you accuse him, he activates his defence mechanism. Once the defence mechanism is activated, he stops listening and attention shifts away from finding a solution. Also, focus on improvements that can prevent mistakes from happening in the first place.
- Don't ask embarrassing questions. Ask only such questions to which others are comfortable replying unless you are conducting a criminal investigation. Avoid awkward personal questions like 'Oh, so you aren't married yet' or 'Why didn't you buy a house?' If someone doesn't reply to your question, it reflects poorly on you, not on him. In personal life and even in business situations, it is essential to know what to ask and, more importantly, what not to ask.
- Even if a question is asked disrespectfully, reply respectfully. This is because history will record your reply, not the question.
- Learn to handle criticism when you are the victim. When you are criticised, don't react instantly. Listen carefully to what is said with an open mind and look at yourself in a mirror. When you think your critics are right, correct yourself. However, don't worry unduly about non-genuine criticism. Do

your best and leave the rest. Criticism is no more than a personal opinion. It stems from the paradigm of the person criticising, not necessarily from the reaction to the situation.

7.13 TENDERING APOLOGIES

- Don't hesitate to accept your mistakes. To err is human. We can't be right all the time. A person who is right only sixty percent of times is considered a great success if he is quick to correct his mistakes the rest of the time.
- Learn to say "I am sorry" whenever you do something wrong or offend someone.
- Apologise freely. Show sincerity in apologies and make them unconditional. Conditional apologies are no apologies. Apologies don't make you small. It raises your stature.
- When you are at fault, apologise even to your juniors.

8
POWERFUL QUOTES

*F*rom time immemorial, many successful people have been speaking and writing about excellence in life. They have condensed the wisdom of their entire life into just a few words. Some of these aphorisms have become celebrated parts of society's lexicon and are so inspirational that they have the power to transform our minds. These timeless truths provide us with a priceless compass pointing towards true success.

Presented below is a precious collection of the most powerful quotes of all time from some of the most incredible human beings in the world who have phenomenal accomplishments to their credit:

	"Be thankful for what you have; you'll end up having more. If you concentrate on what you don't have, you will never have enough." – **Oprah Winfrey**
	"You can only become truly accomplished at something you love. Don't make money your goal. Instead, pursue the things you love doing and then do them so well that people can't take their eyes off you. The money will come on its own." – **Maya Angelou**
	"It's good to have money and the things that money can buy, but it's good, too, to check up once in a while and make sure that, in the process, you haven't lost the things that money can't buy." – **George Lorimer**

"Wealth consists not in having great possessions, but in having few wants."
— **Epictetus**

"You aren't really wealthy until you have something money can't buy."
— **Garth Brooks**

"The real measure of your wealth is how much you'd be worth if you lost all your money."
— **Bernard Meltzer**

"If you need to convince others that you're happy, you have not found real joy. You don't understand true wealth if you need to impress others with material objects.

If you need to correct others, you have not looked in the mirror. If you need to put others down, you have not connected to your higher self.

Know yourself. Be honest with yourself. Don't be a preacher or a judge. Be an example."
— **Eric Allen**

"Education is not a degree or certificate which can be shown to others as proof. Education is our attitude, actions, language, behaviour and personality."
— **Unknown**

"Time is a scarce resource; unless it is managed, nothing else can be managed."
— **Peter Drucker**

"Of all things in the world, the time is the longest and shortest; the swiftest and slowest; the most divisible and the most extended; the most neglected and the most regretted; which devours all that is little and enlivens all that is great."
— **Voltaire**

"Nothing really belongs to us but time, which even he has who has nothing else."
— **Baltasar Gracian**

"Time is very slow for those who wait. Very fast for those who are scared. Very long for those who lament. Very short for those who celebrate. But for those who love, time is eternal."
— **William Shakespeare**

"Don't say you don't have enough time. You have the same number of hours per day that were given to Albert Einstein, Helen Keller, Pasteur, Michelangelo, Mother Teresa and Thomas Jefferson."
— **H. Jackson Brown Jr.**

"If you want to know the value of one year, ask a student who failed a course. To know the value of one month, ask a mother who gave birth to a premature baby. If you want to know the value of one hour, ask the lovers waiting to meet. To know the value of one minute, ask the person who missed a flight. If you want to know the value of one second, ask the person who escaped death in a car accident. To know the value of one-hundredth of a second, ask the athlete who won a silver medal in the Olympics."
— **Marc Levy**

"If I had six hours to chop down a tree, I would spend the first four hours sharpening the axe."
— **Abraham Lincoln**

"If you want to enjoy the luxury of having enough time, time to rest, time to think things through, time to get things done to the best of your ability; remember there is only one way. Take enough time to think and plan things in order of their importance. Your life will take a new zest; you will add years to your life and more life to your years. Let all things have their places."
— **Benjamin Franklin**

"He who every morning plans the day's transactions and follows out that plan carries a thread that will guide him through the maze of the busiest life. But where no plan is laid and disposal of time is surrendered merely to a chance of incidents, chaos will soon reign."

– Victor Hugo (Writer)

"Too many people find their workloads heavy because they are unable to schedule, evaluate and co-ordinate their daily tasks. They keep themselves loaded with or diverted by that, which in actuality is trivial."

– Parkinson

"If you start your day, month or year without a plan, you find yourself reacting rather than acting or pro-acting. Don't become a reactor to your in-tray or your email inbox. Take charge of your time right from the start. Every hour invested in planning produces a dividend of two to three."

– Unknown

"If you (merely) think about it, it's a dream. If you envision it, it's possible. It becomes a reality only if you schedule it."

– Anthony Robbins

"Crystalize your goals. Make a plan for achieving them and set yourself a deadline. Then, carry out your plan with supreme confidence, determination, and disregard for obstacles and other people's criticism."

– Paul J. Meyer

"Get going. Move forward. Aim high. Plan a takeoff. Don't just sit on the runway, hoping someone will come along and push the airplane. It simply won't happen. Change your attitude and gain some altitude. Believe me; you will love it up here at the top."

– Donald Trump

"When I got enough confidence, the stage was gone. When I was sure of losing, I won. When I needed people the most, they left me. I found a shoulder to cry on when I learned to dry my tears. When I mastered the skill of hating, someone started loving me from the core of the heart. And, while waiting for light for hours, when I fell asleep, the sun came out. That's life! No matter what you plan, you never know what life has planned for you. Success introduces you to the world, but failure introduces the world to you. Always be Happy! Often when we lose hope and think this is the end, the almighty God smiles from above and says, 'Relax, sweetheart; it is just a bend, not the end!' Bends are not the ends of life."

– **Sophia Loren**

"We spend at least 50% of our working time trying to get grips with paperwork, i.e. preparing, writing, reading, interpreting, filing and searching. Research has shown that an average office worker has a backlog of forty hours of paperwork on his desk."

– **Declan Treacy**

"Clutter tends to expand to fill space available for retention. A small desk can understandably get cluttered, but if you are a disorganised person, even if you get a desk five or six times larger, it will still get cluttered."

– **Merrill E & D. N. Douglass**

"Productivity is never an accident. It is always the result of a commitment to excellence, intelligent planning and focused effort."

– **Paul J. Meyer**

"Most of us can do three or four times as much as we ordinarily do without lengthening working hours or without driving ourselves mad to the extent that we are exhausted when a day's work ends."

– **F. W. Taylor**

Powerful Quotes

"The average person puts only 25% of his energy and ability to work. The world takes its hats off to those who put in more than 50% of their capacity and stands on its heads for those few-and-far-between souls who devote cent percent."

– Andrew Carnegie

"How effectively you get your day's work depends on the institutional resources supporting your efforts, self-organisation and working habits. All these in combination are the basis for coursing successfully through each day and each successful day lays a foundation for a successful life."

– Joseph D. Cooper

"Many people regularly encourage procrastination by asking, 'What do I feel like doing now?' instead of asking, 'What is most important to do now?' By keeping importance uppermost, you concentrate on what is significant in relation to your goals-not the pleasantness of the moment. When you get totally involved in the activity that is really your 'most important now', what started out to be unpleasant can become pleasant due to the progress you are making towards your goals."

– James Steffin

"Next to being right, the best of all things is to be clearly wrong because you will come out somewhere. If you go buzzing about between right and wrong, vibrating and fluctuating, you come out nowhere; but if you are absolutely and thoroughly wrong, you must have the good fortune of knocking against the fact that sets you all straight again."

– Thomas Huxley

"Help others get what they want and you will get what you want."

– Zig Ziglar

The Twelve Steps To A Life Of Exemplary Excellence

"Before you speak, listen. Before you write, think. Before you criticise, praise. Before you pray, forgive. Before you quit, try. Before you spend, earn. Before you retire, save. Before you invest, investigate. Before you die, give."
— **William A. Ward**

"Transform your life and find true fulfillment with the priceless wisdom of the following ten ancient scrolls:
I) Today, I begin a new life.
II) I will greet this day with love in my heart.
III) I will persist until I succeed.
IV) I am nature's greatest miracle.
V) I will live this day as if it is my last.
VI) Today, I will be a master of my emotions.
VII) I will laugh at the world.
VIII) Today I will multiply my value a hundredfold.
IX) I will act now.
X) Guide me. Help me. Show me the way."
— **OG Mandino**

"Ten principles to success and inner peace:
Have a mind that is open to everything and attached to nothing
Treasure your divinity
Embrace silence
Give up your personal history
There are no justified resentments
Wisdom is avoiding all thoughts that weaken you
Treat yourself as if you are already what you would like to be
You cannot give away what you don't have
You cannot solve a problem with the same mind that created it
Don't die with your music still in you."
— **Dr. Wayne Dyer**

"Watch your thoughts. They become words.
Watch your words. They become actions.
Watch your actions. They become habits.
Watch your habits. They become your character.
Watch your character. It becomes your destiny."

— **Lao Tzu**

"The ten-step formula to solve even the most challenging problems:

Believe that for every problem, there is a solution.

Keep calm. Tension blocks the flow of thought power. Your brain can't operate efficiently under stress. Go at your problem easy-like.

Don't force an answer. Keep your mind relaxed for a clear solution to open up.

Assemble all the facts impartially, impersonally and judicially.

List these facts on a piece of paper. This clarifies your thinking and brings the various elements into an orderly system. This way, the problem becomes objective, not subjective.

Pray about your problem, affirming that almighty God will flash illumination into your mind.

Believe in and seek almighty God's guidance.

Trust in the faculty of insight and intuition.

Go to church or temple and let your subconscious work on the problem as you attune to the mood of worshipping. Creative spiritual thinking has the amazing power to give the right answers."

— **Dr. Norman Vincent Peale**

	"You attain spiritual maturity: - when you stop trying to change others and instead focus on changing yourself. - when you accept people as they are and drop expectations from a relationship. - when you understand that everyone is right in their own perspective. - when you learn to 'let go.' - when you stop craving for fame. - when you stop proving to the world how intelligent and compassionate you are. - when you don't seek approval from others. - when you stop comparing yourself with others. - when you are at peace with yourself. - when you can differentiate between need and want. - when you stop attaching happiness to worldly possessions. - when you become an unconditional giver." **– Unknown**
	The top five most common regrets at the time of death are: 1. I wish I had the courage to live a life true to myself, not the life others expected of me. 2. I wish I hadn't worked so hard at the cost of my health. 3. I wish I had the courage to express my feelings. 4. I wish I had stayed in touch with my friends. 5. I wish I had let myself be happier. **– Bronnie Ware**

9

WHAT SUCCESSFUL PEOPLE DO

*T*he busiest, most successful people always seem to have time to do what they want to do. Thus, not only do they have highly successful professional careers, but they also find time for all the non-business activities they enjoy. What are their secrets? What can we learn from the best practices such successful people follow?

Following is the precious collection of powerful quotes from the most outstanding achievers in the world, highlighting the secrets of their success:

	"I save twenty to twenty-five minutes a day by simply getting up when I wake up. Lingering in bed after waking up is avoidable. Besides, you are not getting any real rest, anyway." – **Arthur Godfrey (Television Personality)**
	"I write between 4 a.m. to 8 a.m. When the house is quiet, I feel alert, fresh and full of anticipation. Today, to do the same amount of work, I need to rise as late as 5-30 a.m." – **William J. Lederer**
	"I get up at 7 a.m. Pillow propped up; I wade through a mountain of national and provincial newspapers and by 9 a.m. I am ready to dictate, frequently remaining in bed until luncheon. It is foolish to stand when you can sit or sit when you can lie." – **Winston Churchill**
	"I show up at my office at 4 a.m. and have a sixteen-hour workday." – **Sam Walton (One of the wealthiest men in America)**

"Without disturbing my family and without interruptions, I get done in two hours, which would take five hours in the office. The automatic coffee maker rings at 6 a.m. I stay in bed with a stack of papers, reports, pads, stamped envelopes and sharp pencils.

If I can't retire early at night, I nap."

– **Unknown**

"I reach the office by 6 a.m. and examine an array of figures on revenues, circulation, etc. The result is a finger on crucial elements involving many highly successful family properties."

– **S. I. Newhouse Jr. (Head of Advance Publications**

"I go for a morning walk for one hour. This is an excellent recharger for starting your day. I listen to my favourite music while walking. I think while walking. After a walk, I cycle, simultaneously checking my email and watching TV news. I do three or four things simultaneously."

– **Kiran Bedi**

"I've adopted the zero-based idea for managing my time. Every quarter, I start from 'ground zero' and re-evaluate all my time use. I run a time log and find out where my time is going. Then I ask myself, 'If I weren't already doing this, would I start now?' If the answer is no, I drop it. If yes, I limit my involvement to the extent that item deserves."

– **Unknown**

"I pick up a few days in a row, start early and work until late in the day with all the speed and zeal I can muster. The volume of work accomplished is so gratifying that it inspires me to increase my basic capacity. After four days of sprinting, I return to a normal schedule, which has now become faster and more efficient. When capacity begins to slip, I schedule a sprinting session again."

– **Carol Davies of Chesterton, Indiana**

"Most entrepreneurs spend time on important and urgent matters. They have to learn to spend more time on what is important but not urgent, like hiring, processes, coaching and mentoring. Spending time on urgent issues gives a lot of an adrenalin rush. In contrast, reviews, coaching and mentoring may feel like boring administrative work but are rewarding. For an entrepreneur, the use of time must move from Quadrant I (crisis and emergencies) to Quadrant II (prevention, planning and improvement). For four years, I tracked how I spent my time. Today, I spend 75% of my time on Quadrant II activities. Whatever I do currently has no impact on this year's earnings but has a long-term impact."

– Rashesh Shah, Chairman, Edelweiss Group

"Years ago, I started dividing my day into fifteen-minute time slots, scheduling programmes for each slot and squeezing into it what might have previously taken twenty five minutes. Thus, I gained an extra hour or more every day. Now, this habit is automatic".

– Dr. Daniel Pawling

"Each time I pick up a paper, I put a tiny dot on the upper left corner. After a few days, it surprised me that some papers looked like they had measles. This helped me correct my time-consuming paper-shuffling habit, which saves eight full days in a year."

– Bernie Rooney

"I put all correspondence and notes for each project into a single transparent envelope. Each morning, I stack a few such envelopes on the desk in order of priority. Then I take a quiet hour in the morning, asking my secretary to shield me from calls and interruptions. I work steadily on these and complete them one by one."

– Donald Burnham

"Full-scale reorganisation of your desk will need two or three Saturdays and a lot of trash bags."
— **Stephanie Winston**

"I phone while I am in the bath—a great time saver."
— **Maureen Lipman (An actress)**

"When I got my first assistant, I was dissatisfied with almost everything he did. It took me so long to explain what I wanted and so long for him to do it half as well, resulting in a waste of time. Then one day, I realised that so long as I would be limited to doing only what I myself could accomplish, I would always be time short, with no real advancement opportunity. I looked for industrious and competent people, even if they were not operating exactly my way. Each pair of hands and brains I trained helped give me more time to develop myself further and move ahead."
— **C. R. Smith (President of American Airlines)**

"To meet your work priorities, you need to think about the best time of day to be unavailable, duly communicating this to team members who have both controlled and response time obligations. Also, develop non-offensive ways to protect yourself from casual callers. Top managers condemn an open door policy and advocate the imperative need for planned unavailability whether achieved by a 'Quiet Hour' or a hideaway or simply staying at home for a few hours of concentration without interruption."
— **Jonathan Coates**

"I have used the following nine-step delegation process with great success:

Select people who have the ability to do the job.

See that those selected understand what you expect.

Let the delegatee know you sincerely believe in his ability to carry out delegated tasks.

Negotiate deadlines.

Secure follow-through commitments from the delegatee.

Follow up.

Provide latitude for others' imaginations and initiatives.

Don't accept reverse delegations and don't do the job for others.

Reward commensurately with results produced."

— **Charles R. Hobbs**

"In all my relationships, rather interactions, I give my best and do my best to live up to what I say. My attachment to my children is complete. However, I remain detached in the sense that I don't expect them to reciprocate my affection. Most importantly, I make a conscious effort not to interfere or pass judgment on the lives they choose to lead. My concern for my near and dear ones will not fade with my detachment.

If you let go of the ones you love, they will never go away–this is the beauty of attachment with detachment. This dictum has developed tolerance in me. When I let people live the way they want to, I learn to accept them for what they are. Most importantly, I learn to tolerate the world around me, which brings me a sense of peace and contentment. Now I realise that we start growing mentally much more only after the children leave the house and we have to tackle the emotional vacuum that arises, along with age-related problems. Those who totally depend on their children's lives to nurture themselves emotionally, need to develop their own interests and hobbies-however mundane they seem to be."

— **Sudha Murthy**

"If you find there aren't enough hours in the day to pursue your necessities, interests, or hobbies, grab the time you have been wasting on sleep. Steal a few hours from the night. The best trade-off of sleep time for working time is exercise. I rise half an hour early to ride a bike. This gives me the energy and alertness needed for my business schedule. The sleep management plan is not really about sleeping; it is about living."

– **Dale Hanson Bourke**

"I have gone through four stages of happiness in my life. The first stage was earning money. However, this didn't give me the happiness which I wanted. In the second stage, I started collecting expensive luxurious items but soon realised that their effect is very temporary and their shine does not last long. In the third stage, I acquired big prestigious projects. I became the biggest manufacturer of steel in India and Asia. Here also I didn't get the happiness which I wanted. Once, one of my friends asked me to donate 200 wheelchairs for disabled children. I purchased and gave these wheelchairs to my friend, but he insisted that I come and personally distribute these wheelchairs to children. When I handed over wheelchairs to children, I saw amazing happiness on their faces and a divine shine in their eyes. They sat on wheelchairs, moved around and played a lot with the wheelchairs. It became like a picnic spot, as if they got something great in life. I experienced true inner happiness that day. When I was about to leave from there, one boy came and held my feet. I bowed down and asked him whether he wanted something else. He said, 'I want to remember your face so that when I meet you in the heavens, I can offer my thanks to you once again.' This reply completely changed my viewpoint about life."

– **Ratan Tata**

10

THE TWENTY COMMON MYTHS ABOUT EXCELLENCE

The common myths about excellence that need to be busted are tabulated below, together with corresponding realities:

MYTH No.	MYTH	REALITY
1	Excellence is synonymous with success.	Excellence is different from success. Success is how good we are in relation to the rest of the world. Excellence, on the other hand, is how good we are in relation to how good we individually can be. Achieving excellence is being our best. Excellence springboards us to greatness.
2	To achieve outstanding success in life and to maximise wealth, we must be self-centered.	To achieve sustainable success in life and maximise our wealth, we must put others before ourselves.
3	Success can't be achieved without a strong attachment.	It is possible to have a strong desire for success yet not have attachments.

4	Excellence in life can be achieved even by superficial transformation.	Radical or paradigm transformation is a must for achieving excellence in life.
5	Monetary wealth and worldly possessions will bring true happiness.	Sustainable happiness can be achieved only when we strike a judicious balance among all elements of true wealth.
6	External circumstances dictate the trajectory of our life.	Our choices dictate the trajectory of our life. Our destiny is in our hands.
7	The clock is more important than the compass.	It is more important to set the direction right.
8	Efficiency means effectiveness.	Effectiveness lies in doing the right things first. Doing things faster is no substitute for doing the right things.
9	Managing time means eliminating leisure and fun from our life.	When we manage our time efficiently, more time will be available for leisure and fun.
10	Managing time will cut us off from our people and make us cold fish.	When we manage our time efficiently, we can spend more quality time with others.
11	Constantly updated and re-prioritised 'TO DO' list hinders creativity and kills spontaneity.	A well-thought 'TO DO' list enables us to accomplish a lot more and that too, as per our priorities. This makes available more time for creative thinking.

12	Most of the day's activity does not need planning.	Planning is an absolute necessity. Every hour invested in planning produces a dividend of two to three.
13	Most people are overworked because of the nature of their job.	Most people are overworked because of non-prioritising, inefficient time management and personal disorganisation.
14	Delay improves the quality of the decision.	Delay seldom improves the quality of the decision.
15	The higher the level, the better the decision.	Lower-level people also make equally good decisions.
16	It is better to do everything ourselves.	The sooner we get rid of the 'do-it-myself' or 'I-can-do-it-better-myself' syndrome, the better. Delegation is the key to success.
17	Delegatee may not do quality work.	A trained delegatee may be as effective as his boss.
18	Delegation absolves responsibility.	Delegation doesn't absolve responsibility.
19	A face-to-face conversation is always absolutely necessary.	In most cases, a well-structured telephonic talk could be as effective.
20	Eight hours of sleep is absolutely necessary.	Most successful people remain energetic and healthy even by sleeping for six hours.

11

PHILANTHROPY: A PRECIOUS PHILOSOPHY

*N*ormally, we relate philanthropy only to financial help. However, this is only a narrow interpretation of the philosophy of philanthropy. Apart from financial help, we all can give many things. Everyone has something to offer: knowledge, advice, wisdom, hope, love or time. The list of non-financial things we can give is endless. Hence, start a philanthropic mission first with non-financial help and then gradually include even financial help in this mission. You don't need a big corpus to start the mission of financial help. You can start on a small scale with your household helper, cook, driver, or needy friends and relatives. Consider using part of the passive income, i.e., income generated from investment for a philanthropic purpose. We have a great attachment to our hard-earned active income or sweat income. However, the level of attachment is relatively less when it comes to passive income; hence, psychologically, it will be easier to part with passively earned money.

Billionaires like Warren Buffett, Ratan Tata, Aziz Premji, Sunil Mittal, and Narayan Murthy have donated millions for noble philanthropic purposes and given back part of their earnings to society.

Consider the following tips to learn and master the art of giving:

- Make service an important goal in your life. It is the most fulfilling investment of time. You will feel purposeful if you can find a way to always be in the service of others. The purpose is to serve. It is about taking the focus off you and your self-interest and serving others. Besides gentleness and fragility, humility is the third prized essential quality of greatness, which teaches us to put others before ourselves.

- Too many people live with a scarcity mentality, believing less will be left for them if they share ideas, wealth, or resources. This is the surest way to a life of little. A candle loses none of its light when igniting another flame. Develop a habit of giving; getting will happen automatically - whether money, happiness or knowledge. One of the primary laws of nature is that the more you give and serve others, the more you get. The universe operates through dynamic exchange. Nothing is static. Life is an echo. Giving creates abundance and triggers the whole process of circulation. In our willingness to give what we seek, we keep the abundance of the universe circulating in our lives. Know that you are just an instrument, taking wealth from one hand and giving it away from the other. You are a conduit-the more you allow giving to flow through you, the more abundance flows back into your life. Give the best and get a great deal back. Giving creates a symbiotic relationship benefiting both parties.

- Consider being a giver in all your relationships. Do something nice for others - however little it may be. Alleviate the sufferings of others. Make a difference in their lives. If someone is in need, lend him a helping hand. Helping someone you like and respect is good, but helping those who hurt you or those you don't even know is a noble act of kindness. True kindness lies in the act of giving without the expectation of getting something in return. Ask not what this world can do for you; ask what you can do for this world.

- Do all good you can do, for all people you can, in all ways you can, as long as you can. Wherever you go and whoever you meet, bring them a gift. The gift need not be expensive; it can be a flower, a prayer, or a compliment. What you gift is not that important; the devotion with which you offer is important. Give away love. Love is a universal need and spans all countries, cultures and faiths. Love is the world's most powerful currency. So is the case with physical touch. A grateful heart is a magnet for miracles. We can accomplish miracles through our giving. Hence, work on your personal programme of self-love, self-respect and self-empowerment and create a huge inventory of what you wish to give away.

- When you give others the things you want for yourself, you have really understood the power of giving. Also, give even in times of hardships. This will help you forget your problems, create breakthroughs and find solutions.
- Give with respect and humility. Give unconditionally. Elevate the self-respect of the taker and dignify him. Once, a poor lady went to a rich lady's house to borrow some sugar. She gave her sugar. After a few days, the rich lady went to the poor lady's house to borrow salt. Puzzled by this, her husband asked her, "Why do you want to borrow salt, though plenty of salt is available with us?" She replied, "I didn't want the poor lady to feel inferior. My act of borrowing from her will make her feel dignified that she also has something to offer to her rich neighbour. Next time she needs something, she will not hesitate to come to us."
- Our destinies will eventually be defined by what we give, not what we get. No one has ever been honoured for what he received. Honour has been the reward for what he gave.
- Acts of kindness, like helping others or volunteering, positively impact your health. People who exhibit higher levels of altruism get a higher release of endorphins. This gives a boost to the immune system and speeds the recovery of the body from ailments.
- Live a simple life. Cultivate the discipline of giving from a young age. This will make it a natural habit.
- Teach your children the art of giving. Let them donate ten percent of their pocket money wherever they choose to give, even if you don't agree with their choice. Then replenish double of what they have given away.
- Find ways to get involved in your social and professional communities. Do some social or charitable work. Give some money to the charity of your choice, or give your time. When you give your time to someone, you give him part of your life. Don't shy away from public service.
- All said and done, the quality of your life boils down to the quality of your contribution to others. Maximise your contribution assets. Leave a great legacy for those around you to savour.

12

CONCLUSION

"We are what we repeatedly do. Excellence is, therefore, not an act but a habit."

– Aristotle

Taking this thought-stimulating book as a guide, you are now ready to develop your own unique Action Plan to accelerate your journey towards a life of exemplary excellence. You can assign priorities to your goals in accordance with your life's mission and design a principle-centered life with a well-proportioned mix of all elements of true wealth.

Key learnings of the book are briefly summarized below:

True Wealth	True wealth is a state of mind. True wealth is having a sense of abundance that we experience rather than possess.
	Don't madly run after success in professional life at the cost of your health. Feed your body with a balanced nutritional, naturopathic diet and your mind with positive thoughts. Allocate time for exercise, yoga, meditation, rest, sleep, holidays, rewarding leisure activities, etc.
	You aren't really wealthy until you have something money can't buy.

Material abundance, success and excellence	Material abundance is not the true success. Material abundance happens to be one of those things that makes the journey of life more enjoyable. But true success, apart from material abundance, also includes an exemplary, passion-driven professional career, good health, a fulfilling family life, enriching personal and professional relationships, knowledge, wisdom, a sound foundation of worthy principles, emotional and psychological stability, spiritual enlightenment, a philanthropically sensitive heart, eventual level of creative freedom as regards all five elements of true wealth and a sense of well-being with serenity and peace of mind. It is an incessant flow of all good things in abundance. The wealth of fulfilment occurs when all the elements of true wealth intersect and are constantly being improved upon. When we are able to continually expand happiness and relentlessly pursue progressive realisation of nobly altruistic worthy goals with effortless ease duly embracing others around us, we achieve excellence. Excellence is a journey and not a destination. The relentless hunger to be the best version of ourselves each day leads us to an exciting and rewarding journey towards a life of exemplary excellence.
Selflessness Quotient	Self-centered people are unlikely to achieve great success even if they possess a high IQ. However, people with a high Selflessness Quotient achieve broad-based, long-lasting success. They establish goodwill first and painstakingly build and nurture a network of friends and associates who become their brand ambassadors. This triggers a positive virtuous cycle and they achieve more and more success effortlessly. Hence, improve your Selflessness Quotient.

Conclusion

Value of time	Appreciate the value of time in your life. Develop a deep personal sense of time. Efficient management of time is the most important prerequisite for living a successful and enriching life - a life of excellence.
Long-range planning	Discover your passion and weave your life around your passion. Establish a strong and nobly altruistic why factor in your life.
	Create an inspiring and empowering PMS and translate the same into an Action Plan covering long, medium and short-term horizons. Dream big.
	Assign priorities to all your activities and learn to put first things first. Eliminate all non-essentials. Subordinate the clock to the compass and shift your focus from urgency to importance. Spend more time on Quadrant II activities. Ask yourself what one thing you could do in your personal and professional lives that could make an atomic and positive impact if you do it regularly.
	Expand your Circle of Influence by proactively focusing and acting only on what you can change.
Daily scheduling	Prepare an exhaustive 'TO DO' list daily, duly assigning priorities to each item. Exploit the power of daily scheduling to close the gap between your compass and clock.
	Schedule at least one quiet hour every day in the high-efficiency morning and use it for creative thinking.

People Management	We can't build a business without building people first.
	Practice total and complete acceptance of people, situations, circumstances and events as they occur. Accept the people or things as they are and not as you wish they should be.
	Never order anyone. Your Leadership Quotient can be considered high if you are able to extract the desired commitment from your followers without using your authority to issue orders.
	Praise freely. Appreciate freely. Compliment freely. Praise in public. Use loudspeaker.
	Avoid criticism. If unavoidable, mix with praise and constructively criticise only the performance and that too in private. Never criticise the performer.
	Help others get what they want and you will get what you want.
	The time efficiency and spiritual maturity with which you conduct yourself in relationships directly affect the quality of your life.
Golden quadrilateral of relationships	Take extra effort and make the relationship with your spouse loving, respectful, peaceful, harmonious and mutually satisfying. Take adequate physical steps to develop fine chemistry with your spouse. Align PMS. Dream jointly.
	Treat the customer like a king. Delight him.
	Align with the boss. Fuse your mission with your boss's mission or corporate mission.
	Invest time training your secretary/assistant and treat them as your greatest allies in improving your time use.

Delegation	Get rid of the 'Do-it-myself' or 'I-can-do-it-better-myself' syndrome. Well-structured outsourcing or delegation is a great time saver. Off-load what you can and then focus on vital items that are truly meaningful to you.
Debt	Live below your means. Live an honourable, debt-free life.
Work-home Boundaries	Don't think about work challenges when you are not at work. Worry not about challenges.
Philanthropy	Use part of passive income for noble philanthropic causes. Philanthropy is the key that unlocks lasting happiness.

May the knowledge and wisdom found in these pages enhance the lives of all those who read them. May you have the blessings of the almighty God in your journey towards excellence. May you always act in such a way that you get what you deserve.

If some of these ideas appeal to you, consider implementing them. Once convinced, you need to seamlessly integrate the above principle-centered approach into your life. Once it becomes a part of your personality and habit in doing, your life will be bountiful and in the end, when you look back over all that you've been through, you can say, "God, I loved my life."

The path to success is supremely exciting, filled with magnificent gifts and fulfilling rewards. This path is open to all. You have everything in you to achieve outstanding success, together with serenity and peace of mind.

See you at the top.

13

APPENDICES

APPENDIX I

TYPICAL PERSONAL MISSION STATEMENT

DATE: _____   REVISION : ____

Sr.	Sr.	MISSION
A		**THE ALMIGHTY GOD**
	1	I shall first merit and then seek divine help.
B		**PERSONAL CHARACTER**
	2	I shall earn income through honest and fair means without losing sight of true wealth and shall never compromise my integrity. In pursuit of this, I shall not hesitate to sacrifice my material fortunes.
	3	I shall demonstrate selflessness of the highest order in all my relationships.
C		**PERSONAL CORE VALUES**
	4	I shall practice and promote non-violence. I shall never hurt anyone by mind, words, or body, nor trouble anyone.
	5	I shall have as few expectations as possible.
D		**PERSONAL ATTITUDE**
	6	I shall maintain a highly positive attitude.
	7	I shall view problems as challenges.

E		**PERSONAL HABITS**
	8	I shall do first things first and manage time effectively through personal organisation.
	9	I shall develop a good sense of humour.
	10	I shall never lose my temper and maintain cool even when others lose their temper.
	11	I shall listen twice as much as I speak.
	12	I shall practice non-judgment.
	13	I shall never spend more than what I earn nor borrow money from others.
F		**HEALTH**
	14	I shall remain a non-smoker and non-alcoholic and promote the same.
	15	I shall take a balanced nutritional vegetarian diet, exercise regularly and do yoga.
	16	I shall take time each day to be silent and to be just myself.
G		**THE FAMILY**
	17	I shall succeed at home first and shall have an enriching and fulfilling family life. I shall spend quality time with my family.
	18	I shall arrange the best education for my children and allow them the freedom to pursue their passion.
	19	I shall provide my family with a decent home, luxury car, etc. I shall also emphasise the importance of contribution assets.
	20	I shall visit important exotic tourist destinations worldwide with my family and build up priceless experience memories.
	21	I shall have adequate life insurance coverage and do prudent post-retirement financial planning to ensure a handsome fixed monthly income/Lump Sum corpus.

H		**PROFESSIONAL FIELD**
	22	I shall reach the top professionally.
	23	I shall facilitate the success of my staff.
	24	I shall read good books about my profession and self-help.
	25	I shall share my knowledge with others.
I		**SOCIAL AND COMMUNITY LIVES**
	26	I shall befriend like-minded individuals in the neighbourhood and community.
J		**HELPING OTHERS**
	27	I shall help needy relatives and friends in medical or other emergencies.

APPENDIX II

PRACTICAL TIME-SAVING TIPS

Time, the third important wealth after physical wealth and social wealth, is one of the most important resources and ranks higher than money in priority. We can't achieve excellence in life unless we manage our time well.

In every facet of life, there is ample scope for saving time. This Appendix enumerates several practical, time-saving tips, encompassing almost all facets of life, from getting up in the morning to sleeping at night. Presented in the form of a prescription, these Dos and Don'ts are readily actionable.

1 GETTING UP

- Rise early. See the sun rising every day. (A recent study on Fortune 500 Company Chairpersons shows they wake up at 6 a.m. or earlier.)
- Steal an hour from the night by getting up early and gain an extra thirty hours every month.
- Establish a regular time for daily rising. This will also help avoid Sunday night insomnia.
- Wake up without the help of an alarm unless you tend to overslip. Also, use a preset kettle synchronised with wake-up time.
- Make yourself want to get up by thinking about the most enjoyable things.
- Get up when you wake up without lingering in bed.
- Establish staggered wake-up times for the family members.
- The pre-breakfast period can give you the treasure of an uninterrupted time slot of ultra-concentration. Moonlight and use this time slot for creative thinking. Be ready like a fisherman holding a fishing hook to catch fish. Keep a pad and pen ready to note down ideas.
- Raise body temperature by suitable exercise in the morning.

2 TIME-EFFICIENT BATHROOM

- Go for a functional, spacious bathroom with two washbasins.
- Provide a phone connection in the bathroom or have a cordless phone. Also provide a portable cassette player, radio and small TV in the bathroom.
- Provide separate personal racks for each family member with a few extra shelves.
- Maintain an adequate inventory of items like toothpaste, soap and shampoo.
- Group items, which are used together. Store frequently used items forward and lower for convenient access and other things backwards and on upper shelves.
- Shave before bath. Use a time-saving electric razor.
- Don't use a bucket. Take a shower and save water.
- Use a high-speed hairdryer.

3 DRESSING UP AND GETTING READY

- Install large, separate time-saver wardrobes for each family member. Prefer a walk-in wardrobe.
- Provide compartmentalised shelves.
- Prefer home-washable, no-iron wrinkle-free fabrics.
- Don't button clothes on hangers. Also, instruct your laundryman not to button clothes except one button.
- Hang ties by colour from dark to light.
- Arrange coordinated colour belts attached to trousers.
- As business attire, prefer dark suits (navy blue, black or charcoal grey). Dark suits reflect sophistication, power and authority.
- Install a mini wardrobe in the office where you can keep a suit, ties, etc.
- Keep removing old and unfit clothes from the wardrobe.
- Eat enough nutritional breakfast to raise blood sugar levels and bring your body to full functioning capacity.

- Synchronise breakfast time with TV news time. Avoid low-content media.
- Keep pills in one place.
- Provide an open plastic tray in the top dresser drawer for emptying your pocket paraphernalia for easy recollection.
- Re-organise your wallet periodically. Remove all unnecessary items.
- Keep the key set in a briefcase. Keep the second set of keys separately.
- Carry an accurate electronic watch with an easy-to-set beep alarm.
- Carry adequate coins and change.
- Use a single credit/debit card (or a maximum of two) for domestic and international transactions.
- Carry a small pocket-size organiser.
- Carry a pencil with an eraser fixed to it. Carry an investment pen. This being expensive is less likely to be forgotten and you will not be stranded without a pen.

4 DAILY PLANNING AND SCHEDULING

- The daily scheduling enables you to accomplish a lot more and that too, as per your priorities. This makes your mind free for creative thinking since you know priority items are being attended to. This is true so long as the daily schedule doesn't induce guilt and you are governed more by your internal compass rather than some clock on the wall. Exploit the power of daily scheduling to close the gap between your compass and clock.
- Plot a chart for two or three weeks to spot the high-efficiency best time and low-efficiency poorest time to facilitate scheduling your 'TO DO' list based on the efficiency level during the day.
- Follow your bio-rhythm. Don't waste high-efficiency morning hours on newspapers, non-essentials, or clearing up little things. Schedule big things on 'TO DO' list (e.g. creative thinking) during high-efficiency morning hours. This will give you a psychological boost, as a head start achieved by a single-mindedness of purpose can make all the difference in your day. Schedule medium-efficiency time for interaction with

others, routine dictation, etc. and low-efficiency time for preliminary sorting and study of routine mail, attending to visitors, phone calls, etc.

- Prepare an exhaustive 'TO DO' list, preferably the previous day evening, so that you have a few items ready to be tackled first thing in the morning. Assign priorities to each item.
- Prepare 'TO DO' list electronically. If you manually prepare the 'TO DO' list, use ink for set items and pencil for flexible items. Use colours freely.
- Don't use multiple 'TO DO' lists.
- Plan your day according to your priorities and not those of others. Control your calendar; else, your calendar will control you.
- Break down big tasks into smaller units and sub-activities.
- Question every repeated action and simplify it. If customers ask some questions repeatedly, answer such common questions in a 'welcome kit' that you send to all new customers. This will save considerable time for the customer care department.

- Allot fixed time commensurate with the importance of the activity to avoid work expanding to fill the time available. Delineate a time limit and stick to it. Optimise each time pocket to get the best out of each minute.
- Allow some buffer time in the 'TO DO' list to handle unforeseen events.
- Drop or postpone whatever you can so that more time is available for vital items.
- Post 'TO DO' list on a wall in front of you or on the corkboard near your desk.
- Don't get overwhelmed by looking at the long 'TO DO' list. Focus on one item at a time.
- Consult 'TO DO' list before you pick up a task.
- Pick up the top priority task from 'TO DO' list and complete it first. Be ruthless and cut away unimportant tasks. Ensure that the tasks that matter most are not at the mercy of those that matter the least.
- Modify 'TO Do' list if a new item crops up or the priority changes. Though a boss or customers can disturb your priorities, anticipating

- their demands or allowing a buffer in your schedule can minimise the impact of such disturbances.
- Don't depend upon your memory. Jot down the moment a thought comes to your mind.
- Squeeze in just one more 'TO DO' item a day.
- Keep quickie tasks handy for picking up in your spare time, like just before lunch or while waiting for visitors to come.
- Remove productivity pit spots that limit your productivity.
- Score your performance on a scale of one to ten. Continually strive to achieve a higher score.
- Be satisfied with what you accomplish without unduly worrying about unfinished items on the 'TO DO' list. Since you have followed the priority, what is left over are low-priority items.
- Transfer pending items, if any, to the next day's 'TO DO' list.

5 MAINTAINING GOOD HEALTH

- Realise that maintaining good health is of paramount importance. Don't madly run after success in professional life at the cost of your health.
- Stay fit and healthy. Stay motivated and passionate about life.
- Build up your health by following sensible guidelines about diet, exercise, sleep and holidays.
- Take care of your body. The human body needs sunlight, fresh, unpolluted air, nutritional food, exercise, rest and sleep. Your food intake and activities should be moderate and balanced. Don't over-exert. If hitting a nail with a hammer requires two units of energy, don't use the whole body to hit the nail. Take care of your body with a disciplined approach and avoid physical abuse to your body. Similarly, take care of your mind. When you do so, a sensory acuity - a sensory sharpness is activated; your body and mind are purified and you perceive the world with enlightenment. Exploit the power of this synergy between body and mind to springboard accomplishments of the highest order.

- If you are an athlete, activate body intelligence depending on the type of sport. For example, a bodybuilder needs to build muscles, or a karate expert needs to create karate intelligence.
- Hunger is a feeling of discomfort or weakness caused by a lack of food coupled with a desire to eat. Listen to your body. Be aware of false hunger. Eat only when you are hungry. Eat to live rather than living to eat.
- Pray before you eat.
- Learn the science of eating. Be mindful of what to eat, what not to eat, when to eat, how much to eat and how to eat.
- Be careful of what goes inside your body - both in terms of quality and quantity. Invitation to diseases is written on the dining table. You feed or fight a disease every time you drink or eat something. You are what you eat. Eat your food as medicine; else, you will have to eat medicines as your food. Have a naturopathic diet with a balanced combination of a soothing, an eliminative and a constructive diet. Such a diet has a positive gut-brain axis effect. The gut-brain axis is a bi-directional system between the brain and the gastrointestinal tract, linking the emotional and cognitive centers of the brain with the peripheral functioning of the digestive tract. Love organic food. Opt for natural foods - foods created by the natural interaction of the sun, air, soil and water. Eat more foods that grow on trees and plants and less of what is manufactured in plants. The selection of food affects the health of the body and mind. Natural foods like fruits and their fresh juices, vegetables and grains maintain a balance in your mind and make your life enlightened, cheerful and filled with qualities like patience, calmness and forgiveness. Use leafy vegetables like lettuce, spinach, mustard greens, fenugreek. Use healthy roots like carrot, turnip, reddish and sweet potatoes. Use herbs like tulsi, curry leaves, basil, mint, fennel, ajwine, giloy.
- Consume about 80 grams of millets per day. Millets are nutrient-rich super food that include diverse small-seeded crops like Sorghum (jowar), pearl millet (bajra) and finger millet (ragi).

Practical Time-Saving Tips

- Eat according to season.
- While a diet high in fruits and vegetables will keep you strong and energetic; bad foods will slow you down and affect your health and moods. Avoid frozen foods or foods cooked before three hours, as these are detrimental to your body and mind. Avoid whole milk products, caffeine, fried foods, snack foods, fast foods, creamy salad dressings, or pastries. Spicy foods may momentarily satisfy your tongue but may harm your body and mind in the long run.
- Let aroma of delicious food tantalise your taste buds. Concentrate on your food while eating. Don't watch TV or mobile while eating. Take small bites. Drink your solids. Chew your liquids. Chew your food slowly and properly. Chew until it is liquefied in the mouth. Finish chewing and swallowing before the next bite.
- Don't overeat. Ekbhokta is maha yogi. Dwibhokta is maha bhogi. Thribhokta is maha rogi. Fill half the stomach with solids and a quarter of the stomach with liquids, leaving a quarter of the stomach empty for churning.
- Don't skip lunch in the office. Eat something nourishing, albeit light, to maintain a high energy level until evening. Eat ample fresh fruits or drink their fresh juices.
- Don't eat lunch alone. Instead, have lunch with your staff, peers, or boss and use this time for business or other useful discussions.
- Drink enough water throughout the day. Start the day with one liter of warm water early in the morning. Never drink water while standing. A glass of warm water forty-five minutes after a meal helps dissolve unwanted fat from the stomach.
- Consider fasting for a continuous duration of twenty-four hours once a month. Fasting could be total or partial. In total fasting, you take nothing except warm water; only fruits and their fresh juices are taken in partial fasting. If this is difficult, try intermittent fasting every day for about twelve hours between 8 p.m. to 8 a.m. Fasting detoxifies your body and offers you several other health benefits. Also, it is an ageless technique to build willpower. If you can conquer hunger with your willpower, you can easily conquer anything else

as well. That is why almost all religions in the world advocate fasting. Whether you fast from religious considerations or health considerations, in either case, the benefits are the same. However, if you have diabetes or other medical ailment, consult your doctor before fasting.
- In addition to fasting of food, we also need fasting of mind. Not losing one's temper is fasting. Eliminating jealousy is fasting.
- Become a willpower warrior. Wage war against impulses that drain your energy and prevent you from reaching your limitless potential.
- Exercise for at least an hour a day, preferably in the morning. Swim, run, walk, cycle, garden, exercise in the gymnasium or have fun at aerobics. Work-out releases beneficial chemicals that give you a mood lift. Top executives, world leaders and other peak performers have recognised the tremendous power of vigorous daily exercise as a tool for self-mastery and life excellence. It also keeps depression at bay.
- Do yoga, meditation, etc. Meditation is your appointment with the almighty God. It is the single most powerful personal development tool.
- Recognise the power of breathing and its relationship with your energy sources. Alternate deep and shallow breathing is a performance enhancement technique. By practising deep abdominal breathing, you will develop a calm, serene demeanour that keeps you cool in the hottest circumstances. It provides relaxation, vitality and energy. By deep breathing, the blood is fully oxygenated and triggers the lymph and your body's sewage system, making your cells more efficient and taking your health to its peak.
- The six best doctors are sunlight, rest, exercise, diet, self-confidence and friends. Maintain them in all stages of life.
- Remember, medicine is not always found in tablets, capsules, syringes, or vaccines. Detoxification is a medicine. Quitting junk food is medicine. Vegetables and fruits are medicine. Fasting, exercise, sunlight, laughter, meditation, prayers and sleep are medicine. Breaking bread with loved ones is

medicine. Friends and enriching relationships are medicine. Being fearless and possessing a positive attitude is medicine. Accepting and staying in the present moment is medicine. Good health comes from peace of mind and peace of the heart and soul.

- Avoid elevators if you have to go just a few floors.
- Pay attention to your postures. Keep your back straight and your head held high. A poor posture harms you physically and mentally. From a physical perspective, slouching puts undue pressure on your lower back and affects circulation and breathing. From a mental perspective, poor posture makes you feel more tired and less enthusiastic. Walk tall. Walk with purposeful steps in a smooth, strong cadence, duly swinging arms. How you sit, stand, walk and act affects how you feel. Don't walk like an aged person. If you act old, you will become old. The essence of youthful living is to prevent an older person from entering your body by thinking and living young.
- A ten-minute strategically allocated break can refresh your mind, relax the body, and lessen the pressure. Take a break when you are tired or feeling exhausted. A tired person is apt to be superficial and may make wrong decisions. During this break, wash your face, take a short walk, do some exercise, run an errand, or meet a friend for tea.
- Get into the habit of taking mental vacations throughout the day. Visit Bermuda for five minutes in the morning. Visualise a swim in the Mediterranean Sea in the afternoon. When you head home after a busy day, imagine skiing down the slopes of the Alps.
- Use a brief power nap as a fresh starter on a busy day.
- Have preventive health check-ups done every year, especially after the age of forty.
- Don't harbour grudges. Don't bottle up your feelings. Let your heart be filled with love and be fully occupied, radiating love that you don't have the space to hold grudges.
- Associate yourself with fitness-minded people. Avoid the company of those who are not health conscious.

- Combining exercise, yoga, breathing practices, relaxation, a balanced nutritional, naturopathic diet, and positive thinking can elevate your condition to one of real excellence where the mind and body unite for lasting good health.
- Learn and be determined to bounce back. The art of bouncing back is simply the physical ability and mental determination to recover swiftly after facing illness, injury or any condition that knocks you down.

6 WISE USE OF TECHNOLOGY

- Realise that wise use of technology can save time and bring a quantum jump into your productivity. Don't be hidebound. Keep abreast and adapt yourself to changing conditions.
- Get the best computer system with ample productivity-boosting and time-saving tools. Buy a high-speed, lightweight laptop. Keep two chargers to avoid carrying chargers back and forth from office to home.
- Buy software with an online tutor. Attend training classes of the software company.
- Don't hesitate to ask your junior for help in technology usage.
- Structure your data storage systematically as a tree. Give self-explanatory folder or file names with dates. For example, 'Time Management PPT 20 March 2018'.
- Keep a set of 'boilerplate' files, i.e. text, graphics, and drawings which are created for one job but universally useable.
- Keep deleting unwanted data.
- Take back-ups every day.
- Automate and digitalise all routine tasks.
- Be aware of the limitations of computers. Computers can't think, weigh alternatives, or make intuitive judgments like humans.
- Be selective in sharing your email address. Use a maximum of two email IDs - one for office emails and the other for personal emails.
- Stop spam and unsolicited emails. Unsubscribe to unwanted emails without procrastination.
- Read the subject header of emails first. Avoid reading irrelevant emails.

- Be selective in response. Every email need not be replied to.
- Take emails just as seriously as other forms of communication. Realise that the contents of the email can constitute grounds for legal action.
- Refrain from recklessly forwarding emails or messages to others. Use the 'Forward All' command with extreme caution. You may make three or four sub-groups and forward emails or messages to the relevant sub-group rather than forwarding them to all.
- Use the best mobile phone with a longer battery life. Use two SIM cards rather than carrying two mobile phones.
- Be conscious of the time spent on the internet, gaming, etc.
- Install a portable printer-cum-scanner-cum-photocopier at home.

7 BREAKING PROCRASTINATION

- Each time you put off doing something, taking up the same again becomes less and less appealing to you. Hence, don't procrastinate. Attack the problem head-on right away.
- Get rid of the fear of failure if that is making you procrastinate. Work out a worst-case scenario or share your feelings with colleagues or the boss rather than carrying the burden of unfounded feelings.
- Never let procrastination root itself. It is the greatest time robber.
- Consider giving up extravagant luxuries of sloth, inertia, laziness, etc. A strong desire and conviction to radically change your routine can help you eliminate procrastinating habits.
- Analyse why you are putting off certain tasks and if you see no good or valid reason, brace yourself and take up the task right away. However, don't confuse reasons with excuses.
- Analyse why you dislike a particular job and work on converting such dislikes into likes.
- Alternate tough and easy jobs.
- Divide and conquer. If you procrastinate because the task is too large, divide it into smaller units and add milestones for tracking progress. Identify and take the first

step right away and mark a file or folder that should become part of your open project files. Spend one hour daily, preferably during the quiet hour, until you complete this task.
- Consider delegating or outsourcing dull, boring, or distasteful tasks to gain precious hours for vital tasks. Delegate data collection.
- If you have been procrastinating on some task for a long time, assign the task to your assistant and plant seeds now.
- Give in to procrastination by doing nothing for fifteen minutes, then clear everything off your desk and get on to work on hand for an hour with ultra-concentration. Go ahead with what you have without waiting for the last piece of information.
- Make a deadline commitment to yourself.
- Strengthen your resolve and publicly broadcast it.
- Imagine how great you will feel when the task you have been procrastinating for months or years gets completed. Paint a positive picture of the outcome in your mind.
- Reward yourself handsomely upon accomplishments.
- Allow no exceptions to your new habits.
- Set up barriers to procrastination.
- Make it a habit to be cut-throat in tearing down all time-wasting habits. Reduce at least one time-wasting habit every week and replace it with a new time-saving habit. Keeping track of accomplishments will boost your confidence.
- Reserve a small amount of time for prospective procrastination items.

8 CLEARING AWAY THE DESK CLUTTER

- Learn and practice the art of good deskman-ship. If your desk is cluttered, you spend much time looking for buried documents. While a cluttered desk sends a negative message, a tidy desk sets an example of a model desk and makes you proud.

- Go for a spacious, functional office rather than a status symbol office. Create the right ambience. Pay attention to physical comfort, aesthetics and lighting. Provide Bluetooth speakers, listen to your favourite soothing piped music and get into the groove. Music can have a powerful effect on your emotions. You'll get a real feel-good vibe.
- Have a location for each task. Handle mail from the desk, make calls from your side chair or dictate sitting by the window. This way, your mind gets conditioned for that particular task and will not get distracted.
- Set aside a definite block of time to tackle the problem of the cluttered desk head-on.
- Slice the cleaning operation into small pieces.
- When too many loose papers are piled up on your desk, especially when you return after a tour, gather them into a single pile or a box and then categorise them suitably for action.
- Eliminate those items that are dispensable. Discard as much as you can.
- Worship your waste paper bin with as many sacrificial offerings as you can.
- If you are unsure about certain items, move them into an inactive storage area and discard them if not used for a year. However, keep documents like bank statements and income-tax returns till their statutory retention periods.
- Don't treat the desk as a storage place. Use it only for work in progress. Clear the desk of everything except one item on hand.
- Avoid sorting papers by piling them on the desk. This may clutter the desk again. Similarly, have papers filed daily instead of allowing them to pile up.
- Place priority materials on top the night before.
- Place most frequently used items easily accessible.
- Deal with each piece of paper as soon as it arrives and handle it only once. Never allow it to taste your desk and settle down there.
- TRAF your papers immediately. (Throw them away. Refer to someone else. Act on them. File them.)

- Use time-saving pre-punched stationery.
- Don't keep files horizontally. Keep files in a hanging file folder in a file cabinet.
- Once you clear existing clutter, have your preventive maintenance programme to avoid cluttering the desk again.

9 HANDLING PAPERWORK

- Go for a paperless or less-paper office.
- Think of the cost of your and others' time before you create a paper.
- As a thumb rule, if you can handle an item in twenty people - minutes or less, do it in person or on the phone.
- Eliminate unnecessary paperwork like covering letters.
- Encourage employees to take risks. Let them learn by doing rather than dilly-dallying or remaining indecisive and hiding behind papers.
- Avoid self-protector or self-congratulating memos and motivate others to avoid the same. Give incentives for cutting down the paperwork.
- Avoid the temptation to look for good news. Be brave to handle unpleasant news.
- Trust people to report exceptions.
- Get reports on audio or videotape.
- Control access to the photocopier, which will help to reduce paper explosion.
- Clear at least one terminally troublesome piece of paperwork a day.
- Establish a 'Ritual' whereby you have a Blitz day every month. Get large sacks or boxes and fill them with accumulated junk.
- Think green. Tie up with a local paper recycler to come every week. This will help you and others ruthlessly throw away unimportant papers.
- Don't recycle confidential papers; shred them in a shredding machine yourself.
- Conduct zero-based paperwork planning every quarter.

10 HANDLING CORRESPONDENCE

- Have a secretary open and sort posts by major groups.
- Pull out papers that require action on top priority.
- Decide which item is to be dealt with first in the context of your priorities and not those of senders. Don't go by the urgent label put by the sender, the mode of communication used, or reminders sent by them. Respect the sentiments of senders of the communication, especially if they are your customers, but not at the cost of delaying your top priority task.
- Be selective in replying to correspondence.
- You can answer 80% of posts when first read. This will avoid re-reading.
- A quick handwritten note on the original letter can save time. Keep the original and send back the photocopy. Never return the original to the sender.
- Circulate one copy to three or four concerned people or put it on the bulletin board. Request people to check the bulletin board periodically.
- If lengthy and time-consuming calculations are required, separate the same from the body of the letter and go ahead with the letter.
- Be brief. Avoid big sentences.
- Use bulleted points rather than long sentences.
- Make your writing reader oriented.
- Prepare the draft in double space.
- Attach the letter under reply and accompanying papers with the draft.
- Train the secretary to notice the slightest reference to related materials you might need and bring the same along so that the final version is through faster.
- Correct minor misspellings in pen and avoid reprinting.
- If a car is coming to receive you at the airport, ask your secretary to send urgent correspondence through the driver.

11 DICTATION

- Realise that dictation is a valuable time-saving skill. Whereas you can write at the most thirty words per minute, the dictation output is over 150 words per minute. Hence, master the art of dictation and get rid of your phobia about dictation.
- Start dictation practice with brief letters involving a few sentences. This will give you the confidence to dictate long letters.
- Use a portable Dictaphone freely.
- Listen to your tape-recorded voice and objectively study your speech style for improvements.
- Consolidate your dictation.
- Decide objectives, collect thoughts and write on a piece of paper before you dictate.
- Have the references ready before you dictate. Don't procrastinate dictation just because some data or information is not available. Proceed with dictating the first draft, leaving blanks for unavailable information your secretary can collect.
- Spell unusual words for the benefit of your secretary. If you get stuck on some word or idea, say 'something, something' and continue with the dictation and fix it when the draft comes.
- Practice until your dictation skill is sharpened to the stage where the first draft becomes final.

12 WRITING

- Before writing, ask yourself whether it is absolutely necessary to put it in writing or if a phone call will suffice.
- Instead of writing everything yourself, delegate your writing to your secretary (who can write routine letters), to your assistant (who can write articles or prepare PowerPoint presentations) or to your spouse (who can write social correspondence).
- Standardise routine letters. For forwarding a document, use standard postcards with fillable

blanks. While conducting a survey, provide check-off boxes which others can tick off.
- Make a checklist for letters you write often.
- Instead of writing the entire letter from scratch, borrow paragraphs or sentences from your best letters retained topic-wise in a folder. However, guard against a tendency to copy and paste blindly.
- Write the subject of the letter boldly.
- Structure your letters properly.
- Make your letters appealing by making them short and snappy, with lots of spaces, bold types, italics, short paragraphs, short sentences, bulleted points, titles in colours, etc.
- Cover only one topic per memo.
- Don't cover too many demands or requests in a single letter. The reader is more likely to grant only a few (which are least harmful to him) and conveniently ignore others.
- Support your contention with the strongest argument first. Also, don't give too many points to support your contention, thinking it will strengthen it. If you give too many points, a few points are likely to be relatively weak. The reader is likely to pick up the weakest point and reject your contention based on the weakest point, conveniently ignoring other strong points.
- Make your writing brief, crisp and to the point and reader-oriented.
- Believe that many letters need not be longer than a few sentences or, at the most, one paragraph.
- Consider using cryptic telegraphic language. Since telegrams are charged based on the number of words used, people use words sparingly. Use each word with the cost-consciousness of telegrams.
- Ensure neat penmanship. Write clearly to save minutes down the line.
- Regularly send handwritten notes to your customers to strengthen the bond.
- Fold your letters properly so they do not need turning around for reading upon unfolding.
- Use window envelopes to avoid typing the addresses on envelopes.
- Avoid multiple staples or excessive cello tape on envelopes.
- Make letterhead complete with the full address (not only Post Box No.), pin code, phone, fax,

website, email address and location guidance.
- Don't use paper to discuss or argue.
- Clearly state the required action and mark it directly to the person concerned.
- Develop a habit of documenting your success stories or failures or lessons learned for the benefit of others and publish the same suitably.

13 HANDLING ASSIGNMENTS

- Learn to eliminate undue performance pressure. Do your best to meet the requirements of your boss or customer without spending unduly extra time making it unique or better than others.
- Don't overenthusiastically start working on the project yet to be fructified or yet to be assigned to you.
- Insist on clear and unambiguous assignments. Ask questions and clarify doubts.
- Read every word if the assignment is written.
- Don't start full-scale report preparation unless the recipient approves a one-page outline.
- Keep dated notes.
- Execute your assignment plan flexibly.
- Structure the report properly. Use charts or graphs freely in the reports.
- Give your recommendations and conclusions in the report. In case of a lengthy report, prepare a one-page Executive Summary.

14 DEADLY PRESSURE OF DEADLINES

- Every task deserves a deadline (even if the same is weeks or months away), either imposed externally or decided internally. Tasks having deadlines are less likely to be put off. Set deadlines and race against time.
- Set deadlines that are neither impossible to achieve nor easy

to meet. The idea is to build a challenge, not to cause frustration. As a thumb rule, allow 85% to 90% of the time they would ordinarily require.

- Don't fix or accept arbitrary deadlines.
- Don't fly blind. Don't hurriedly accept any deadline, especially from the customers, without estimating time or checking your calendar/organiser. Buy time to think. You can always say, "I will check my calendar and revert." Then, revert promptly.
- Avoid the 'Yes-man' syndrome. Learn to say 'No'.
- Be brave enough to say that the assignment has to wait its turn if it lands in your lap at short notice unless it affects customer satisfaction.
- If the assignment requires an input of data from others, seek the same in advance, specify the date when you need the same, and dovetail it to your deadline.
- Let others know what your deadlines are. This public awareness will put extra pressure when the going gets tough and prevent you from missing the deadline.

- Begin well before the deadline. Don't wait until the last moment.
- Don't be a perfectionist at the cost of missing the deadline. Don't make the perfect the enemy of the good. Decide input of efforts and an accuracy level commensurate with its end-use. Go for a sensible approximation that is good enough for all practical purposes. Don't allow unimportant details to drag you down. Don't agonize over your work beyond the point where the extra effort no longer produces a proportionately worthwhile improvement in your final product.
- Maintain a good track record of meeting deadlines. Be a confident professional who keeps up his commitments. This will inspire others.
- Reward yourself handsomely upon meeting the deadline.
- Anticipate in advance if you are likely to miss the deadline. Be candid with the person waiting for work and request him to extend the deadline. Alternatively, ask for help from colleagues and share part of the work.
- Evaluate the risk of missing the deadline. If the risk is low, you may

miss the deadline, but sincerely apologise to the person waiting for your work. If you miss customers' deadlines, offer discounts or concessions to maintain goodwill.

- If you continuously miss the deadline, analyse the reasons and conduct honest introspection. The reasons may include:
  - Unclear or ambiguous scope or unclear or ambiguous spelling out of the assignment.
  - Underestimation of time required for the assignment or arbitrary deadlines or the tendency to accept even non-workable deadlines due to lack of courage to say 'no'.
  - Accepting deadlines without checking the calendar/organiser.
  - The tendency to procrastinate.
  - Absence of external pressure or follow-up.
  - Non-availability of data, information, or inputs.
  - Non-dovetailing of the deadlines with deadlines of other departments or non-cooperation by other departments.
  - The tendency towards perfectionism.
  - Midcourse changes in assignment scope.
- Evaluate how your staff are performing in meeting the deadlines. Share the track record with them and give them objective feedback. Praise them in public if they consistently meet the deadlines. Reprimand them privately if they frequently miss deadlines. Identify whether they thrive in a pressurised situation or buckle at the first sign of pressure.

15 CUSTOMER: THE KING

- Treat the customer like a king. Adopt the customer-first philosophy because the customer is the very reason for the existence and survival of your organisation. If your customer goes to your competitor, your organisation's very existence will be endangered.
- Understand and respect the customer. Understand his feelings and emotions. He has unlimited needs, desires, wants

and aspirations, but pretends to have limited resources. He looks for value for each dollar he spends. Hence, the organisation that provides value to the customer is likely to win the customer's heart sustainably.

- Satisfy the present and future needs of the customer and continually enhance his satisfaction. Delight him.
- Sell certain satisfaction. Don't sell a product.
- Don't contradict the customer on facts. Don't defend something for the sake of defending. Acknowledge and accept the customer's statement, then give convincing logic to justify your stand. If you admit some of the shortcomings that the customer is pointing out, you establish credibility. This will give you a platform to bounce back aggressively when you have the upper hand.
- Besides expecting the best product quality, customers also look for the best service. The concept of quality is not limited only to the quality of the product or service but is quite comprehensive and starts with how your telephone operator answers the customer's call. Other things being equal, customers will go where they will get better service. Hence, provide the best service to your customers.
- Drive your organisation into customer-centric mode rather than internally oriented. Rise above inter-departmental issues and pay attention to customer requirements.
- Develop personal rapport with your customers. Apart from official communication, open up channels of personal/ informal communication. Open an emotional account with them. Talk to them frequently. Meet them on social occasions. Meet them even if there are no issues to be discussed or there is no formal agenda. Don't selfishly limit your relationship only to a particular transaction. Develop a transformational relationship rather than a transactional relationship. Each meeting with the customer should take your relationship to the next level. Enquire how your organisation is performing in meeting their expectations and what more needs to be done to enhance satisfaction.

- Repeat orders from your customers are one of the most appropriate measures of organisational excellence.

16 BUILDING WINNING TEAMS

- Have near and dear ones on your team. Don't get this wrong. The message is not advocating nepotism. It stresses the need to treat your team members as if they are your near and dear ones. Undoubtedly, you must constitute your team objectively, selecting the best members suited for that particular task based on merit, but after forming such a team, treat them as your near and dear ones to bring the best out of them.
- Ensure your team is homogeneous. A heterogeneous collection of individuals can't make a winning team even if they are star performers in their individual capacities. You may have the greatest bunch of individual stars in the world, but the club will not be worth a dime if they don't play together. A successful team has many heads but one mind.
- Inspire people to great heights by promoting harmony, teamwork, and trust. Create a conducive work environment through love and professional respect. Breed creativity. Commend their contributions. Guide them. Groom them. Share your wisdom. Create abundance by encouragement. Act as a catalyst and help them unleash their peak performances. Raise the level of the game of all your team players. Get the best out of everyone by awakening what lies half asleep in them. Travel that extra mile and draw extraordinary performances from even ordinary people.
- Uplift the morale of your team. Morale is a state of mind. It is that intangible force that will move the entire team to give their last ounce to achieve something without counting the cost to themselves. High morale makes them feel they are part of something greater than themselves. Endurance is the essence of morality; for this, it must have spiritual, intellectual and material foundations. Spiritual first

because only it can stand real strain. Here, the word spiritual conveys a strong belief in the cause, not its strictly religious meaning. Next is intellectual because reasons and feelings sway men. Materials last because the highest morale can be met even when material conditions are lowest. There must be a great and noble objective about which each team member is convinced. They should own it and strongly believe in its attainability. Each team member should feel that what he does matters directly towards attaining this noble objective. The method of achievement must be active and aggressive.

- Adopt a goal-based approach rather than a strategy-based approach. Once goals are mutually agreed upon, allow the team to decide the suitable course of action. Let them execute their plans flexibly so long as they operate within the general framework of the organisation's rules.
- Catch people doing things right. Encourage the use of their talent for the common good.
- Take your team into confidence and keep them informed about what is happening. Keep a very little secret. Secrets always breed distrust and they have a funny habit of leaking out and that too at the most inappropriate time and in a garbled and distorted manner. When something has been decided, announce it at the earliest before the grapevine can bear it at you.
- Develop a habit of acquainting yourself with the thoughts and ideas of your team.
- Create a giving and sharing environment among the team. Give your time, energy and knowledge generously.
- Build your staff into a competent management team - a high-performing, winning team, always ready to face challenges and strive to increase productivity. To excel is human nature. Often, this latent greatness needs to be merely sparked into life by leaders.
- Be aware of group dynamics. Introverted people tend to go by the group's thoughts, keeping aside their individual opinions. Provide an encouraging ambience so that even introverted people are inspired to give their opinions. Specifically, invite or provoke them to give their

opinions. Let a few extroverted people not bulldoze the rest of the team members by forcing their decisions.

17 THE ART OF SERVANT LEADERSHIP

- Leadership is the art of inspiring others to give their best and the courage to use this art.
- Leadership exists at team, operational, strategic, national and global levels. Develop necessary attributes depending on the level of leadership.
- Your success as a manager depends on your technical knowledge and competence, but leadership demands many more attributes, like the ability to inspire people and commercial savviness. Leaders inspire the entire team. For this, they must self-inspire themselves. Be an inspirational leader, not a manager. Also, be a can leader.
- The leader must be confident, resourceful, active, careful, hardy and quick-witted. He must possess unwavering courage, definitiveness of decisions, self-control, a keen sense of justice, sympathy, empathy and understanding. He must be both gentle and brutal, at once straightforward and designing, capable of both caution and surprise, lavish and rapacious. He should be generous and mean, skilful in defence and attack and there are many other qualifications - some natural, some acquired that are necessary to be a successful leader.
- Be a charismatic leader, though it is not the essence of leadership. Charisma is a kind of personal aura. It is visible in arresting eyes and audible in a compelling voice. Charisma is personal magic or charm which arouses unusual devotion from others. They attract a special kind of personal loyalty and enthusiasm.
- An office order or a circular may appoint you as a leader, but you are not a leader until your appointment is ratified in the hearts and minds of those who work for you. All leaderships are in the gift of followers.

- Adopt the philosophy of servant leadership, the essence of which lies in prioritising growth and well-being of others rather than self-interest. It hinges on generating a positive influence on employees rather than authoritatively controlling them by toxic leadership tactics. Create not followers but partners in the common enterprise.
- The leader must deserve and earn the confidence of the team members. Team members should feel they will get a fair deal from their leader with the required resources and good working conditions.
- Keep lines of communication open at all levels – both formal and informal. Ideas and disagreements should flow freely in all directions- upward, downward and sideways.
- Lead by example - often sharing the difficult conditions, hardships and physical toils of team members.
- Leaders jointly develop and paint the picture of the future with their followers, making them visualise the bright future. They consciously aid their individual development. They do so as much by their example as by words. Their leadership are evidence-based.
- A leader should be able to put himself on an equal footing with the others involved, relying on the authority of knowledge and personality to gain respect. Such a stance requires considerable inner confidence. Your followers can notice its existence and even lack of it.
- Be consistent and predictive. Consistency pays. Consistency means you act the same way or in a similar way time after time when situations are identical. It means the absence of double standards. Your consistency makes it easier for others to follow your leadership.
- Leadership potential can be developed. Learning to lead and learning to swim are analogous. Most people can be taught to swim, but a few will reach Olympic standards.
- Leadership is at a premium because so many people are reluctant to make irrevocable decisions, are tepid in their enthusiasm, timid in their self-belief and many others are afraid of the burden of responsibility and undecided about their direction. Leadership means

- taking tough calls on things that once were non-negotiable.
- Avoid interfering with others' work. A department head who has the itch or craving to run every other department in preference to his own is unlikely to succeed sustainably.
- Each employee should have only one boss. He can take advice from many, but only one person should have the power to discipline him, tell him off, or reward him.
- Engage specialists or staff officers but keep them under the administrative control of line managers. Specialists may have a narrow vision and are so obsessed with their expertise that it is difficult to expect a customer-driven approach.
- Introduce a personal touch to your working style. An organisation is not a legal entity. It is a living entity with a spirit and soul of its own.
- Dismantle the fence between workers and the top management. Be on the same side of the fence. A wise leader discards his ego. His interactions with juniors are free of positional entitlements.
- For dos and don'ts of leadership in general and servant leadership in paricular, refer to Appendix III.

18 THE ART OF DELEGATION

- Get rid of 'Do-it-myself' or 'I-can-do-it-better-myself' syndrome. If you insist on doing everything yourself, human limitations will govern your growth. Your career and life will be restricted by the limited quantum of work you can do yourself.
- Realise that you cannot add the 25th hour into your day, nor can you add a third hand to your body, but you can add hundreds of hours to your day or hundreds of persons to assist you by delegating or outsourcing.
- Get rid of the fear of insecurity that those who work for you will compete with you or may topple you.
- Recognise and overcome delegator's barriers like indispensability, insecurity, and lack of confidence in staff. Analyse your predicament

in delegating and work to eliminate the theme.

- Realise that delegation is an art and you can perfect the same by practice once you overcome initial resistance. Until you put this into practice, you will find it easier to work yourself and continue to do so.
- When a new task comes up, ask yourself questions like:
  - Should this be done at all?
  - How can this be simplified?
  - Should I do this myself?
  - Who else can do this?
  - What is a better alternative use of my time?
- Strive to delegate everything someone else can do, keeping yourself free for high-level creative and strategic thinking.
- Delegate routine tasks even if you could do them quickly yourself.
- Don't delegate assignments that your boss wants you to keep confidential.
- Delegate a wide range of assignments. However, avoid piecemeal mundane handouts that may bore the delegatee. Make delegation interesting for the delegatee by delegating the challenging task or building on challenges. Allow him to use his brain.
- Don't look at delegatee merely as a resource to offload your work. Create powerful synergy through a shared vision.
- Find persons with unused or underutilised abilities.
- Find the not-so-obviously qualified.
- While allocating the assignments, keep in mind an individual's strength, aptitude and abilities.
- Delegate even to an individual with a weakness. Work on his weaknesses and convert them into strengths by providing support or guidance. Impart training if the job is novel.
- Interview your staff to shortlist potential candidates when you want to delegate a major job. Be objective in choosing someone whose talent matches the job requirements.
- Distribute assignments objectively on a fair and equitable basis with no bias. Give considered and careful thought before allocation and avoid the embarrassment associated with withdrawal of the assignment. Ensure everyone has a fair workload at all times and equal

opportunity for advancement in their career.
- Consider the workgroup effect while delegating.
- Time the delegation appropriately. Instead of delegating work on Friday afternoon, delegate on Monday morning.
- Don't delegate at the 11th hour, but give the delegatee adequate time.
- Don't delegate by shooting out a memo. Show courtesy and discuss before you delegate. Even if you feel issuing a memo is necessary, do so only after pre-speaking personally. There is no substitute for a one-to-one candid personal talk in the delegation process.
- Praise before you delegate. But ensure the praise is sincere. Try phrases like "I know how good you are at organising systems; I would like to use your expertise in helping to…" or "You have been doing so well that I want you to take up the task of."
- Cover the following in your opening brief to delegatee when you delegate:
  - Explain what exactly you want him to do.
  - Explain what you think is important to know for him as background information.
  - Sources from where he can get the relevant data.
  - Outline the larger perspective explaining the bigger picture for the organisation or the department and delegatee's career growth and how this task fits into the same.
  - Explain what needs to be done to accomplish the task.
  - Explain both the scope and the limits of the responsibility as to how far the delegatee can go in the corporate structure.
  - Explain the coverage and limits of the authority so that the delegatee neither feels too timid nor steps on toes.
  - The frequency at which you would follow up.
- Use delegation as a means of showing trust.
- Involve delegatee in planning and decision-making.
- Let the delegatee tell you how to do the job rather than you telling him. Never thrust your ideas on him. At the most, you may suggest two or three possible courses of action

or options and allow him to think through all the pros and cons. Then, let him choose one he thinks is the best. This will avoid passing blame to you in case of failure. Of course, your skill as a leader lies in indirectly influencing him in such a way that he selects the option of your choice but feels that he has chosen the option.

- Put down ideas or thought-stimulators for delegatee rather than merely delegating or directly giving solutions. However, frame the ideas or thought stimulators intelligently so that it leads him to find the final solution that is in your mind or which you think he should adopt.

- Use phrases like "What, according to you, is the solution?" or "If I were you…" rather than you giving solutions. If the delegatee excessively depends upon you for a solution, the most effective what-if phrase is 'If I were dead, what would you do?' However, use this sparingly.

- Demand solutions, not problems. Don't solve the delegatee's problems; make him solve them and find answers.

- Be open and receptive to new ideas. Don't pre-programme or close your mind, which creates prejudices and prevents an unbiased perspective. Don't shoot down a suggestion before you have heard it in full. Instead, encourage new ideas through incentives, awards, public recognition, etc.

- Share your ability. Invest time in teaching a task. Mentor and coach the delegatee.

- Start with short-run delegation.

- Delegate only the first step if the task is novel or complex. However, outline the entire project to the delegatee for a complete understanding. Evaluate the results of the first step and proceed with the next step.

- Test delegatee's readiness. The best time to test his readiness is while you are away.

- Tailor delegations carefully to minimise unpleasant consequences and mistakes.

- Give the delegatee a chance.

- Be prepared for errors. Don't mind if the delegatee fails once in a while. The best way for the delegatee to learn and grow is through real-life

experiences, which means taking chances and making errors.
- Develop closeness with delegatee, which breeds team spirit.
- Improve the overall work environment. Listen to their grievances about the work environment with empathy but without bias or pre-judgment.
- Provide resources. Appreciate that the delegatee is very sensitive about the non-availability of resources like a desktop printer, especially if his peers have it.
- Give confidence to delegatee that you want them to succeed and grow rather than merely getting work completed by any means.
- Make sure others recognise the delegatee as your deputy. If required, intervene so that the delegatee does not get the frustrating feeling that he has a responsibility but no authority.
- Follow up intermittently and ensure the delegatee is on the right track to deliver on time. Delegation doesn't mean you completely isolate yourself until the deadline. Different categories of delegation require different degrees and levels of involvement from the delegator. However, don't over-manage or interfere.
- Be available when the delegatee wants you. Give appointments to him on priority. Provide timely guidance, comments, suggestions and approvals to enable him to complete the task on time.
- Inform the delegatee in advance if you are going on a long tour so that he can grab the time window by hastening.
- Depute delegatee to some of the internal and external meetings instead of you attending all the meetings. Ask the delegatee to submit a concise report of the meeting to you. This will save you valuable time and give good exposure to the delegatee.
- Evaluate the results of delegated tasks objectively.
- Don't accept the reverse delegation. Delegatees may use various techniques to throwback work in your lap, which include:
  - "We've got a problem", and he asks you to solve the problem for him. Insist, he solves the problem himself. Don't fall into a trap by saying, "Let me think about it." He would love this

and leave your room whistling with joy.

- "I want to discuss this at your convenience." Realise that he wants to gain extra time. Make him think again and ask him to come back only if he cannot solve it. Remind him that the ability to solve problems has a major weightage in the performance appraisal scoring system of the organisation.
- "I leave this file with you for your approval whenever you are free." He is smartly nurturing your ego to get additional time. Don't touch this hot potato. Either discuss immediately (even if this amounts to admitting you are not busy) or ask him to come with the file at another pre-fixed time.
- "You only can handle this, or you do this much better than I do." Don't fall into this ego-nurturing trap. Use his technique back at him by saying, "You are quite intelligent. You are capable of doing better than me." This way, he will not come back to you, as he would not like to admit that he is incapable.

- Avoid withdrawal of assignments as far as possible. If unavoidable, handle it tactfully and gracefully, maintaining the self-respect of the delegatee. Guard against even the slightest damage to his self-respect that could happen unintentionally. Don't take withdrawal action in isolation, but wait till an opportune time and combine the withdrawal with the allocation of a new assignment to minimise the negative effect of withdrawal on his morale.
- Rotate delegation among your staff. Also, re-delegate to develop teams.
- Use a bit of productive and healthy rivalry among the competing staff so that one can outshine the other, but step back if a hostile or killer attitude develops. Healthy competition is fine, but aggressive competition may lead to grudges, which can be destructive.
- Sponsor delegatee for relevant seminars and conferences.

19 OUTSOURCING

- Realise that well-structured outsourcing is a great time saver.
- Consider and evaluate the option of outsourcing before delegating.
- Spend more quality time on direct, revenue-generating and billable work, which has scope for higher profits. Outsource most of the ancillary, non-billable, or low-billing work.
- Use vendors, contractors, consultants, freelancers, for outsourcing.
- Take 'Make or buy' and 'Do or outsource' decisions after considered thought. Consider buying as many things as possible from others and restrict your self-production to only those where your expertise adds quality or value. Similarly, do only those activities that are your core competence and consider outsourcing the rest.
- Pay adequate attention to purchases and subcontracting. Whereas a dollar increase in topline contributes only a small fraction to the bottom line, a dollar saved on purchases or subcontracting straightaway adds like amount to the bottom line.
- Apart from saving time, outsourcing offers many other advantages, which include:
  - Low costs as outsourced workers charge lower salaries and wages.
  - They don't use your office space and equipment.
  - You are not required to invest your scarce capital.
  - No long-term commitment.
  - Less paperwork.
- Start outsourcing with a small task if you hesitate to outsource a major job.
- Select the vendor or subcontractor after considered thought and due diligence duly evaluating all parameters. The cheapest is not necessarily the best.
- Don't make Purchase Orders or Contracts so weak that they make you vulnerable to time-consuming legal battles, nor make them too stringent such that it hampers the performance of the vendors or subcontractors. Of course, you can always relax stringent contract conditions or give some concessions as work progresses. However, take other departments of your organisation into confidence at the contract-forming stage. If this is not

done, they may block your proposal to relax contract conditions or give some concessions.
- Instead of relying on a single vendor or contractor, engage two or three vendors or contractors so that possible blackmailing is avoided.
- Deserve and earn the status of 'preferred customer' from your vendors or contractors. The rating you get from your vendors and contractors primarily depends on how well you treat them as human beings.
- Develop healthy relationships with your vendors and contractors so that you can rely on them to help you in crisis.
- Treat your vendors and contractors as partners in your business in letter and spirit. In their growth lies your growth. While multiplying your business with self-efforts is quite time-consuming, it is relatively easy and much faster through vendors and subcontractors.
- Don't allow your vendors and contractors to fail. Guide, assist and support them. Their failure is your failure as well.
- Don't allow differences or disputes to grow bigger. Resolve them amicably by dialogue in a nascent stage. Differences are never settled while passion rages. They are never permanently settled by conflict. One party may be temporarily subdued by power, but the sense of wrongdoing will remain; the fire of passion may slumber, ready to break out again on the first occasion. Resolving differences or disputes by dialogue will remove all causes of hostility. It will cease conflicts and humanity will go hand in hand to do its work and reap its just reward.
- When there is a dispute, both parties get worked up, shifting their attention from the subject of the dispute (which is the matter in dispute) to the object of the dispute (which is the other party). You start generalising the behaviour of the party and start hating him as a person. You start thinking about what he has done to you and others in the past. Is dispute resolution possible when you are so much worked up against him as a person? A mediator can solve the dispute because he focuses on the subject of the dispute and delinks it from personalities.

- Avail part-time outsourcing help when there is a temporary increase in workload, like annual account closure.
- Consider outsourcing research and development activity. For example, you may outsource the innovative design of the next-generation improved version of a machine component to a vendor supplying this component currently or to a prospective vendor.

20 THE SECRETARY

- Realise that your professional success, among other things, to a large extent depends upon the quality and time efficiency of assistance rendered by your secretary/assistant.
- Treat your secretary and assistant as your greatest allies in improving your time use. Exploit their full potential to revolutionise your time use.
- Hire the best. Expect the best. Pay the best.
- Prefer a female secretary because of their inherent aptitude for orderliness and housekeeping.
- Have a brief daily morning and afternoon conference at a fixed time. Inform her if there is a change in schedule.
- Let your secretary know what you expect.
- Ask her what she can do from what you are doing now. Encourage her to assume more and more jobs utilising her strengths fully.
- Foster responsibility. Give your secretary complete responsibility for many routine jobs together with commensurate authority.
- Let your secretary answer as many of your routine letters as possible. Initially, check these letters before release, but once you are confident, allow her to handle them independently.
- Give her a variety of assignments, including plenty of new challenges and learning experiences. Give credence to her intuition.
- Depend on your secretary's sense of orderliness and housekeeping. Allow her to develop herself in her own way.

Practical Time-Saving Tips

- Don't keep piling assignments upon assignments. Allow your secretary to develop a priority list of her chores.
- Go easy on the buzzer. Consolidate your interruptions and vice versa.
- Don't make your secretary wait for you.
- Encourage your secretary to state her needs.
- Be on the same page with your secretary while using terms like emergency, urgent, etc.
- Keep your secretary informed about your whereabouts during local and outstation travel unless the destination is required to be kept confidential.
- Don't assume that what you have asked to be kept confidential will be kept confidential. Test her abilities to keep business secrets confidential by some harmless secrets before relying on her for high-risk secrets.
- Invest time in training her. Transform her into a professional assistant.
- Give vertical knowledge, covering all aspects of a job from start to finish rather than piecemeal and superficial horizontal knowledge.
- Let your secretary know the internal structure of your organisation. For example, she should know who handles shareholders' grievances so she can direct such mail to the right officer.
- Train your secretary to block interruptions from the phone and internal and external visitors.
- Train your secretary to act as a second pair of eyes for you. However, guard against willful spying.
- Encourage others to deal directly with your secretary.
- Back up your secretary.
- Resist the temptation of cutting down your secretary's speech or bearing down heavily on her.
- Avoid harping on her weaknesses.
- Don't tyrannize your secretary / assistant or vice versa.
- Ensure a cordial working relationship between your secretary and your assistant, emphasising that their work is complementary. Intervene if their relationship is strained. Meet them informally once in a while. Establish common goals so that overlapping or conflicting efforts are eliminated.

- Have built a library for references and other books.
- Investigate new methods, efficient gadgets, etc. and keep them up-to-date.
- Sponsor enrollment of your secretary as a member of a professional association and nominate her to relevant seminars or conventions, individually and in groups, to foster team spirit.
- Avoid promoting incompetence.

21 DEALING WITH YOUR STAFF

- Help your staff to do a better job through proper guidance and motivation. Show interest in them. Appreciate them. Praise them. Work produced by them is the measure of your efficiency and success.
- Don't interfere unnecessarily or arbitrarily with your staff's individual rights and liberties. Resist the impulse to act important. Don't misuse your authority. Don't dominate or over-power your staff.
- Avoid excessive supervision. Too close supervision may help reduce errors but has a morale-diminishing effect and discourages initiatives.
- Decentralise decision-making. A person on the job is best equipped to make appropriate decisions rather than the boss sitting hundreds of kilometers away. According to the principle of an iceberg of ignorance, senior executives see only 4% of problems; the remaining 96% are hidden from them.
- Realise that if a boss is honest and fair, people will be willing to put up with many of his shortcomings.
- Encourage your staff to express their views. If required, pretend ignorance. Encourage even dissenting opinions. Don't surround yourself with a yes-man kind of staff.
- Encourage your staff to take the initiative.
- People work with redoubled energy when entrusted with challenging work.
- Treat all your staff equally. Don't favour a few of them. Preferential treatment upsets morale. Not only should you not favour anyone, but

- you must also appear to be doing so.
- Consult your staff before making a decision. Rely more on opinions and judgment and less on facts or statistics, as statistics could sometimes be presented selectively or out of context to mislead us or to advocate a certain course of action.
- Involve your staff in policy formation. If there is no participation, they may not implement the policy wholeheartedly or may even sabotage it.
- Your staff should be made to feel that their work is important and that they matter. This is job enrichment.
- You don't have to accede to all requests or demands of your staff. Learn to say no but say so tactfully.
- Phone your staff directly rather than through your secretary.
- Ensure that your staff understands what you expect.
- Ask how long the assignment should take and negotiate a deadline with them.
- When your assistant wants to see you, either see him immediately (he probably needs only a minute from you) or give him an appointment, but don't make him hang around. The more valuable you consider your assistant's time, the more valuable they are likely to make it. Answer their communication promptly so they don't interrupt you to get answers.
- Let your staff know the value of your and their time.
- Go to your assistant's desk once in a while. That way, you are in control of discussions and he will always remain alert.
- Give due credit to your staff for their success. Do this in public.
- Remain level-headed when something goes wrong. Hold your fire. Find out why it happened. Go to the root cause. Attack the cause, not the man.
- Cultivate humility. Publically accept the responsibility for the mistakes of your staff as you have selected them.
- Meet your staff on social occasions. Befriend them.
- Allow those behind you to go ahead. Allow your staff to grow in the organisation's hierarchy and become more prominent than you are. If a person trained by

you is growing bigger than you, it enhances your stature.

22 DEALING WITH THE BOSS

- Align with your boss. Co-mission with your boss. Fuse your life's mission with your boss's mission or corporate mission. Let your life's mission marry your boss's mission. Make the boss's priorities your priorities. Dis-alignments between your life's mission and your boss's mission are likely to cause stress, tension and unhappiness.
- Do more than the boss expects.
- Deserve and ask for more work from the boss to exploit your full potential. This will avoid job burnout and also enhance your value in the eyes of peers and your staff.
- Don't embarrass your boss. Don't give unpleasant surprises to him. Avoid doing anything which requires your boss to defend you. This can cause your boss to lose face with his peers and superiors.
- Consult your boss when required. Don't subject yourself to unnecessary strain just to prove that you can handle and cope with any situation on your own. However, do the homework and think thoroughly before you approach him.
- Occasionally, ask questions to your boss. When you ask questions, you are putting others on a high pedestal. This builds good rapport.
- Avoid any direct confrontation or head-on collisions with the boss. Realise that your duty allocation, your salaries and perquisites, your promotion, your career, and your mental peace are all in the hands of your boss.
- Consider a job change if the relationship with the boss is strained beyond a point.
- Educate your boss tactfully. Make occasional tactful suggestions when you see a possibility that your boss might improve his time use and avoid a tendency to infringe on your planned schedules.
- If you get a chance, gift your boss a book on Time Management on his birthday.

- Broadcast your commitment to time management and let him know of your progress in improving concentration span or quite-hour implementation.
- Keep your priority or 'TO DO' list visible.
- Don't feel shy about admitting your limitations if your boss repeatedly expects you to carry out tasks in impossible time frames. Keep a record of the actual time v/s estimate of the boss. If he habitually or intentionally underestimates the time required for the assignment, showing him such data will help.
- If your boss keeps you waiting after calling for a meeting, take some quickie tasks with you or wait a while and ask the boss's secretary to call you back when the meeting is ready to start.

23 DEALING WITH CHRONIC TIME-WASTERS

It is very difficult to control others' behaviour, especially chronic time-wasters or troublemakers. This is outside our Circle of Influence. Having accepted this ground reality, we must find a suitable strategy or manage our behaviour to deal with them. Different categories of chronic time-wasters or troublemakers may require different strategies. (Refer APPENDIX IV)

24 TELEPHONING

- Realise that the telephone could become a great time saver if properly used, but it can also waste much of your time if misused. Don't become a slave to your telephone or a victim of telephone tyranny.
- If you can't meet someone in person, the next best option is to telephone him rather than a memo unless too many points are involved. In such cases, use brief bullet-pointed fax/email rather than long telephone calls.

- Locate the telephone in the home and office at an easily reachable location.
- Update your phone with the latest available time-saving facilities like speed-dialling, call-waiting, call-forwarding, timer, answering machine, conference calling, cordless instrument, speakerphone and voice messaging.
- Use a hands-free speakerphone, operator-type headset, or Bluetooth to facilitate multitasking.
- Avail professional teleconference calling facility with global reach. It is simple to set up and easy to use.
- Maintain only one telephone diary rather than multiple diaries. Write the telephone numbers in pencil.
- Save contacts of your mobile phone.
- Note frequently called persons' available time to avoid 'occupied' or 'out' response.
- Treat callers the way you would treat guests in your home or office. Answer the phone with enthusiasm in your voice and show your appreciation to the caller. Be pleasant while receiving a call - no matter what your mood is. Let your anger, impatience, or boredom not be transmitted through a telephone cable. If you are having a bad time, ask whether you can call him back and propose a specific time.
- Convey authority on the line by standing up. This will further instil confidence in your voice. Never answer or make calls in a sleeping position.
- Answer the calls on the first or second ring.
- Don't leave your phone unattended. Instead, cover yourself by activating the answering machine or call forwarding to the receptionist. Inform her when you are likely to return.
- Don't call someone more than twice continuously. If they don't answer your call, presume they have something important to attend to.
- Identify yourself to the callers and prompt them to identify themselves.
- Avoid offensive screening questions which put the caller in an embarrassing position. Avoid questions like, 'Do I know you?' or 'Will the boss know where you are from?'
- Inform the caller if you are recording the call, transferring the call, or

putting him on speakerphone or on conference with others and also inform who is listening to him.
- Avoid putting the caller on hold as far as possible. If unavoidable, take his permission and ensure the hold time doesn't exceed one minute. If the hold time is likely to be longer than a minute, ask if the caller would prefer that you call him back. Promise to call back at a specified time and do so.
- Have your secretary screen all calls and appropriately redirect them to your staff or other departments. You don't have to answer all the calls yourself.
- Give your secretary three lists of callers who can be connected straight away, to be connected after confirming and to be avoided tactfully. Update these lists periodically.
- As far as possible, don't avoid calls from creditors. Also, take extra care to be courteous and kind to them.
- Block spam calls ruthlessly. Register your mobile number on the national 'Do not call list' by dialling a designated toll-free number.
- Make the best calling time known by printing it on your visiting card.
- Be out of the office rather than at the conference.
- Train your secretary not to say you are not in but when you will be available. She should take a precise message with adequate information for calling back (at a specified time) and expect her to give relevant phone numbers and papers for returning a call. Call back punctually.
- Think before you dial. Don't pick up the phone the moment a thought comes to your mind. Instead, note down the thought and schedule all outgoing calls together.
- Schedule time to call important persons and note them down in your organiser.
- Place action requesting calls in the morning so you get the result by the end of the day.
- Note down points to be talked about before making a call. If items are three or more, announce at the beginning that you have multiple items to be talked about and then take them up one by one and tick off as you get information. Stick to the point. Clock your calls using a stopwatch. Believe that no

call needs to be longer than three minutes.
- Always get the names of persons supplying information and note them down in your organiser. This will help you reach them directly next time and will also develop personal rapport.
- Develop friendly relations with secretaries of frequently called customers. When you visit the customers, meet their secretaries as well. Carry your company memento or some gift for them.
- Leave a precise but brief voice message if the party you are calling is out.
- Learn to say 'No' in a non-offensive manner. It is easier on the phone.
- Refuse to be put on hold. Instead, call back in your phoning period. If reaching someone is difficult, keep some paperwork handy for attending while holding on and in any case, don't hold on indefinitely.
- Don't mix business calls with pleasure.
- Develop non-offensive ways to protect yourself from casual callers. Handle politely but firmly open-ended 'How-is-everything?' type social calls by saying, "Everything is pretty fine but terribly busy. I am just rushing to town to attend a meeting. Thanks for calling." Thus, learn to reduce socialising without becoming antisocial.
- Practice winding up conversations fast by saying, "I know you have lots to do, so I will let you get back to work now, bye." or "It has been great talking with you, bye."
- Practice techniques like setting a time limit or signalling the ending with phrases like "The last point before we hang up …."
- If someone hangs on for half an hour or longer, often using you as a substitute therapist, short cut him by introducing your problems into conversations.
- Don't disconnect the phone and more so, never disconnect when someone is speaking. Instead, if at all you want to disconnect, do so only when you are speaking.
- Don't interrupt someone who is visiting you on a long-standing appointment to entertain a casual caller who just decided to ring you up. Instead, avoid him politely and call him back at an appropriate time.

- Explain to your visitors in advance if you are likely to be interrupted by an important call.

25 FACE-TO-FACE CONVERSATION

- Do it in person when dealing with people. However, avoid excessive drop-in, one-on-one types of meetings.
- Avoid the temptation to talk of pleasantries, non-essential preamble, trivialities, and irrelevant conversations for extended periods.
- Remove and help others in removing fat from the conversation. For example, instead of saying, "I would like to begin by telling you that the assumptions I have made for this report are: say, "The assumptions for this report are:"
- When a speaker gives you extraneous background, politely sidestep by saying, "I know you have put a great deal of hard work into developing this, but can you tell us what are the key benefits of your proposal?" This way, you acknowledge his efforts and while remaining cordial, you get to the business at hand.
- Give full attention to the other person. Guard against time-wasters like taking time for a coffee break before getting down to the business.
- Give and obtain feedback and summarize conversations at small intervals.

26 MEETINGS

- Critically examine the very need for a meeting. Examine the possibility of a teleconference, videoconference, webinar, or circulating business or idea notebook instead of a meeting.
- Apart from the meeting itself, the pre-meeting and post-meeting stages are also important. Make meetings time-efficient and successful by planning and managing all the stages of the meetings.
- Identify the meaningful purpose or theme of the meeting, like solving

a problem or arriving at a decision and categorise it accordingly so that planning and preparations are focused.
- Keep the direct and indirect costs of the meeting in mind all the time.
- Bunch your meetings.
- Cut meetings down to size - reduce the number of meetings you attend.
- Make a selective attendant list who could contribute to the purpose as a resource person, like a technical expert, legal expert, or idea man. Optimise the number of participants. When you receive an invitation to participate in a meeting, ask what contribution is expected from you or ask, 'Can we not discuss this informally over a cup of coffee in your office?'
- Decide in advance when the meeting will start and end and inform participants beforehand.
- Go for breakfast meetings or schedule the meeting before lunchtime or towards the end of the day to prevent it from dragging.
- To facilitate the conduct of the meeting in a time-efficient manner, decide on a suitable venue, seating arrangements, projection screen, etc., beforehand. Have all the gadgets checked before the meeting starts.
- Don't volunteer to hold a meeting in your room. Don't get stuck as the host of the meeting. Try to have it in someone else's room or conference room.
- Consider removing all chairs if really looking to shorten the duration of the meeting.
- Prefer a seating arrangement in the shape of a round table that symbolizes equality and induces team spirit. (During India's long freedom fight, three landmark meetings were organised on round tables and have been popularly described in history as the round table conferences.)
- Issue an agenda beforehand. Involve the participants by inviting comments and suggestions from them. Remind them once again one day before the meeting date. This way, no one will indulge in adding a new point to the agenda during the meeting.
- Consider circulating relevant reading materials, popularly known as Approach Papers, along with the agenda. Invite participants to submit Approach Papers. Insist all

participants read Approach Papers. Well-prepared Approach Papers can bring all the participants on the same page, making it easier to move forward in the desired direction.

- Itemise the issues you want to cover and present them as posers rather than statements. If issues are presented as statements, the participants are likely to harden their stand, thinking that the organiser of the meeting wants to dictate his pre-decided views. However, issues presented as posers, when decided after deliberations, will have a stamp of consensus.
- Sequence the agenda in the proper order of importance and how you would like to cover it. Discuss vital items first. Start meeting on a high note by taking up non-controversial items initially.
- Allocate time for each agenda item based on its importance and inform the participants beforehand. Make someone responsible for each item of the agenda with an accountability mindset.
- Learn what you can about the people who are attending the meeting.
- If required, pre-speak individually and advocate or lobby your views. By pre-speaking, you nurture their egos and avoid possible knee-jerk reactions during the meeting.
- Identify and isolate anyone with conflicting views by either trying to get him on your side beforehand or mustering enough support to counteract such conflicting views.
- Diagnose and treat hidden agendas that influence participants' thinking and may prevent some from contributing.
- Use the meeting as an opportunity to meet and get to know the people you work with, especially if you work on a long-distance basis.
- Have the meeting audio or video recorded. However, the audiotapes need not be transcribed; just preserve them for future reference in case such a need arises.
- Keep required stationery, extra copies of the agenda, and supporting/additional information likely to be needed in the meeting room.
- Prepare well for the meeting and insist that participants come prepared.

- Despite late arrivals, start meeting on time. Avoid meeting tardiness. Minute absenteeism, late arrivals and read when offenders are present. Collect a small sum, say $25, from latecomers and use money so accumulated for a get-together on a weekend.
- Do away with extended, aimless pleasantries.
- Start meeting briskly and make a start impactful.
- Request the operator not to divert calls during the meeting.
- Demand a competent leader who can keep the meeting moving ahead briskly, everyone involved, and decisions being made.
- Avoid digressions yourself and control digressions attempts by others.
- Keep meeting on target by using a board with a poser posted on it.
- Respect the chair. Speak after permission of the chair. Don't interrupt others.
- Keep meetings free from arguments. Avoid debate over who is at fault for a delay or a mistake. Instead, such cat-and-dog fights get down to the business of the meeting.
- If you have to leave early, prepare the Chairman and others for this beforehand. Ask permission to leave when the agenda relevant to you is completed. For this purpose, insist that agenda points relevant to you are bunched up together.
- Hijack the chair and run the meeting yourself if such a need arises.
- Learn and practice the art of good Chairmanship. If you are chairing a meeting:
- Be a clear and rapid thinker, an attentive listener, impartial and impersonal, a referee and a leader, patient, tolerant, kind, friendly but brisk and business-like.
- Establish ground rules for attendance, participation and behaviour.
- A Chairman should not speak much himself. He should just start the show.
- Don't worry if you are not a fluent speaker. What counts is your ability to put a case clearly in the meeting.
- Give positive or negative feedback by expression or movement of the head, body language, etc.
- Recognise and appreciate the contributions of participants.

Practical Time-Saving Tips

- Control over participation by a few ego-driven extrovert participants firmly but gracefully in a non-offensive manner.
- Give less assertive, shy, or introverted people a chance to be heard. Prompt or provoke them to speak.
- Be cruel when some expert is invited to attend the meeting. He may throw his weight around and go on too long. Get an Approach Paper from him in advance. Then say, "Nice approach paper. Does anyone need to add anything?" in a firm tone of voice, obviously expecting a negative answer. If someone tries to object, use phrases like 'Has anybody any objection?' or 'Are you objecting? You are not. Right? Next business…' and the meeting can move on.
- Don't allow meetings to be used for discussing bilateral or personal issues or settling scores.
- Encourage participants to answer after careful thought and discourage the tendency to give off-the-cuff answers to impress others or to score points.
- Tighten focus with specific, pointed questions. Prevent it from becoming a disorganised forum.
- Keep track of time. Keep reminding about leftover time.
- Harness all available skills to arrive at a decision.
- Appoint one knowledgeable person to take minutes. Consider preparing interim speed minutes covering only the decisions, assignments and deadlines. Ensure everyone gets a rough copy of the speed minutes before they leave the meeting.
- Summarize frequently at small intervals.
- Wind up on a positive note. Conclude the meeting with an impactful punch that participants can remember as a takeaway from the meeting.
- If one more meeting is absolutely necessary, schedule the same before winding up when all are present.
- Promptly circulate the final minutes of the meeting, briefly covering proceedings of the meeting and decisions taken and take follow-up action.
- Focus on the human aspects of the meeting to reinforce the team spirit among the participants. Add

richness to business life by having brief social talks before or after the meeting.
- To assess the real importance of a meeting, cancel or skip one or two scheduled meetings. Also, skip unproductive meetings or depute your assistant to attend the meeting.

27 HANDLING OUTSIDE VISITORS

- Fix visitors' time slot, preferably in the evening between 4 to 6 p.m. during the low-efficiency period. Permit visitors only after appointments and that too during the above specified time slot.
- Train your secretary to handle visitors respectfully, like guests in a reputed five-star hotel.
- No visitor-internal or external should directly come to you but come only after screening by your secretary. Train your secretary about who can walk in, who can wait and who can be attended to by others. Do the needful gracefully, as the other person's self-esteem is a prized possession.
- Have your secretary interrupt through the intercom or personally instead of visitors directly interrupting you.
- Find the right person to handle the visitor.
- Don't block visits of aggrieved creditors. This may lead them to doubt your intention regarding the release of payment to them and precipitate matters. Agree to meet them so that they can vent their feelings. Handle them with extra care, courtesy and tactfulness. Discourtesy or unkindness, even if unintended, may add fuel to the fire.
- Greet the visitor by standing up. Stand firm. Believe that if someone comes to your office to see you, that person is honouring you. Give him a hearing no matter what he wants.
- Remove all extra chairs and avoid padded chairs.
- Remove paintings and artworks, which could give visitors topics to start irrelevant non-business conversations. Signs and pictures should relate to your organisation or your personal goals.

- Whenever someone drops, keep a pen or paper in hand as a sign to get back to work soon.
- Cut down visitors' interruption time by three steps. First, as soon as a person arrives, pleasantly ask specific, pointed questions like "Exactly what can I do for you, Sir?" Don't allow time to start on weather, cricket score, or office gossip. Second, direct all your attention to the reason for the interruption. Take action or dictate in the visitor's presence to register his request so that he does not repeat the same. Third, finish up while control is still with you by saying, "I am glad we settled this. Now I can get back to this report". Then, with a smile, start working on the report. Thus, it is not necessary to be rude; just be firm and use smile freely.
- Don't work while the visitors are there.
- Keep a large timepiece that the visitors can see. It should beep every thirty minutes. If required, look at it periodically or set the alarm.
- Serve coffee to important visitors and order (rather request) at the beginning to avoid waiting only for coffee. Serve coffee to unwanted visitors in a waiting lounge rather than in your cabin.
- Maintain a business-like stance. Be quick and alert. Be ruthless with time but gracious with people.
- As far as possible, don't let visitors go empty-handed. Give minor concessions or yield to a few of their low-ranking demands so they can return to their office with some achievement. However, this should not lead them to believe that they need to visit you to get something done.
- Use body language like moving to the edge of your seat, closing your datebook, or shuffling papers.
- Hint closing by statements like "I guess that sums it up" or "I certainly appreciate your dropping in."
- When the moment comes for a visit to end, stand up. When it is your turn to speak, express thanks as you walk towards the visitor. He will also probably be standing then.
- When a visitor overstays, ask your secretary to buzz or say on the phone that you will be through in a minute.
- When your secretary sends a card of a habitual talker, meet him in a

corridor or on your way out of the office.

- For those customers who interrupt frequently, consider scheduling regular weekly or bi-weekly meetings so that issues are consolidated for such scheduled meetings.

28 AVOIDING INTERRUPTIONS

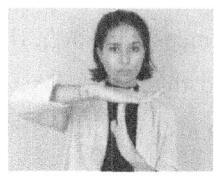

- Encourage a brief written note in preference to personal interruptions.
- Encourage reporting by groups.
- Avoid interruptions by closing your door and disconnecting the phone.
- Draw a line and stick to it, someone taking offence notwithstanding.
- Re-arrange office furniture to avoid eye contact with by-passers. Stop by-passers and buck-passers. Avoid those who are just dropping and sticking their heads off the door. Avoid playing visitors yourself to others.
- Don't let others cut you down to an eight-minute attention span. When interrupted, note down what you were doing. Then, pick up again without delay and from where you left off without repetition.
- Consolidate or accumulate tasks and do them together once instead of several times a day.
- Avoid wasteful or aimless wandering around the office or plant to get the feel of things. Avoid wasteful chatting with employees.
- Avoid or delegate non-vital visits to the branch office, plant, or site.
- If interruptions are getting you down, take a day off, go to some quiet place, work on something big and accomplish it.

29 THE QUIET HOUR

- Reduce the noise level in the office. Target low decibels. Soundproof your room. Avoid cabins having transparent glasses.
- Sell the idea of Quiet Hour to your department, the entire organisation and others.

- Insist your organisation adopts a Quiet Hour Policy. (Those who have tried this report great enthusiasm and a quantum jump in output.)
- Let the entire office have a Quiet Hour together with just one telephone operator fielding calls. Enforce it strictly and make no exceptions.
- Have your own Quiet Hour even if no one else in your organisation cooperates with you by coming to the office an hour earlier.
- Talk to your peers and try to win their support for Quiet Hour. If not, at least seek their help in not disturbing you in your Quiet Hour.
- Post the Quiet Hour sign on your door and remove the same when the time has elapsed.
- Pick up one top priority task during the Quiet Hour and tackle it with a single-mindedness of purpose.
- Communicate about Quiet Hour to customers, vendors and others, but don't let them assume it is your nap time or some other frivolous use of time.
- Educate your staff, fellow workers and outside contacts about Quiet Hour.
- For a real emergency, be available through a secret code.

30 CONCENTRATION SPAN IMPROVEMENT

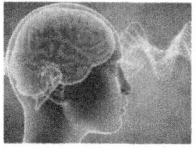

- Assiduously cultivate the art of concentration.
- Improve concentration span by:
  - Quiet surroundings.
  - Clear desk.
  - Putting away the laptop and mobile phone.
  - Setting a timer and working in blocks like 11 a.m. to lunchtime with no interruptions.
  - Writing specific goals for the period of concentrated work.
  - Shutting your eyes. (This will remove many distractions as over 80% of our sensory input comes from our eyes.)
- To enhance your concentration, read a passage in a book you have never explored. Then, try to recite it verbatim for five minutes.
- Stare at the second hand of your wristwatch for 120 seconds. Practice in a row for twenty-one

days and your mind will not waver during the routine.

- Focus on a burning candle to improve your concentration. Find a tranquil spot at a quiet time. Light a big candle, making sure the room is otherwise dark. Look at the candle's flame for as long as you can without blinking. Study the shape of the flame, its colour, its texture, its movements, etc. Don't take your mental focus away from the flame. If it drifts off to something else, gently pull your mind back and concentrate deeply on this beautifully empowering light.

31 READING AND SPEED READING

- Knowledge is power. People who have achieved outstanding success are not necessarily more intelligent or skilful than others. What separates them is their desire and thirst to acquire knowledge through reading.

- Readers are leaders. A few hours of study can give you the benefits of years of experience of the authors. When your knowledge increases, you have a sense of independence and an added source of strength. Reading will give you brilliant ideas about improving every aspect of your life and take your life to new heights.

- Empty your cup. A full cup can't accept anything more. Unwillingness to learn can cause stagnation and can come in the way of promotion in a job or advancement in life.

- Read five or six newspapers a day. Don't read every story. Know what to read, skip and clip out for reading at another time.

- Select the reading materials that give the best return on your time investment. Decide for yourself what you want to read. Don't give this right to the senders of the reading materials. Control the inflow of the reading materials coming to you. Without procrastination, stop and unsubscribe magazines or newsletters you do not read. Similarly, speak to people whose reports are not relevant to you and

Practical Time-Saving Tips

- have your name deleted from their mailing lists.
- Build your personal library at home and in the office. Be generous yet selective in your collection. Consider reading reviews of the book before buying the book. Buy books related to your professional field, General Management and self-help. However, don't do tsundoku. (Tsundoku, a Japanese term, is used to describe the act of buying books but never reading them.)
- Train the librarian to extract a table of contents of magazines and circulate it. Get the relevant magazine and retain a photocopy of the required article, file it topic-wise, and read at an appropriate time when that topic comes up to avoid multiple readings. Return the magazine so that its circulation is not blocked. Check your stack of pending reading materials periodically and get rid of materials that are no longer relevant to you.
- Train your secretary to screen reading materials coming to you.
- Delegate reading to your secretary, assistant, spouse, kid, or even a paid reader.
- Organise cooperative reading with your colleagues and distribute reading among yourselves. Exchange relevant articles of common interest with colleagues, peers, and others. Train your secretary to share such articles with concerned persons.
- Preview reading materials before reading. Read with a specific purpose, not aimlessly.
- Keep good readings handy for reading during local and outstation travel time or while waiting.
- Set aside a specific reading time of at least fifteen minutes each day. Read when freshest. Before you sit down to read, ensure you have a notepad, pen, pencil, eraser, highlighter, etc. Light a candle beside you when reading in the evening. It is most relaxing and creates a wonderfully soothing experience.
- Use a card to focus attention on the reading spot. Improve total eye span. Concentrate on the first sentences. Avoid word-by-word reading. Train your eyes to take whole phrases at a glance and skip unimportant words or ideas–zero in on the juiciest meat. Have the confidence to dismiss the trivial.

- Highlight freely in colour. Respond constantly to your reading by analysing, criticising, admiring, etc. Pause and summarize.
- Force yourself to read faster. Practice speed reading. Take a professional course on speed reading or read a book on this topic.
- Recognise that different reading materials require different levels of attention, concentration and speed. Light readings (like a newspaper) require a speed of 5 to 6 words per second. Average readings (like a routine report) require a speed of 3 to 4 words per second and heavy readings (like a new investment proposal or a research report) require a speed of 2 to 3 words per second.
- Don't move your lips as you read, for it limits reading speed. (Some children and even grown-ups do this!)
- Don't suspend reading if you come across some unfamiliar words. Check such words later. Don't backtrack. Write notes on the margin in pencil where you are stopping for ease in restarting. If a report is long, write notes on the margin. In case you need to reread the report, read these notes.
- Retain information in the subconscious mind through repetitive layered reading.
- Document your Action Plan to implement the learnings of the readings.
- Have eyes checked regularly and change glasses periodically.
- Do write reviews on the books you read. Be generous in appreciation but extremely cautious and unbiased in criticism. Realise that the author has spent countless hours writing a book. Your unthoughtful criticism may harm the author irreparably. On the contrary, genuine appreciation will motivate the author to write more. Reviews will also help other readers to decide about reading the book or skipping its reading, depending on their areas of interest.
- Share the knowledge gained from reading.

32 LOCAL COMMUTING

Practical Time-Saving Tips

- Select the best mode of transport considering time, comfort, and cost in that order of priority.
- Avoid peak rush hours by starting early from home or leaving late from the office.
- Consider pooling the vehicle with office colleagues or neighbours and use this time for business discussions. Two office colleagues staying nearby can pool their cars- one taking out the car on odd dates and the other on even dates.
- Consider using the service of a driver rather than self-driving.
- Maintain your car in up-to-date condition. Keep the emergency kit and refill it periodically.
- Use local time effectively. Turn your car into a university. Keep relevant books, audiotapes, a notepad, a pen, a pencil, a highlighter and a city map in the car. Use morning commuting time for reading and evening commuting time for relaxation or meditation. Read relevant books or listen to motivational audio or videotapes. Be a committed audiotape user. Most self-mastery programmes are now offered in this format.
- If you are continuously on the move, use an office-on-wheel kind of fully equipped van with a built-in desk, sofa, television, VCR, pantry, bathroom, etc.

33 BUSINESS TRAVEL

- Make destination-wise trip files for frequently visited destinations. Weed out trip files periodically to eliminate outdated materials, irrelevant information, destinations no longer of interest, etc.
- Prepare lists of take-along items for an overnight trip, a trip for a few days and a longer stay and have respective travel kits ready to go at all times.
- If you are a frequent traveller, keep one suitcase with clothes and take-along items in the office.
- If you visit a single destination thrice or more in a month, retain luggage there so that you don't have to carry luggage with you every time.

The Twelve Steps To A Life Of Exemplary Excellence

- Seek answers to the following questions before making a trip:
  - Is the trip necessary?
  - Can I do it by post, telephone or video call?
  - Can I get them here instead of me going there?
  - Can someone else make it?
  - Would an associate be able to handle the business?
- Delegate routine travelling to your deputy as also preliminary meeting with a customer. You can then travel only for the final meeting, but to maintain continuity, take him along.
- Don't miss important family celebrations because of travel. Inform your boss in advance when you can't travel, for example, on a child's birthday.
- Examine introducing some extra productive stops without going out of your way. However, don't plan too many things for one trip.
- Write the objectives of the trip and prioritise them.
- Send a business agenda in advance. Do the necessary homework and prepare well for the business meeting.
- Prepare a list of those you are planning to meet with contact details. If you invite them for lunch or dinner, find their favourite restaurant and food choices from some source.
- Arrange the traveller's cheque and foreign exchange beforehand.
- Before taking up an international tour, ensure you have adequate medical insurance.
- Carry a separate folder for each place you have to visit.
- Carry a permanent folder containing company letterheads, your Power of Attorney, etc.
- Carry a small alarm clock, a torch, a map and other relevant information. Identify the work you can do during travel and carry papers accordingly.
- Know where you are going.
- Engage a good travel agent who can find time-efficient and cost-effective travel options. Sometimes, surface travel could be a better option than flying.
- Use the same airline, as far as possible, to get frequent flyer privileges like priority checking.
- Prefer direct non-stop flights and cut down on layovers and plane

Practical Time-Saving Tips

- changes. Also, take connecting flights of the same airlines, keeping enough time between two flights.
- Take flight with a full-course meal so that you do not have to take extra time for a meal.
- Call for reconfirmation of the meeting before travelling.
- Leave an itinerary with your secretary and family.
- Reach the airport well in time. After collecting the boarding pass, spend some time at the bookstore to see the latest and best self-mastery books and tapes.
- Drink water every hour to fight jet lag. Adjust to the local time. If it is lunchtime, eat even if you have just eaten to reduce jet lag.
- Select an important task while airborne. Don't stop working when the plane lands.
- Try for airport meetings wherever possible.
- Try for business lunch meetings wherever possible so that you can acquaint with your associates in a relaxed atmosphere.
- Schedule appointments, keeping the city's geography in view and avoid crossing the town three or four times.
- Set an appointment with a fixed time. Leave enough time between appointments. Don't over-schedule. Don't write the appointment time in your schedule; write when you must leave.
- Ask for an English-speaking driver at the time of booking a car.
- Use a car in the best condition, equipped with a GPS navigation aid, radio, tape, etc.
- Reach at least ten minutes before time.
- Don't unpack everything in a hotel room.
- Call home daily. If your kid is used to listening to bedtime stories, read a story over the phone.
- Buy gifts for the family from each destination you cover.
- Take out at least one hour to just relax and be yourself. This is much easier when you are on tour.
- Dine at off-hours for faster service. Don't hesitate to tell a restaurant boy you are in a hurry. Ask for a menu with cocktail orders, and order a meal when the cocktail arrives. Then, when dessert time comes, ask for a bill with that final order.

- Use room service in hotels and integrate breakfast with dressing up or packing.
- Inform the reception about your checking out fifteen minutes in advance.
- Upon reaching your office, thank everyone you met for their kind courtesy and confirm the key points of business discussions.
- Take the necessary actions promptly that you have committed. As regards actions expected from others, follow up in a non-offensive manner after allowing a reasonable time.

34 SEMINARS / WORKSHOPS

- Seminars or workshops help you to learn powerful techniques and strategies that others have spent years learning and refining.
- Find what exactly they will cover, and pre-study the material to see its usefulness.
- Get to the seminar early and skim the course materials. Note down your doubts or questions and clarify them during the seminar.
- Listen carefully to important ideas that appeal to you.
- Use lunch breaks for meeting delegates, networking, business discussions, etc.
- Practice what you learn step-by-step.
- Document your Action Plan to implement the learnings of the seminar.
- Circulate the learnings of the seminar to colleagues and peers and give a PowerPoint presentation to them. This way, you will not only refresh your learnings but will also be able to master the topic.
- Review materials, notes, and your progress on your Action Plan a few weeks after the seminar.

35 THE ART OF PUBLIC SPEAKING

Practical Time-Saving Tips

- Learn and master the art of public speaking, especially if you are inspiring to be a charismatic leader. Learning the art of public speaking will sharpen your abilities to think clearly, logically and rapidly on your feet under pressure.
- Don't allow hesitation to speak in public to become a bottleneck to reaching the top.
- Make some great public speakers or good orators your role models. Visualise a picture of such a person. Stand like him. Talk like him. Make eye contact like him. Smile like him. Crack jokes like him. After achieving a certain level of expertise, slowly introduce your unique originalities.
- Read books on public speaking.
- Join the best course in public speaking. Such courses teach the art and science of public speaking and provide a platform for public speaking practice with expert comments. Carefully considered, these comments can give valuable input for improving your public speaking skills.
- Practice plenty of impromptu speeches to build up self-confidence.
- Spend adequate quality time preparing your speech. The shorter the speech, the larger the time required for the preparation. Study the topic thoroughly, especially controversial aspects. Do the necessary homework. Think about possible questions and prepare to answer them.
- Pay due attention to all three sections of your speech, viz., the beginning, the core and the conclusion.
- People always look for their self-interest. People will listen to you only if they find your speech beneficial to them. Hence, design your speech to satisfy their needs. Identify the Dominant Self-Interest Motive (DSIM) of your audience. Demonstrate genuine concern for the benefit of the audience. Your speech should appeal to them.
- Package ideas in a form that avoids any overtones of sermonizing or self-importance.
- Pay attention to body adornment. Your clothing style should suit your personality, physique and complexion. Dress neatly. Don't roll up your sleeves. Ensure no wardrobe malfunction.

- Drink a glass of warm water before you start your speech to maintain a honey-like smooth voice.
- Make sure mike is working. Knock from side-not from the front. Adjust the mike below the chin. Stand six inches (fifteen cm) away from the mike.
- Stand tall and firm. Plant legs firmly on the ground. Ensure equal weight on both legs and shoulders up. When you stand tall, you will feel you are an expert on the topic and as a result, you will speak with authority. Visualise yourself as the authority on the subject. Look confident. Look successful.
- Pay attention to mannerisms. Avoid behaviour that irritates people.
- Transmit energy to the audience with a firm handshake, tone of voice, vibrations of your thoughts, posture, carriage of your body, etc.
- Present your ideas forcefully and powerfully, but maintain delivery unfailingly gentle. Speak loudly, but don't shout. Learn voice projecting. Open your mouth and throw words. Vary the tone and pitch of your speech as required. Learn where to increase pitch and where to give pause so that people can understand. Let your voice reflect the authority.
- Pay attention to every word you use, the language, the grammar, the tone of your voice, the gestures you make, your facial expression, body language, etc. Use all these to enhance your image as a speaker.
- Consider starting your speech with a relevant short story, a powerful quote from a famous person, or impactful humour. The story, quote, or humour should be factual, familiar, and capable of convincingly conveying your proposal and its benefits. Make your beginning sensational.
- Add ample humour in your speech to break the monotony. Humour is one of the best techniques for getting favourable attention. An impactful and appropriately timed humorous punch can make you a popular public speaker. Make sure your humour is socially acceptable and non-offensive.
- Widen your span of analogy. The audience will comprehend your message if you give some analogy or example to which they can relate.
- Use short sentences. Use small phrases.

Practical Time-Saving Tips

- Speak slowly. Pause and look at your audience when you want them to grasp some important point. Be visible and audible to all rather than a select few.
- Maintain eye contact with the audience.
- Smile freely. Use a big smile when you have to say 'No'.
- Service your audience. Make them understand your message clearly and instantly.
- Plant questions in your speech to directly focus on the desired point, but don't allow anyone to answer. Don't pause after the question, but continue with your next sentence in the same breath. Still, if someone answers, take control back into your hands immediately.
- Announce in the beginning that there will be a question-answer session at the end. Don't entertain questions in the middle of the speech. Do this gracefully in a non-offensive manner. Use a smile freely. Also, don't allow more than one or two questions per speaker. Consider planting your people to ask the first question if no one wants to break the ice.
- Study the psychology of the audience. Never ridicule the audience. Avoid counter-questions. Don't argue with the audience. Show genuine respect for them. Praise them. Be generous. Establish a connection with them. Reach their heart. Win their heart. Develop a rapport with them. Handle troublesome participants tactfully.
- End your speech with DSIM punch showing the principal benefits of your proposal, which they can carry as a take-away.
- Avoid thanking the audience. It is unprofessional.

36 DEVELOPING AN ENRICHING RELATIONSHIP WITH YOUR SPOUSE

- Choose your life partner wisely, as it is the most important decision of your lifetime. The marriage relationship offers 90% of all your support, happiness and fulfilment. The most desirable qualities are

- affection, integrity, intelligence, a sense of humour, temperament and compatibility. Move slowly and let no one press you into an uncomfortable decision.
- Realise that developing an enriching relationship with your spouse goes a long way in your professional success. Take extra effort and make this relationship loving, respectful, peaceful, harmonious and mutually satisfying.
- Praise your spouse. Compliment your spouse. If you say five positive things to your spouse for each negative one, you have a good chance of a successful and lasting relationship.
- Be compassionate. Know all the details of your partner's story.
- Give in sometimes. Learn to compromise. Realise that you have to change first.
- Resolve issues, if any, and move ahead. Pray or meditate on the issues. Don't keep them unresolved.
- Take adequate physical steps to develop fine chemistry with your spouse. The better the chemistry with your spouse, the better the quality of your personal and professional lives.
- Dream jointly. Share your vision with your spouse – both for common goals as a family and personal goals in an individual capacity. If you are inspiring to elevate to the top post of your organisation, make your spouse a partner in this dream and live this dream jointly. This way, she will appreciate your viewpoint if you have to work hard. Explain to your spouse that if you have to go to the office on some Sundays, it is a matter of pride for her, as he is in great demand.
- Limit your workweek to 60 hours. Avoid bulging briefcases. Be smart about what you carry home.
- Spend quality time with your spouse and children. Pay due attention to them. Get the family together in the morning for breakfast and at night for dinner,
- For at least fifteen minutes every day, spend quality time with your soul mate. Get involved in deeply meaningful interaction and strengthen bonding. Similarly, set aside at least one day every week to be alone with your spouse. Turn off the television and switch off phones. Focus all your attention on your life partner and enjoy the

company of this very special person in your life. Make an appointment for a grand dinner with your spouse on Saturday night and keep it as scrupulous as a business meeting.
- Make your weekend colourful, refreshing and guilt-free by planning in advance.
- Help your spouse with some household work, especially muscular work.
- Be with your spouse when she needs you the most, like during pregnancy or illness.
- Strengthen relationships by working more on common interests and keeping aside other areas.
- Use your spouse as a sounding board for important decisions in your life. Your spouse can give you invaluable feedback and insightful suggestions.
- Allow your spouse to pursue her interests and passion. Provide support and encouragement. Attend the programme she is conducting or organising even if you don't like or enjoy the same.
- Chart a social calendar every month in consultation with your spouse. Don't ignore in-laws in social calendars.
- Go on vacations. Don't boast of going without a break for years. This is a sign of trouble - not commitment. Relaxing on a beach, under the sun, with waves pounding at your feet, is a marvellous way to relieve some of the pressure that invariably builds up in the work environment. Don't go for a hectic ten-day eight-country European tour; introduce some idleness to your vacations.
- Plan some of the business travel along with your spouse. Attend some of the seminars along with your spouse.
- Build a library at home with books of common interest and read books jointly.
- The most appropriate index for measuring marriage success is the willingness of your spouse to be with you for the next seven births.

37 PERSONAL CHORES

- Opt for electronic transfer of your salary and other receipts in your bank account.

- Consolidate your banking. Have a joint bank account. You, your spouse and your parents should avail the nomination facility for the bank accounts and update the same as required.
- Maximise the use of Internet banking. Take due safety precautions.
- Open a joint Demat Account rather than physical shares, bonds, etc.
- Examine investing in mutual funds rather than various stocks.
- Streamline your document storage for ease of retrieval. Consider using a suitable platform for availing services of a digital locker.
- Deposit valuables and important documents in a safe deposit vault (duly retaining photocopies) or use an unassailable, fire-resistant digital home locker.
- In a diary, list important information like bank account numbers and keep it handy and safe.
- Put bills in a folder at a fixed place as soon as they arrive. Opt for paperless bills.
- Pay regular bills by direct electronic debit.
- Keep pre-stamped envelopes and postal stamps.
- Use a rubber stamp or sticker for your residence address.
- Avail paid services for tasks like ticketing, renewals of passports and driving licenses.
- Hire a tax consultant rather than filing your income tax return yourself.
- Teach finance to your children. Explain to them the value of education and money in life. Cultivate the habit of savings and explain to them the mind-boggling power of compounding. Open bank accounts for them or include their names as joint holders in your account. Teach them banking operations, ATM cash withdrawals, etc. Cultivate the best habits in them. Explain to them the importance of being happy rather than becoming rich so that when they grow up, they know the value of things, not the price.
- Keep your spouse and adult children informed about your financial investments. Capture details of your financial investments in one electronic file (could be named

'Your family should know') and periodically update the same.
- Avail of services of a reputed certified financial planner for major investment decisions.
- Jointly work out fund requirements with your spouse for goals like the child's education and marriage and start saving and investing money at an early stage.
- Ensure adequate health insurance is in place for you and your family.
- Ensure adequate life insurance cover for the bread-earning member of the family.
- Do prudent post-retirement financial planning to ensure a handsome fixed monthly income/ Lump Sum corpus for you and your family. This will help you maintain the same standard of living that was prevailing before retirement.
- Consider the preparation of a will. Don't postpone the preparation of the will because of apprehensions about future revisions. The will can easily be changed or replaced by a fresh, updated will at any time. Consult a reputed professional lawyer to help you in preparing the will.

38 HOUSEHOLD CHORES

- In our lifetime, we spend about six years doing chores. Hence, do these chores efficiently.
- Instead of spending your precious time on tedious chores, channelise your energy into your work to earn a better income so that you can hire some professional agency to do jobs like vacuum cleaning, carpets or window cleaning. Keep your eyes open for household tips.
- Prepare a list of household chores duly categorised based on their daily, weekly, and monthly frequency. Allocate responsibilities on a regular or rotating basis to all family members. Weekend is the time to unwind and recharge your batteries and prepare for the peak performance of the subsequent week. Hence, in the weekend 'TO DO' list, allow plenty of time for rest and relaxation and protect it ruthlessly.
- Teach children about household chores through how-to-do sessions.

The Twelve Steps To A Life Of Exemplary Excellence

- Use a 'job jar' for unpleasant chores that no family member readily agrees to do. Every Sunday, write one such chore on a slip of paper and drop it in the jar along with a few blank slips. Whosoever randomly gets a non-blank slip does the chore.
- Use time in relation to energy levels and the importance of the task. Don't aim for perfection.
- Use mail rather than doing things in person.
- Have a categorised master list of purchases.
- Shop once a week or even less. Avoid weekends and peak hours for shopping.
- Consider teleshopping or online shopping.
- Shop only twice a year for items like clothes. Also, avoid the festival rush.
- Buy pre-wrapped gifts, including extras for people you may remember later. Carry enclosure cards for gift recipients so they can go right into the gift packs and be delivered directly from the shop.
- Choose good service shops near the office or home or on the commuting route and regularly use the same shop to get better and faster service.
- Anticipate the child-care crisis and have a backup ready.
- Bunch your medical and other appointments. Also, combine your appointments with your spouse wherever possible. Take appointments on the way to the office or back home.
- Keep items like umbrellas extra—in the office, at home and in the car.
- Don't be glued to the tube, but watch selectively and instead read, exercise or rest.
- Keep tools together and return them to the same place after use. Don't put things down - put them away. Keep everything in place and have a specified place for everything.
- Entertain guests with a relaxed dinner rather than a tense seven-course meal.
- Accept invitations selectively.

39 DEALING WITH STRESS AND CRISIS

242

- RELAX
- Use waiting time for relaxing.
- Don't curse the entire city while waiting for a prolonged period at a traffic signal or level crossing. Instead, use this block of time positively for relaxation rather than as a negative time drag.
- Stress is simply a response you create in interpreting the event. You can control stress by controlling your interpretation of the events.
- Learn to control your emotions. It is emotional upheaval that drains off energy; not the hard work.
- Learn to see beauty in imperfection. If you can't see beauty in imperfection, you will get tense and personal excellence can never happen in tension.
- Avoid self-pity.
- Avoid credit card debt traps as also unaffordable EMIs. Instead, exploit the mind-blowing power of compounding by inculcating the habit of commencing saving a pre-determined amount from an early age and doing so regularly with a disciplined approach. Instead of defining savings as income minus expenditure, redefine the amount available for spending as income minus the pre-determined amount of savings. The Rolex can wait. The BMW can wait.
- Develop a future-oriented outlook with a positive attitude. A future outlook with improved skills increases confidence and makes one optimistic.
- Take problems as challenges to your capabilities so that overcoming them gives satisfaction rather than nervous tension. Don't underestimate problems or get carried away or bogged down by them.
- Get tasks and concerns under control by charting out, allocating time, delegating some, and eliminating others.
- To keep your mind nimble, use it often. Solve crossword puzzles or riddles.
- Indulge in hobbies. This will take your mind off your work. Take up painting, singing or any activity that satisfies your creative side.
- If a change has been turbulent in your organisation, try stabilising the work schedule to reestablish normalcy. Take a relief day or a long weekend.

- Have dual offices- a regular office and a small secret office where you can go to unwind and work away from the crowds for a few hours when work pressure overwhelms you.
- Avoid emergencies by planning ahead, anticipating and solving potential problems in advance.
- Identify reasons for a crisis like inadequate planning, improper estimates of time, a tendency to enjoy crisis, or a tendency to sweep things under the rug and take appropriate corrective action.
- Identify the sources of the crisis. If there is a weakness in a particular department, improve the same structurally from a long-term viewpoint.
- Learn to anticipate and try to catch a crisis in its early controllable stages. Recognise the symptoms that precede the full-blown crisis and diagnose the underlying root causes. Crisis, especially related to human resource grievances, is best handled early because when human beings bottle up their feelings, they get irritated and make mountains out of molehills. Hence, nip the issue in the bud.
- To prevent crisis:
  - Catalog a set of routine remedies for the recurring crisis.
  - Delegate responsibility for various types of crisis.
  - Plan alternatives.
- In case of an inevitable emergency, imagine yourself as a professional doctor handling the emergency in a super cool, calm and organised manner with an unemotional and rational approach.
- If you think you are entering a crisis, shut the door for five minutes and be alone by yourself. Let your anger reach the pinnacle and then relax. Let your body go limp and stop thinking. Take a deep breath. When you open the door, things will look a lot different and you will have a more rational approach and you will act positively rather than emotionally. This short mental vacation helps in reducing stress and tension. Don't under-react or over-react, but take the following steps:
  - Don't lay blame.
  - Stop worrying.
  - Think back.
  - Do as little as possible until the pressure is entirely off.

- Lower the temperature and creatively find some common ground for moving forward.
- Plan a step-by-step programme.

• When there is a crisis, calibrate your words carefully. When things are hot, the next few words you speak are crucial. It can either start rolling the ball for a peaceful solution or lead to an explosion.

40 THE ART OF SLEEPING

• Realise the importance of quality sleep in our life. In our lifetime, we spend nearly 1/3 of our life (about twenty five years) sleeping, yet 30% of people have to struggle to sleep well. According to one estimate, in the U.S.A., twelve million sleeping tablets are required every night to put Americans to sleep. Sleep is not an optional lifestyle luxury but a non-negotiable biological necessity and a natural, restorative process. After a day's hard work, one would think that any person would be able to sleep peacefully, but apparently, we have even lost the art of sleeping. The disruption of deep sleep is an underappreciated factor that is contributing to memory decline in ageing and other ailments.

• Arrive at the optimum sleep duration you require by trial and error. An optimum sleep means arising afresh on your own without the help of a wake-up alarm.

• Don't sleep immediately after dinner. Ideally, allow about a three-hour gap between dinner and sleep to ensure proper digestion of food.

• Start winding down an hour before bedtime.

• Avoid alcohol or even stimulants such as caffeine. Use decaffeinated coffee.

• Take a bath with water heated to 40° C and add one tablespoon of mustard powder to normalise and tranquillize circulation. Be sure the bed is already prepared and hop right in.

• Ensure a single bed is at least 40 inches (100 cm) wide and a double bed at least 60 inches (150 cm) wide. (This is, of course, assuming normal size spouse!)

• Ensure the mattress is neither too soft (such that you have to wake up to turn over) nor too hard (such

- that it exerts pressure on your body).
- Spray the scent of your choice in the bedroom.
- Create a monotony. Eliminate noise. Avoid excitement as it prevents sleep.
- Don't work, watch television or argue with the spouse in bed. (Arguing with the spouse is strictly prohibited at all times!)
- Practice yoga sleep.
- If you can't sleep, go elsewhere, turn on a light and read something boring till you feel sleepy.
- Resist the sleeping pill temptation.
- Sleep like an innocent, cute baby.
- To sleep well, first collapse physically. Practice this several times. Let go of every muscle in the body. Carefully relax each body muscle. Deliberately let your arms, legs, and trunk muscles go.
- S T R E T C H
- Focus on the quality of sleep rather than the quantity of sleep. It is a myth that eight hours of sleep is absolutely necessary. (Our parents drummed this myth into us, probably because they needed at least an eight-hour break from us.) Many of the world's greatest achievers slept fewer than six hours without compromising their health and well-being.
- Reduce your sleeping time in steps of fifteen minutes each, preferably by rising early and not by going to bed later.
- The best trade-off between sleep time and non-sleep time is exercise.
- If you feel tired, you do not necessarily lack sleep. Being tired is just as often a symptom of stress, depression, or poor nutrition.
- Avoid ruminating. Don't think about work challenges when you are not at work. Avoid needless worry over trifling matters. Worry is a misuse of our power of imagination to create something we don't want. And 99% of the things you worry about don't even happen. What worries you, master you. Worry implies that we don't trust the almighty God is big, powerful, or loving enough to care for what's happening in our lives. Stop worrying about what can go wrong. Instead, get excited about what can go right. Worrying causes stress. Prayer causes peace. Worry less, pray more. Eliminate worry by compartmentalising it.

APPENDIX III

DOS AND DON'TS OF LEADERSHIP IN GENERAL AND SERVANT LEADERSHIP IN PARTICULAR

- Be domain expert
- Be charismatic
- Don't demand respect; deserve it
- Don't focus on gaining authority
- Develop stewardship
- Create a burning desire to serve others
- Serve with humility
- Create a powerful vision of the future
- Lead by example
- Lead with integrity
- Prioritise ethics over monetary gains
- Privilege and empower people
- Empathise
- Know thyself
- Be confident and decisive
- Be consistent and predictive
- Challenge yourself
- Solve the issues
- Dissolve ego
- Remain calm
- Hold your tongue
- Value your and other's time
- Pursue, follow up
- Allow time for healing
- Network and build community
- Share your knowledge generously
- Learn to handle failure with grace

APPENDIX IV

DEALING WITH CHRONIC TIME WASTERS

CATEGORY/(SYMPTOM)	STRATEGY
Boredom (Complaining - hangdog look)	Give a larger workload with some juicy projects.
Too many ideas (An idea a minute and eagerness to instantly share with you)	Insist that he puts down the idea on a piece of paper or let him present the same at the scheduled meeting.
Lack of confidence (Dilly-dallying and afraid to take a stand)	Offer praise and encouragement to enable him to improve his self-image.
Excessively confident (Enthusiasm and ego)	Insist that he puts down the idea on a piece of paper or let him present the same at the scheduled meeting.
Thoughtlessness (Lazy, careless, inconsiderate)	Reprimand firmly in private. If required, give ultimatums in private.
Hostile aggressive (Critical attack)	Remain cool. Stand up to the person, but do not fight. Let him blow off steam or say you are leaving the room and returning in five minutes.
Complainers (Exaggerate woes and expect sympathy)	Don't agree or disagree; just be non-committal.
Indecisive (Analysts or being nice who fear making enemies)	Give evidence duly reinforced with facts and figures or give a deadline for decision-making.
Unresponsiveness (Afraid)	Let him know you are friendly and non-threatening and demonstrate so.
Know it-all (Phony expert)	Appreciate some of his knowledge first and where he is erring, show your own facts and figures and logically convince him.

APPENDIX V

THE JOURNEY TOWARDS A LIFE OF EXEMPLARY EXCELLENCE: QUANTITATIVE SELF-APPRAISAL

STEP No.	INTROSPECTION-PROVOKING POSERS
1	**Put others before yourself**
	Am I always thinking of myself?
	How many times a day do I utter self-centered words like I, me, my, mine and myself?
	How can I use more and more people-centric words, like we, us, our, ours and ourselves in my daily conversation?
	Am I going out of my way to help my family, friends, neighbours and colleagues? (In the initial stages, it is ok even if this help is non-financial.)
	What steps should I take to gradually improve my Selflessness Quotient and eventually bring it to nine out of ten?
	Do I have enough fire in my belly to relentlessly keep pursuing excellence even when the going gets tough?
2	**Discover your passion and weave your life around your passion**
	Have I discovered a) what stirs my soul and what resonates with me? b) what makes me feel I am totally in harmony with why I showed up here in the first place? c) what is the cause for which I can wager myself with confidence and dive in wholeheartedly? d) which activities make me lose track of time when engrossed in them?
	Am I weaving my life around my passion?

The Twelve Steps To A Life Of Exemplary Excellence

3	**Establish a strong and nobly altruistic why factor in your life**
	Why am I doing what I'm doing?
	What is the predominant purpose of my life? Is this purpose altruistic, i.e. non-self-centric?
	Is this purpose strong and noble enough to keep me driving even when the going gets tough?
4.	**Focus more on self-improvement and build up an impeccable character**
	Have I attained spiritual maturity to accept others as they are?
	Am I focusing more on improving myself instead of trying to change others?
	Am I focusing on building an impeccable character?
5.	**Don't focus only on monetary wealth; focus on all elements of true wealth**
	What are my current weightages for each of the five elements of true wealth?
	What should be desirable levels of weightages for each of the five elements for me based on the unique scheme of things in my life?
	How am I currently placed as regards achieving mastery in each of the five elements of true wealth?
	What steps should I take to attain the highest levels of freedom in each of the five elements of true wealth?

6.	**Create an inspiring and empowering PMS and set nobly altruistic worthy goals**	
	Have I planned where do I want to be after five years from now?	
	What are my non-negotiable core values and principles?	
	Am I prepared to forgo monetary gains to uphold my core values and principles?	
	Is my PMS inspiring and empowering enough to motivate me to accelerate my journey towards a life of exemplary excellence?	
	What steps should I take so that my PMS is aligned with that of my spouse?	
7	**Select a legendary role model and a mentor**	
	Have I identified a legendary role model whose accomplishments match my vision?	
	Have I started cultivating good atomic habits which my role model possesses? Am I thinking and acting like him?	
	Have I identified my best mentor?	
8	**Transform your life the butterfly way**	
	Am I mentally and physically ready to embrace a butterfly-like paradigm transformation?	
	Am I prepared to break free from the illusory veil of the egoistic mind and free myself from attachments to the physical body and material world?	
	Am I prepared to transform my thoughts, mindset, attitudes, rituals, routines, habits, desires, actions and lifestyle to facilitate a paradigm transformation of my life?	
	What steps should I take to ensure a seamless paradigm transformation of myself?	

9	**Spend time on what is deeply important to you**
	Have I developed a deep personal sense of time?
	Am I eliminating all non-essentials and putting first things first?
	Am I subordinating the clock to the compass?
	Am I focusing on Quadrant II activities?
	Am I exploiting the power of daily scheduling?
10	**Sharpen your people management skills and commercial savviness**
	Where am I currently placed as regards developing people management skills?
	Have I developed enough traits that are essential for servant leadership?
	Does my communication style have overtones of orders?
	What steps should I take to improve my people management skills and master them?
	Where am I currently placed as regards commercial savviness? Am I blessed with an ovarian lottery? If not, am I prepared to do whatever it takes to acquire these skills? What steps should I take to sharpen my commercial savviness and master it?
11	**Work hard with a single-mindedness of purpose and climb one step at a time**
	Am I prepared to work hard with a single-mindedness of purpose?
	What steps should I take to come out of my comfort zone and stretch myself beyond elastic limits?

12	**Make your today a better day than yesterday and leave behind a great legacy**
	Am I doing justice to the potential the almighty God has gifted me with? Am I the best version of myself?
	Am I continually upgrading my intellectual capacity and spiritual enlightenment?
	Am I increasing my value manifold every day?
	Am I better today than I was yesterday? Will I be more thoughtful, optimistic, determined, focused, intentional, and purposeful in the future than I am right now?
	What additional steps should I take to make today a better day than yesterday?
	How do I wish to be remembered? What legacy should I leave behind?

Total Max. Score = 200	
Score Evaluation Matrix	
<75	You are yet to start your journey towards a life of excellence. Large gaps exist in most of the steps.
76-150	You are in the early stage of your journey towards a life of excellence. Gaps exist in a few of the steps.
151-175	You are in the middle of your journey towards a life of excellence. You are performing reasonably well in most of the steps. You may have to focus more on high-weightage steps.
>175	You are in the advanced stage of your journey towards a life of excellence. You have demonstrated excellence in most of the steps. You need to consolidate your position and keep relentlessly accelerating your journey towards a life of exemplary excellence. This may lead you to make legendary contributions as you approach the score of 200.

NOTES:

1) Taking the help of introspection-provoking posers, thoughtfully arrive at your current score for each of the above steps on a scale of one to ten.

2) Multiply these scores by the corresponding weightage and arrive at your total current score. For Step nos. 5 and 10 the weightage is 3. For Step nos. 1, 3, 6, and 9 the weightage is 2. For the rest of the steps, the weightage is 1.

3) Taking the help of the Score Evaluation Matrix, ascertain your current status in your journey towards a life of exemplary excellence.

4) Prepare a time-bound Action Plan, which is essentially a self-improvement plan. Though an Action Plan can show the results or outputs you want to achieve, the focus should be more on the inputs, i.e. structural-level changes or transformations that you need in yourself to achieve planned results. Such changes or transformations must comprehensively encompass your thoughts, mindset, attitudes, rituals, routines, habits, desires, actions and lifestyle.

5) Every year, re-evaluate your score and feel the difference in your life.

6) Generously share your personal experience with others and motivate them to implement this twelve-step process in their lives.

14

BIBLIOGRAPHY

1. Shiv Khera
   'You can win'
2. Zig Ziglar
   'See you at the top'
3. Lauren Robert Januz & Susan k. Jones
   'Time Management for Executives'
4. Mike Levy
   'Get Yourself Organised'
5. John Adair
   'Inspiring Leadership'
6. Napoleon Hill
   'Think and Grow Reach'
7. Stephen R. Covey
   'The Seven Habits of Highly Effective People'
8. Swami Sukhabodhananda
   'Personal Excellence through the Bhagavad Gita'
9. Robin Sharma
   'Mega Living'
10. Robert H. Schuller
    'Success is never ending. Failure is never final'
11. James Clear
    "Atomic Habits"

ABOUT THE AUTHOR

$\mathcal{M}$. U. Shah, a Civil Engineering graduate, has a scholarly, distinguished academic career and an illustrious professional journey. He has worked in India and North Africa on various prestigious infrastructure projects and has been accredited with several exemplary achievements.

A distinguished alumnus of The National Institute of Construction Management and Research, he is the recipient of a Lifetime Achievement Award.

An inspiring speaker, a trainer and a passionate writer, he has authored several papers on technical and managerial topics. He has officiated as the Editor of Gammon Bulletin for over twenty-five years. He is an active member of prestigious professional bodies like the Institution of Engineers, Indian Concrete Institute, Indian Roads Congress, and International Road Federation and has been nominated on various technical committees. He has chaired and co-chaired several technical sessions in seminars and conferences.

He has also participated as Faculty for various training programme in India and abroad. His flagship workshops on the topic of 'Excellence' are immensely popular. So far, over 2500 participants have attended these workshops.

Another book by the Author: **Compounding Monetary Wealth Together With True Wealth**

Made in the USA
Monee, IL
03 May 2026

49438450R00148